WORLD DIRECTORS SERIES

Film retains its capacity to beguile, entertain and open up windows onto other cultures like no other medium. Nurtured by the growth of film festivals worldwide and by cinephiles from all continents, a new generation of directors has emerged in this environment over the last few decades.

This new series aims to present and discuss the work of the leading directors from across the world on whom little has been written and whose exciting work merits discussion in an increasingly globalised film culture. Many of these directors have proved to be ambassadors for their national film cultures as well as critics of the societies they represent, dramatising in their work the dilemmas of art that are both national and international, of local relevance and universal appeal.

Written by leading film critics and scholars, each book contains an analysis of the director's works, filmography, bibliography and illustrations. The series will feature film-makers from all continents (including North America), assessing their impact on the art form and their contribution to film culture.

Other Titles in the Series

LARS VON TRIER

Jack Stevenson

 Publishing

Watkins College
of Art & Design

Tak for hjælpen til Peter, Helle, Klaus og Troels. Det var dejligt, at I gad kæmpe jer gennem de grå dage i Hillerød blot for atprøve at lære mig det mærkelige danske sprog. Uden dét ville jeg ikke have kunnet skrive denne her bog.

First published in 2002 by the
BRITISH FILM INSTITUTE
21 Stephen Street, London W1T 1LN

The British Film Institute promotes greater understanding
of, and access to, film and moving image culture in the UK.

Illustrations: BFI Stills; Danish Film Institute (DFI): pp. 3, 22, 29. 34, 36, 42,
55, 62, 77, 79, 81, 83, 105, 117, 124, 135, 179, 184, 190

Design by Ketchup
Set by D R Bungay Associates, Burghfield, Berks
Printed in England by The Cromwell Press, Trowbridge, Wiltshire

British Library Cataloguing-in-Publication Data
A catalogue record for this book is available from the British Library

ISBN 0–85170–903–6 (pbk)
ISBN 0–85170–902–8 (hbk)

CONTENTS

AUTHOR'S NOTE

Heretofore most information available on Lars von Trier in the English language has been, while not censored in the classic sense, heavily filtered. The information reported by the range of publications and media organs that concern themselves with him adds up to create something less than a complete picture of the man, as they only focus on highly specific and limited aspects of the story – a story that also has a language bridge to cross.

The film journals analyse and interpret the artist's creative achievements, the trade publications focus on the businessman's acumen and the director's sense of professionalism, and the steady stream of proclamations from his studio, Zentropa, are concerned with marketing the product of their biggest name (and co-owner) and burnishing his public image. The Danish tabloids, in turn, focus on the man's personal life. Large segments of 'the story' from the last two sources never make it out of the Danish language, or if so, usually only in 'approved' versions.

Considering the fractured and incomplete nature of the story that has thus far been made available to English-language readers, I have written this book with two main objectives: to construct a fuller portrait of the man by delving into the massive bank of information thus far largely confined to the Danish language, and to make that story accessible to a wide readership by telling it with a style that has narrative flow. My aim is to give weight to all aspects of the story, rather than, for example, to put the focus on exhaustive critical analysis or a re-interpretation of his works. This already exists, and is ongoing, in film literature.

Nor do I intend to deify or besmirch Lars von Trier. To join in the heated and emotional debate that swirls around this controversial and polarising figure is not appropriate for me, as the author of this book, although the book certainly takes full stock of the situation, as it should.

Although I've resided in Denmark since 1993, I still have an outsider's perspective to the story which has enabled me to remain relatively objective

— not an easy thing to be when one is writing about Lars von Trier from a Danish perspective. While discussions with various Danes have aided me in my efforts to solve the riddles of culture and mentality that are central to the story, I am particularly indebted to Maren Pust, a journalist, editor and teacher active in the Danish film milieu for many years, for her invaluable and indefatigable assistance. She provided a wealth of insight and ideas and gave me much needed feedback throughout the whole long process. Suffice it to say that this book could not have been written without her input.

INTRODUCTION

Most of you holding this book first heard about Lars von Trier when his film, *Breaking the Waves*, broke through to international success in 1996. In Denmark, however, the shy fellow with the mischievous tight-lipped smile had already been a 'pebble in the shoe' of Danish film-goers for fourteen years – going back to 1982 when his film school graduate project, *Images of a Relief*, opened for the paying public at the Delta cinema in central Copenhagen.

Not that this fifty-seven-minute-long film figured as any kind of precursor to *Titanic* (1997): it received mixed if largely sympathetic reviews, was hardly a box-office smash and remained pretty much 'a student thing'. Von Trier was no overnight success and the path his career would take would be anything but predictable, thanks in no small part to the many decisions he would make that ran against the grain of commercial logic. His evolution as a film-maker, his road ahead, still had many twists and turns and cul-de-sacs in it, but he insisted on taking the time to explore all these detours and develop his craft and his vision.

No, an overnight sensation Lars von Trier was not. But he was something else right from the start. An enigma. And that he has remained. He is the antithesis of your average successful film-maker who owns a home in LA and spends his time travelling the world festival circuit, wearily but politely hosting press junkets for assemblies of fawning scribes. He hates 'the Circus'. It almost seems he fears this kind of fame.

Yet today he is the best-known Danish cultural export since Victor Borge. He is probably the most provocative, unpredictable and polarising film-maker in the West, if not the most visionary. He is the rarest of entities in modern film: a 'name' director with 'clout' who makes 'big' films for an international audience, yet who remains an uncompromising film artist and keeps a tight grip on that rarest of powers – total artistic control. He's never been a 'hired hand' director and he's never done adaptations of other people's stories. He makes his own stories. He is hailed today as one of the leading proponents of a modern, pan-European film aesthetic, a maker of the kind of movies that many people hope will counter the juggernaut of the Hollywood studio system.

Almost nothing takes place today in Danish film without Lars von Trier somewhere in the picture. He is a catalyst, a facilitator, a complainer, an irritant and an inexhaustible source of good stories and controversy. He is both a frustration and a blessing to Danish journalists, and for Danish film-makers he casts a shadow they cannot escape. It almost sounds as if he's not human, but from the picture one gets in Denmark, he is all *too* human. He is the most relentlessly exposed personality in Danish film, and at the same time its central mystery. His personal life is grist for the mill of the yellow press, while his art installations and media 'concepts' are endlessly chewed over by intellectual film and art critics. He is the film-maker who has become famous for not playing 'the Game', while all the while playing a million little games, putting us on, taking us for a ride. Although far from Denmark's only great director, he is the main reason that Danish film is today experiencing its second 'golden Age'.[1] He has helped make film one of Denmark's most visible export commodities.

Yet despite the international acclaim he receives today, a certain scepticism has shadowed him throughout his career – *particularly* in Denmark.

At regular intervals various critics figured they had him pegged as a fraud. 'Lars von Trier makes meaningless films that pretend to mean something,' they said in so many words. The punk Provo had become, to use Celine's scathing invective, 'middle-class respectable'. He is a spoiled brat who threatens to leave the country if he doesn't get his own way,[2] and couldn't care less about the film awards we heap on him. He's vanity incarnate, comparing himself not only to Carl Th. Dreyer and Ingmar Bergman but to Edgar Allan Poe[3] as well. He's just jerking our emotions around for his own amusement in his irritatingly ironic post-modern way – he couldn't feign sincerity if he had a gun pointed at his head. He's an inveterate fabricator and fantasist who might very well have lied about his entire life story.[4]

Von Trier would probably be the first to mischievously admit that all of this was at least half true, even if it wasn't. He's comfortable playing the role of charlatan.

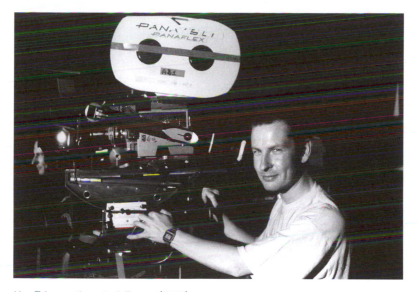

Von Trier on the set of *Europa* (1991)

He's less comfortable playing the role of genius. And even if he isn't *really* a genius, at least he's been proclaimed as such by enough people to make the idea stick, going back to the days when no one outside Denmark even knew he existed. If, as the popular conception would have it, genius is erratic, enigmatic and tormented, von Trier fits the bill. If a genius is arrogant but at the same time insecure, visionary but also dysfunctional, he would seem to qualify.

While the question of genius is, in and of itself, an empty semantic exercise, the tag of genius has charged the debate about von Trier, predisposing some to wildly acclaim any film he makes while inclining others to greet his work with a reflexive suspicion or hostility. Perhaps in part this is because we tend to be uncomfortable with *living* geniuses. Dead ones are easier to quantify, celebrate, come to terms with, to have definite and firmly fixed opinions about.

But who *can* be comfortable with the idea of being a genius? He seems, naturally enough, eternally discomforted by it all. He hates explaining himself, he hates interviews, he hates the crowds, the Circus. In that sense, film was the worst profession he could have chosen, although he hardly 'chose' it in any kind of premeditated way.

Discomforted but not fearful. When it comes to the subject of failing, of being a 'has been', of possibly making a 'bad film', he has no fear at all. Odd for somebody with so many phobias and insecurities. But about his creative judgments, he is utterly fearless, if not always utterly secure.

This fearlessness, or perhaps rather indifference, is interpreted by many as arrogance, and here the chorus of doubters strikes up again. What do you call it when a twenty-eight-year-old neophyte refuses to accept anything less than the world's top film prize – the Cannes Film Festival's Palme d'Or – for his first feature film (crewed by a bunch of film students)? And when he does win a prize, he usually doesn't even show up to claim the trophy. This is an insult to all those who demand of the successful that they take their success seriously, that they learn to say 'thank you' properly when they receive their awards and that they don't, for example, embarrass the entire country back home by calling the foreman of the jury a 'midget'.

It is with a mixture of both pride and chagrin (at the moment, mostly pride), that Danes view their eternal problem child, the boy from Lyngby who went out into the wider world and conquered. For ultimately, despite his flirtations at various points with all things German and French, and despite the fact that he supposedly possesses some very 'un-Danish' traits, he is as a person very much a man of his generation and culture, and as a film-maker very much a product of the way the Danish film business functions.

On the surface, Danish culture appears to have been as successfully 'Americanised' as any in Western Europe. Danes in general speak good English. They don't share the official French antipathy to it, and they imbibe American pop-culture on a par with anyone. But below the surface, Danish social norms and language (spoken virtually nowhere else) are relatively impenetrable, and Danes exhibit a lot of traits that run very much counter to the codes of behaviour common in America and Britain, for example. Imagine a country where there is virtually no such thing as a political sex scandal, and where sexual preference or gender is hardly ever an issue in public life. Imagine a country where the tabloids treat the royal family with kid gloves, where people *want* their sky-high tax rate maintained, and where even the right of extremists to express their opinion is considered sacred.

Whether the Danish character is imprinted more by a progressive liberalism or a sense of blasé is open to debate, but in any case it can safely be said this is no scandal culture when compared to the likes of the American or British models. One the other hand, to call it a free and open society would be hotly disputed by those – including many Danes – who see it as a cloistered and close-minded culture where everyone 'knows his place'.

Lars von Trier, the classic Dane in many respects, is a product of these ambiguities. It is within this culture that the famously home-bound director functions and searches for inspiration and themes, themes that often end up somehow connected with his childhood. It is therefore essential to tell the story from a Danish perspective, and to shoot it in CinemaScope, so to speak – to consider his films within the wider context of their origins.

Contradictions and paradoxes crop up throughout the story and I can't imagine there are any neat answers to them. How, for example, can you be a rebel when your parents never set any rules to rebel against? How can you rebel against the Danish film establishment when from practically your very first student film you've been acclaimed a genius, the saviour of Danish film come to earth ... and when today you *are* the Danish film establishment? Why do you take so many chances when your whole life is a desperate search for security? How can you be provocative when you come from a country so easy-going that nobody can be provoked? How can such an apparently temperamental and dysfunctional artist make so many of what have turned out to be brilliant business decisions?

One
The Early Years

Childhood

The lives of Lars von Trier's parents were, like most of those of their generation, deeply affected by World War II.

Denmark was occupied in 1940 by the Germans without a great deal of
bloodshed, and thereafter, generally put, the country as a whole didn't cover
itself in glory in regards to its resistance to the Nazis. But there was a resistance movement, and Lars von Trier's mother, Inger Høst, twenty-five years
old when Denmark capitulated, was a member of it.

The daughter of civil servants, Inger became a member of the Danish
Communist Party in her youth and during the Occupation became involved
in the publishing and distribution of illegal periodicals. This earned her a
place on the Germans' list of those to be executed. She fled across the
Øresund Strait to safety in neutral Sweden in the autumn of 1943, at the
same time that Danish Jews were also secretly being evacuated en masse to
the same destination.

It was in Sweden that she met her husband-to-be, Ulf Trier, a tall man
with bushy eyebrows who was in his mid-thirties. Ulf, of partial Jewish heritage, had also been forced to escape to Sweden. They were married and
returned to Denmark after Liberation Day, 4 May 1945.

In December 1945, they had a son whom they named Ole. At that point
the family lived in Fuglebakke-Kvarteret, a middle-class neighbourhood of
modest brick terraces on the outskirts of Copenhagen that Danes would
term a suburb.

Ulf, a staunch social democrat, had received a Masters degree in political economics and would go on to spend his working life as a civil servant in
the Social Ministry. Inger Høst, a self-confident and independent woman,
who kept her maiden name after marriage – very rare at the time – also

earned a Masters in the same field, and in 1951 found employment in the Social Ministry as an office supervisor.

On 30 April 1956, Ulf and Inger had their second son, and they named him Lars. Lars Trier.

By now they had moved to a rural, suburban village north of Copenhagen called Lundtofte, about three kilometres outside the market town of Lyngby. Their new home was a two-storey brick villa on Islandsvej (Iceland Street) in a nice, wooded residential quarter, literally a stone's throw from Ørholm Station. It was not really a 'station' at all, but rather an open-air stop on the regional train service that served the more sparsely populated districts outside Copenhagen.

Across the tracks from Lars' childhood home lay Ravneholm woods, a wilderness area laced with streams and ponds which had been nicknamed 'little Switzerland' in a fit of civic exaggeration. It was here in these leafy, pastoral environs – far removed from any hint of the grimy urban squalor that characterised the Vesterbro or Nørrebro neighbourhoods of Copenhagen, about forty minutes away by train – that Lars grew up. And it was here he would return later in life when seeking spiritual solace and creative inspiration. The area was not 'old money' but it did have upper-class insinuations and represented the better life that those with good jobs could expect in a still very much strapped postwar Denmark.

The Trier household was a typical civil servant's home. It had books, art, a piano. The overall atmosphere was one of acquired progressiveness. A sense of liberalism and tolerance prevailed alongside a pronounced distaste for the sentimental or vulgar excesses of popular junk culture. Ulf was as far from an Orthodox or practising Jew as one could get, and the progressive-humanist philosophy both parents subscribed to was devoid of any religious overtones.

Lars unfailingly uses the term 'cultural radicalism' when he describes his upbringing, and it is a term with very specific inferences in the context of postwar Danish society. Cultural radicals were a certain kind of people. They went in for jazz and classical music, not schmaltzy, popular ballads or Sunday morning radio sing-alongs. They preferred to take their vacations in Paris rather than driving the autobahns of Europe with a camping trailer, a popular pursuit of 'average' Danes in the late 1950s and early 60s. They would go to the theatre, to the opera and to films, but only *good* films. Their favourite painters included the likes of Asger Jorn and Picasso. One would never find kitsch exotica or mass-produced paintings of clowns, babies or cute puppies hanging on their walls. In regard to literature, well-known Danish authors like Hans Scherfig, Otto Gelsted and Hans Kirk were read by cultural radicals; in fact, Inger knew these writers personally and they were occasional visitors to the Trier home. Solid Danish-design furniture was in, wall-to-wall carpeting and television was out (although they might deign to own the latter). Children were to be spared from the old-fashioned methods of discipline, and let in on the complexities of life. They were to be dealt with honestly. This was a new age.

It was people like Inger and Ulf, committed welfare-state bureaucrats, who in the 1950s would plan and implement the social reforms that set the liberal, progressive tone of Danish society in the 60s and 70s.

Ulf, forty-nine years of age when Lars was born, was an 'old' father and not the type to kick a football around with his son, yet Lars was very fond of him. Ulf was a practical joker and played the clown to entertain the boy. But it was his mother who dominated the atmosphere of the home. A strong-willed and self-assured woman, she was at the same time committedly *laissez-faire* when it came to disciplining or setting rules for young Lars. It was left to the boy to decide if he needed to go to the dentist, whether he should do his homework and when he ought to go to bed.

These extraordinary freedoms produced a child who felt anything but free, burdened as he was with the heavy responsibility of making all his own decisions, of having to instantly be a grown up. On top of it all, he felt a duty to the whole planet. 'I was very much afraid of the atom bomb. Every single night before I went to sleep I would engage in a mass of rituals to save the world.'[1]

On a spiritual level, he was denied many of the fantasies young children take refuge in.

My parents were eager to tell me that Santa Claus didn't exist. When everything must be so explainable and open, it is hard to be a child. It was only as an adult

that I could permit myself the luxury of believing in Santa Claus. I was taught
there was no deeper meaning to be found in existence. When one is dead, one is
dead. A person is just a pile of molecules.[2]

To make matters worse, Lars was sent to Lundtofte School, a place that in his
opinion was very strict and old-fashioned, even for that time. School routine consisted of standing in eternal lines, moving in lock-step and sitting
down on cue. One needed to get permission for everything, even going to
the toilet. He was fond of gazing out the window.

> Every single day I sat there and hoped I would become a gardener, since I could
> usually see two gardeners out there weeding. I was convinced that it must be the
> luckiest thing in the world to be able to do that. They did exactly as they wanted
> while I sat there and suffered.[3]

This collision between a home-life with no borders and a school life with
too many was fairly traumatic for him. On top of it he was often bullied and
harassed at school. He was not into sports, he was not a physical boy in that
sense. He attempted to be a Boy Scout but without success. Considered
something of a 'problem child' as he progressed through the grades, he was
sent to a psychologist on a number of occasions. A consensus emerged that
he had 'adjustment difficulties'.

As an adult, in the company of journalists, he would often speculate on
the effects that such an angst-ridden childhood had on his personal and
creative development. Lacking discipline at home and hating the type he got
at school, he had to make his own games, form his own rules and create his
own inner discipline. 'This shows in the amazing work discipline I have,' he
would reflect. 'I work the whole time ... the positive thing I got from this situation was a strong belief in my own creativity – almost like a gift given to
me at the cradle.'[4]

For her part, his mother did what she could to cultivate creative instincts
in her son, praising him to the heavens every time he drew a line on a piece
of paper. At the age of seven he even dictated a little crime novel which his
parents transcribed.

Earliest film-making

At about ten, Lars got his hands on his mother's little Elmo standard-8 movie camera. He was immediately fascinated by all the mechanical possibilities. It could run backwards and be adjusted to different speeds, and you could take single shots, and double-exposures by reversing the film and running it twice through the camera. It was a very basic mechanical challenge he took to eagerly. It was a fascinating play toy.

His uncle, Børge Høst, who was about forty at the time, played a more active role in encouraging his interest in film. Høst had, in 1945, co-founded the Copenhagen Filmstudio (film club), and in 1956 had helped to establish the Union of Danish Film Directors. By the mid-60s, he had directed a number of highly regarded documentaries and short films on topics as diverse as nuclear science, Islam and the historic Danish frigate, *Jutland*. He was involved in film on just about every level, as a teacher, a director, a technician and a bureaucrat.

He shared with Lars what enthusiasm and experience a ten year old could absorb, and he gave him some of the raw goods as well: an old film splicer and a stack of old 16mm prints that Lars could mess about with and cut up.

Lars converted a little shack in the garden into a makeshift film studio where he began to cut and edit and manipulate film and get a feel for its physical properties. He coloured black-and-white film by hand and experimented with colour dyes. When other boys his age dreamed of getting a bicycle or a BB gun, he wanted a real editing table. Instead of building a tree house, he dreamed of building a camera crane. Considering his natural affinity for mechanical tasks, given the component parts, he just might have done it.

One of his first films was a little found-footage item he constructed from some loose reels his uncle had given him. He took a documentary about cockroaches and some footage from Dreyer's *The Passion of Joan of Arc* (1927) (the scene where she is being interrogated by the inquisitors) and spliced them together in a cross-cut montage, and then he hand-coloured some of the pictures.

At eleven he made a primitive 8mm animation film, entitled *Turen Til Squashland* (*The Trip to Squashland*). Made by stop-motion, the piece was barely two minutes in length but all considered was quite an accomplished piece of work.

In 1968, at twelve years of age, Lars answered a notice in a local paper that was advertising for child actors to participate in a youth-oriented TV series. 'He presented himself and explained that he could do this and that,' recalled the director, Thomas Winding, many years later.

> He was small, frail, nervous and very 'with it' ... he was grown in many of the ways that some children are, for both the good and bad. He was in control of his own life and didn't trust anybody. He was not particularly charming, but a good and focused boy. He had an incredibly good feeling for pictures – where he should stand in the picture and how it would look. One of the requirements was that he must be able to ride a horse. All of it he could do well, he assured us.[5]

He got the part.

The four-part series, entitled *Secret Summer*, was a Danish-Swedish co-production shot in the Lyngby environs that summer. The plot dealt with two somewhat neglected kids who find themselves together on a boring summer vacation. The boy, Lars – played by Lars – is sullen and contrary, particularly towards his strict father, played by the twenty-eight-year-old Jens Okking. Then he meets Maria, a fanciful girl who tries to pull his leg by telling him that she is involved in a spy case. She was played by a Swedish girl named Maria Edström who coincidentally would go on to become one of Sweden's top film critics.

The shooting went well enough, and Lars even filmed a bit on the set with his S-8 camera. But it quickly became clear that he could not ride a horse. In fact he was rather scared of them. That caused problems.

The day the first episode aired, on 4 January 1969, the Danish daily, *Aktuelt*, ran an article on the show which included a still from the series: a reticent looking Lars astride a bicycle. He wore a mop-top hairstyle, something akin to a Beatles cut. (No doubt getting a haircut was one of the last things his parents ever forced him to do.) Reporter, Lars Hoffman, wrote that his schoolmates teased him for becoming a 'movie star', but Lars claimed he didn't care. 'I'm the one who earned the money, and I got free from school for three weeks while we filmed.'[6]

He was paid 3,000 kroner for his work in *Secret Summer*. He spent the money on an electric organ that he planned to use for the music in his forthcoming films. Would this film-crazy kid become an actor, asked Hoffman? 'That I don't know, but surely I will have something to do with film.'

That same year (1968) he made a film entitled *Nat, Skat* about a bank robbery. The title is word play which translates both as *Good Night, Dear* and *Night Treasure*. The following year he made two more films, *En Røvsyg Oplevelse* (*A Dead Boring Experience*), which was a drama dealing with everyday subject matter, and a fragment entitled, *Et Skakspil* (*A Chess Game*). All three of these films were 8mm and approximately a minute in length.

He followed these up with a somewhat more ambitious 8mm-sound film in 1970, the seven-minute *Hvorfor Flygte Fra Det Du Ved Du Ikke Kan Flygte Fra? Fordi Du Er En Kujon* (*Why Try to Escape From That Which You Know You Can't Escape? – Because You Are a Coward*). The plot kicks off in dramatic fashion: a boy is run over by a truck. A second boy sees what has happened but runs away in fright, down along a steep stairway and on into the woods, to a stream where he swims away in panic. Meanwhile we see the dead boy lying on the sidewalk with his head swathed in mummy-style bandages, and – in a mystic touch – surrounded by candles burning on the paving stones. We hear a priest praying as he rises up, pursues and catches the fleeing boy. Lars' pals played the parts, as per any other film that he made that required actors after a fashion. It was a way for Lars to be social and in control of the game. Among his small circle of friends, he was the one who usually decided what they would do and how they would do it.

School continued to be a torment for the boy, and in 1970, after being officially registered for the start of seventh grade, his name was abruptly deleted. He had dropped out, from all evidence on his own decision.

At least now he had more time to dedicate to reading, drawing and to what would constitute his final 8mm production: *En Blomst* (*A Flower*, circa 1971), a seven-minute black-and-white sound film. The plot is fairly basic: a boy finds a flower bulb in a ditch where construction work threatens to kill it. He plants it out in nature where it flourishes and grows into a flower. One day when the boy goes out to take a look at it, a warplane streaks across the sky and crashes in a great explosion. The boy lies lifeless and bleeding on

the ground, and by the side of him is the flower, broken. A hallelujah chorus sounds.

In the summer of 1972, sixteen-year-old Lars visited his uncle's family
in Dar Es Salaam, Tanzania, where Børge taught at a film school. This has (to
date) remained the only trip he ever made outside Europe.

In the autumn of 1973 he (or perhaps his parents) figured it was time to
get his proper education over and done with, and he enrolled at the Virum
Statsskole in HF.[7] After a couple months, however, he either dropped out or
was kicked out, perceived by the teachers to be a difficult and arrogant
young man constantly in opposition. Years later he would admit as much,
that he was utterly impossible and neurotic in these school settings.

After this he did various odd jobs. He spent some time working with a
crew that laid concrete floors and as a messenger boy in his mother's office.
He was rejected for military service – obligatory in Denmark – on grounds
of his earlier psychological problems. At this point his parents must have
been wondering what would ever become of him.

About 1974 he began to paint in earnest, developing what might be
termed a hyper-realistic style inspired in large part by Edvard Munch whom
he was much taken with. He sent some paintings to Den Frie Udstilling (the
Free Exhibition),[8] but they were not accepted.

His self-portrait from 1975 is rendered in cold greys and blacks that
evoke a morbid and haunted feel. Colour is selectively limited to the blue in
the eyes and the red of the blood that runs in a single long drop out of the
corner of the mouth. The hair is grown long in front and drawn behind the
ears except for an unkempt strand that dangles casually down, a touch of
studied dishevelment. It was the look he was cultivating himself at the time.

His new look also included a tendency to dress in long coats and scarves,
a uniform which, when draped over his tall, thin frame and accented by the
riding boots he had taken to wearing, resonated with vague overtones of a
decadent, almost fascist elitism. It was no doubt something of a rebellion
against his dyed-in-the-wool social democratic parents.

1975 was a busy if not very successful year for Lars, a year of lots of output and effort met by lots of rejection. He tried to get accepted into the Art
Academy, the Journalist School, the National Theatre School and the Film

School where his uncle had even been a teacher – all without luck. He sent a novel-length manuscript, *Bag Fornedrelsens Porte* (*Behind the Gates of Degradation*), out to publishers. It was also rejected.

He made another attempt to complete his education and in 1976 he took all the HF final exams as a privatist (a student educated at home or outside the normal school structure). He passed. 'It was incredibly easy,' he later recalled, 'you only had to know the rules, then you could just read up for the HF exam in a week. I passed, but only just.'[9]

University

In September of 1976, at the age of twenty, Lars enrolled in the film department at Copenhagen University. He was already an avid film buff prior to this, familiar with whole slabs of classic film history with an accent on the European masters. While American films were now much in vogue among his mates, he was far more passionately taken with European filmic traditions such as neo-realism. His fellow students as well as his teachers were impressed by what he already knew, although as a person they found him inscrutable: distant yet passionate, ironic, yet sincere. Not an easy person to get to know.

Despite what one might assume were his attempts to provoke his parents with the vaguely fascist/elitist style of dress he favoured prior to admittance to university, politically he had always been a communist after his mother's lead, a DKU-er (member of the Danish Communist Youth Party). He demonstrated against the World Bank and even participated as a twelve year old in a demonstration in front of the US embassy, thrilling as a nearby demonstrator hurled a stone at Old Glory.[10] A reflexive anti-Americanism was part-and-parcel of the world-view he had grown up with, and which the 68-ers (as they were known in Denmark) – student radicals or hippies – had bequeathed to his generation. But here at university, in this heavily politicised/leftist environment, he got what he termed a 'A KAP overdose'[11] (Kommunistisk Arbejderparti – Communist Workers' Party), became determinedly apolitical and began to go around in a lounge suit and tie as a kind of new provocation.

While he held himself at arm's length from theory and analysis, he still apparently grasped the issues in other ways. He claims he never opened a book the whole time he was there, and that when he wasn't working on one of his own films or chatting with his favourite teacher, Martin Drouzy, he was bored. Drouzy, a fascinating character in his own right, had been a Dominican monk in France before moving to Denmark in 1953 and finding work as a film critic. In 1972, he became a teacher in the University's film department which was established in 1967. He published a book on Buñuel and taught classes on Bergman, but his burning passion was for the work of Carl Th. Dreyer. With his heavily French-accented Danish, and an engaging manner that was at once humorous, frank and subversive, he became well known and liked by everyone in the Danish film milieu, and there is no doubt that he had a profound influence on Trier. There can also be no doubt that if they talked at any length, Trier certainly had to open a few books to keep up with him.

Early on at university, Trier made contact with Film Group 16. Formed in 1964 to produce 16mm films and spread the philosophy of personal, experimental film-making, they had, by the time Trier contacted them in 1976, turned into more of a discussion group, but they still had their equipment.

They met to decide whether Trier could join them and by that get access to their hardware. There was some opposition to the idea, but he was accepted. It was primarily with and through them that he made his two university films. They would form the bulk of his cast and crew. He also persuaded a teacher or two to act in these productions, although the films had no official connection with the University.

Film-making at university

Film Group 16 functioned as a classic collective: they would meet to talk about proposed films as a group, what they were about and how they were going to be made. But Trier's two films were never discussed. He was not about to 'discuss' his films. He knew what he wanted. Period.

His first, *The Orchid Gardener*, made in 1977, was financed by various odd jobs he did, such as mowing lawns and working as a projectionist at the Klaptræet cinema. His mother also threw in some money. He additionally worked for a spell as a labourer at the F-16 airline hangar in Værløse. Apart from the several part-time jobs he held, this was virtually the only 'real' job he ever had, that is to say the only job outside the film world.

The Orchid Gardener was about an emotionally dysfunctional, creatively blocked painter who suffered from an overwhelming angst. Trier played the lead, Victor Marse, a Jew with a typically long nose. The film dealt with Marse's problems with identity, particularly sexual identity. Marse had to dress up in various disguises (as a Nazi and a woman, for example) in an effort to relate to the love of his life, Eliza. Unable to connect with her either sadistically or affectionately, he instead goes out to abuse a little girl who is pushing her doll carriage. The viewer only sees Marse buttoning up his trousers.

Marse's utter failure in life (and art) leaves him sprawled naked on the floor in front of a canvas marked only by his bloody hand prints. He finally abandons hope of connecting with people and connects instead with his orchids, as a gardener (played by Drouzy). The very same occupation that held out the promise of escape and peace not so many years ago to a grade-school-bound Trier.

This was the first appearance of the somewhat stereotypical Jewish characters that would crop up in his early films. As he would say a few years later, 'I am very taken with my Jewish background. Jewishness has something to do with both suffering and historical consciousness which I miss so much in modern art. People have left their roots, their religion behind.'[12]

After *The Orchid Gardener*, Film Group 16 more or less disbanded although it would regroup two years later in fragmentary form to help him make his next film, the thirty-one-minute *Menthe – La Bienheureuse* (*Menthe – The Blissful*), a kind of Marguerite Duras-inspired adaptation of *The Story of O.*, which he shot in French in 1979.

The film takes place almost exclusively in a barren white-walled room that is supposed to be the inner-sanctum of a monastery. Two women are present in the room – Menthe and her mistress, who is the dominant partner in this sado-masochistic relationship and whose voice narrates the film. She tries to persuade Menthe to travel south with her to warmth. She attempts to manipulate her with the recollection of shared memories, many of which are of a sexual nature. The film is full of symbolic images, such as a black snake which slithers across a white sheet. It ends when an older woman comes to the cloister and leaves with Menthe. A pair of hands open an envelope and take a letter out: Menthe herein explains in terms of her religious faith why she must leave.

'That film was more of a study in style, because I'd seen too much Marguerite Duras,' Trier would later comment.[13]

These two films were shown to a small clutch of acquaintances and participants – his first 'public', albeit non-commercial, screenings. They were considered by some the attempts of a fledgling film-maker to find an aesthetic, and by others to be the expressions of a distressed and neurotic young man. They made virtually no impact in a wider sense, but some within the close-knit Danish film scene were starting to pay attention to this unusual fellow.

The film-maker himself looks back fondly at these primitive early efforts.

> I always tell young people that it is very, very important to show your ignorance, to make a fool of yourself at the start. Most of the directors that are worth seeing today made fools of themselves at the start, and those are some of the most interesting films to see because when one makes a fool of oneself, that's because one bares or exposes oneself ... the more skilled a director becomes, the better one becomes at controlling oneself. 'A little bit but not too much.' But it is in these uncontrolled and exposed films that one finds the essential core of what that director is all about. A director can become so good at his craft that his films become completely boring to watch.[14]

Film School

After three years at university, Trier again applied for admission to the Danish Film School. Founded in 1966 with an accent more on broad-based artistic development than on the technical trades, it was, in its first years, perceived to be somewhat adrift, lacking leadership and vision.[15] In 1975, Henning Camre, who had been director of cinematography on many of the central works of 70s Danish cinema, was appointed headmaster, and the school became more professionally oriented and gradually began to achieve a reputation as one of the best film schools in Europe.[16]

Students were to concentrate largely on a single craft: directing, scriptwriting, cinematography, sound, producing or editing. Each speciality was considered a 'line' that the student would follow throughout the three-year duration of his or her enrolment. Trier applied for admission to the directors' line. Normally at that time only four new students were admitted every year to each line, making it difficult to gain entry to the school. In Trier's year, however, eight students were admitted to the directors' line as a kind of experiment.

This time Trier had a 'real' film to bring along to the application inter-view – *The Orchid Gardener* (*Menthe* was not yet completed). It made a clear impression on the selection committee, which, in addition to Camre, included Ulla Ryum, who taught dramaturgy, Mogens Rukov, who was to found the manuscript department, and Anne Wivel, the student represen-tative. Trier was both shy *and* self-confident during the interview, making it clear that he had not come so that they could pass judgment on him, but rather so that he could see if he would choose to go there.

Part of the application procedure consisted of giving each applicant a 16mm camera with five minutes of film. They then had two hours to go out and make a short film edited 'in camera'. To make best use of the limited time, the other applicants went around in the nearby vicinity of Christianshavn, while Trier went off to the well-heeled environs of Rungsted and shot his little film there – a voyeuristic, spy-like exploration of the accoutrements of the rich world, where in the midst of horse stables, villas and luxury cars one also spies a crumpled porno magazine on the ground. Trier's test film was not necessarily better than those of the other applicants, but it did look different.[17]

Trier was accepted. He began in the autumn of 1979.

The old white-painted brick compound that housed the Film School was also the site of the Danish Film Institute and Film Museum. They shared some facilities as well as an old cobblestone courtyard. Like the University, the compound was located on Amager, a large island separated from Copenhagen proper by the main shipping channel.

Unlike most of his fellow students, Trier had already been making films for a few years and was very focused and motivated right from the start. It was clear to the teaching staff and the other students that he definitely had talent of some sort, but he was hard to figure out. He was a bundle of contradictions: shy but also provocative, respectful towards his chosen craft but also colossally self-confident. He was at once outspoken, stuck-up and shy.[18] Some simply found him to be arrogant and exclusive. And his apparent obsession for not only German Expressionism but for all extremes of German culture and history was not, so to say, politically correct at that time in that milieu.

The school was organised in such a way that the students were obliged to work together, to cooperate and assumedly cultivate a spirit of solidarity. This was in line with the traditional belief in the importance of 'the group' which is so central to Danish society.[19] In fact one of the most serious charges that can be levelled in the workplace is that one can't get along with one's co-workers. This was also the end of the 1970s when so much was done in collectives, with lots of discussion and debate. How could a loner like Trier thrive in such an environment? Well, in any case, he survived. On the other hand, to infer he was the lone disruptive egotist at the school would be misleading inasmuch as the film world, and by extension the Film School, attracted those with big egos and big plans. His fellow students were not abnormally reticent themselves.

Trier now began to make some sporadic impressions on the Danish film establishment. In the summer of 1980, he found work as a trainee on the set of a Nils Malmros film, *Kundskabens Træ* (*The Tree of Knowledge*). He didn't demonstrate particular eagerness, remembers Malmros, but at least he had access to a Volkswagen bus that they needed. A film journalist, Morten Piil, recalled chatting with Trier on the set.[20] Piil had also previously been a consultant with the Danish Film Institute from 1975–7, a job that entailed the granting of development and production funding to specific directors.[21] Piil found Trier's views on the state of Danish film to be remarkably straightforward. 'Who had I chosen to give subsidies to when I had been a consultant?', he asked. Jørgen Leth and Nils Malmros. OK, but who else? X and Y ... ? They got the finger very forcefully. A very conceited fellow, I thought.'

At this point the unknown Trier made a glancing impression on another Danish film-maker, Christian Braad Thomsen, when he visited the Film School to give a guest-lecture in 1981.

> As I lectured, I noticed a student sat there with a strangely transported or fascinated smile, which at first glance could seem flattering. Then I discovered he had a Walkman on and was listening to something completely different. I thought in irritation that such an arrogant bloke would hardly get far in the film world.[22]

Trier's social behaviour was characterised by this same sort of aloofness, to pick a positive adjective for it. Journalist Jørgen Ullerup years later recalled a visit by young Trier to one of the many wild parties thrown by his collective which was located on Vesterbrogade in Copenhagen. 'He came in without a word and sat himself down by a big cupboard in the corner of the room and sat there like a statue with a gloomy gaze. In the middle of the night he got up and left again without a word.'[23]

He was not widely known as a funny guy in those days. He seemed to dwell on another plane of reality. One of his close friends at the school, fellow director-line student Åke Sandgren, recalled:

> Already at that time he had a strong and stubborn personality … The rest of us knew we would somehow make films. *He* already knew what kind of a filmic universe he would create. He had no wall between the idea and the practical implementation. He had no fear of making decisions.[24]

Trier's stubborn streak could grate on the teachers. 'I believe first and foremost that he used the school as a sparring partner,' recalled one of them, Mr Gert Fredholm. Fredholm remembered that Trier managed to get resources and support from the School for his own films, underway at the time. It was kind of hushed-up as it was quite unusual and could smack of favouritism, 'but he was so energetic, it was hard to refuse him'.[25]

One evening Fredholm tried to close up an editing suite where a bunch of students were working late, Trier among them. They protested so energetically that finally the teachers got fed up. Fredholm accused them of behaving like the gentry of Sealand.[26] They might all just as well have 'von' for a middle name, he added angrily.

Hence was born Lars von Trier.

When one of his school productions was shown soon after, 'Lars von Trier' appeared on the bill. 'We didn't really know if he was in jest or not,' recalled one of his mates. 'One could never be sure about Lars.'[27] This new moniker quite properly suited his theatrical sense of posed Germanic elitism and self-invention. It also rang smartly of the fake royalty that jazz musicians like Duke Ellington and Count Basie, and film-makers like Joseph von Sternberg and Erich von Stroheim, had draped themselves with.

This was the story that went around. On the other hand, one of his paintings from 1975 is signed 'von Trier', so ... ?

If von Trier was using the school as a sparring partner, then the guy at the receiving end of most of his swings was headmaster, Camre, who, to begin with, 'was not popular with the students, and didn't try to be', as his good friend, the Danish director, Jørgen Leth would later remember.[28] Provocations on von Trier's part ranged from trying to get Camre to allow him to make a porno film as a school project to his refusal to work with fellow student and feminist, Bente Clod, from the manuscript line, pursuant to a plan that the directors would shoot films written by manuscript students. Logical enough, but von Trier refused to work with her. Camre was furious and threatened to throw him out of the School. Some say Camre was constantly on the brink of throwing him out.[29]

On the other hand, Camre at least occasionally defended von Trier as an artist. Morten Piil recalled that after a screening of one of von Trier's student films, where the audience almost died of laughter, Camre took it with elevated calm: 'This Trier works with a goal-oriented consciousness which will eventually find a serviceable mode of expression. Wait and see.'[30] Camre would later recall being impressed by von Trier's initiative and his ability to get others in motion as well as himself, and denied that he was either wild or unpredictable.[31]

Two teachers at the Film School with whom von Trier had a particularly good relationship were Mogens Rukov and Ulla Ryum, both of whom had sat on the selection committee that had approved his application for admission. They assisted him in various ways and helped support his projects, and Rukov has continued to advise on his scripts to this day.

Carl Th. Dreyer

Von Trier continued to faithfully attend screenings at the Danish Film
Museum. It was not hard to get to since the cinema was located in the same
cobblestone courtyard as the Film School, which also used the room for lec-
tures and screenings. It was here in this cinema (seating around 150) that
von Trier developed his great and enduring enthusiasm for the films of Carl
Th. Dreyer.

What he loved about Dreyer was 'his very beautiful, pure-bred style
which has a little Hammershøi[32] in it … and the minimalist themes and
dialogue'.[33] But he was also fascinated with the man himself, proclaimed a
genius around the world but misunderstood and unappreciated in
Denmark, punished for leaving the country in the early 1930s, going to Paris
and thinking he was somebody. Thereafter upon his return in 1934, broke
and disillusioned, he was obliged to work as a beat reporter penning daily
'life in the city' columns. For the last thirty-two years of his life, from 1936
until his death in 1968, he lived with his family in a very modest two-and-
a-half room flat in the quiet Copenhagen neighbourhood of Frederiksberg,

Carl Th. Dreyer (r) on
the set of his last
film, *Gertrud* (1964).
Gertrud was a
favourite of von Trier's
which he often chose
when asked to
present a 'director's
choice'

and slept on a fold-out bed.[34] Von Trier would refer to him often over the
years. 'I respect him because he always went against the spirit of the times.
I have a lot of respect for rebels, and I think he was certainly that. Or, if you
will, a martyr. To a high degree he suffered prejudice.'

Dreyer was quite proud that his style varied from film to film. He once
enthused:

> A Danish critic said to me one day that 'I have the impression that there are at
> least six of your films which separate themselves completely from each other.'
> That touched me, for that is exactly what I am attempting to do – to find a style
> which is perfect for the individual film ... that atmosphere, that treatment, the
> people and the topic.[35]

This would also become von Trier's *modus operandi*.

Dreyer would remain an inspiration, a hero, a role-model and a kind of
indefinable mystical figure for von Trier. During work on a TV adaptation of
the never-filmed Dreyer script, *Medea*, in 1988, von Trier claimed to have a
telepathic connection with him. He even claimed his golden retriever,
Kajsa, was also in spiritual contact with Dreyer and would howl at the mere
mention of his name.[36] He would acquire the tuxedo Dreyer had originally
purchased in Paris in 1926 during pre-production on *The Passion of Joan of
Arc*, and wear it on special occasions, as if to literally drape himself in the
mantle of his predecessor's greatness. He cast some of Dreyer's old actors,
and he employed Dreyer's old cameraman – even wanting him to use the
same camera he used on Dreyer's films.

Film School productions

Four short video films and a four-minute documentary, *Lolita*, also shot on
video, made in 1979 and 1980, constitute von Trier's first practical exercises
at the School. Neither of the first two fictional video productions are titled.

Video Production 1 is a three-part work that deals with death and is the
most accomplished of these early video pieces. Scene one shows a close-up
of an apparently dead woman's face as voice-over narration gives an inven-
tory of the various outward indications of death (rigor mortis, etc.) with scientific dispassion. Scene two is subtitled 'I See Myself a Couple of Meters

Away', in reference to the out-of-body experience reported by those who have almost died. The main scene is shot from a bird's-eye view down on a crumpled automobile. The driver is dead behind the wheel. Another person tries to extinguish the fire under the hood. Hands from heaven reach down and try to pull the dead man up. Family photos, apparently from the dead man's childhood, shimmer past. In scene three we are back gazing upon the image of the female face. In sombre tones the scientific voice talks about putrefaction and how the processes of death re-introduce the corporeal remains back into the eternal cycle of nature. Eventually we realise that the girl in the picture is not dead but just leaning her head back to enjoy the sun at a bathing spot.

Video Production 2 takes place in the waiting rooms of an airport. We see a panorama of planes in their berths, giving the expectation of movement, of travel. The film is told in voice-over narration via the monologue of a girl who has arranged to meet a male friend here. He hasn't shown up yet. The girl's monologue develops into a somewhat existential reflection on how one leaves a trace in the world. She compares graffiti with fossils, and so forth. She waits. He never shows up. The meeting was necessary for her to confirm her existence. 'When nobody meets you, you might as well be somewhere else,' she concludes.

In Video Production 3, *Masjas Anden Rejse* (*Masja's Second Journey*), a couple prepare for their second honeymoon. The first was ruined by an awful experience with the flight which left the woman, Masja, with a fear of flying. She believes she has now overcome this fear because she has handed over responsibility for herself, and therefore also her phobias, to her husband. But in sado-masochistic fashion her husband uses the memory of her fear to force her out of her sense of security and to re-experience the erotic connection they had back when they were first wed.

Video Production 4, *De To Gamle Mænd, Med Alt For Unge Koner* (*Two Old Men With Wives That Are All Too Young*), begins with a young man and a young woman sitting in the back seats of separate cars which drive along a highway. At an intersection the two cars stop and the fellow entices the girl to roll her window down. She asks him to tell her a story. He tells her the story of the two old men with wives that are all too young, a well-known erotic fable wherein two old men in Renaissance Italy fail to deflower their lovely young brides, but through a screwball mix-up manage to make love to each other's wives. The story over, the man and the woman touch each other's lips with their fingers before their cars begin to drive off again, the man just able to bequeath to her a toothbrush before they turn off in different directions.

In the documentary exercise, entitled *Lolita*, von Trier, camera in hand, follows a number of little girls around as they make their way to school. The result is a no doubt intentionally exaggerated tribute to the art of voyeurism. In voice-over, the male narrator proclaims his love for all these girls, and states that while they all have different names, they should all properly be called Lolita. He proceeds to test the viewer's sense of decency – or sense of humour – by telling about a girl he saw go between two parked cars and take a pee. Politically correct he still wasn't.

Von Trier would later say that he used most of his time at the Film School to work himself from the texts over to the pictures. These efforts are apparent even here in his earliest Film School exercises, primitive as they may be, as he tries to work away from the beginner's technique of telling the story with voice-over narration, to telling the story through an organic interplay between images and dialogue. Perhaps if anything, he worked himself too far over to the pictures.

Nocturne

In 1980 he also shot his first 16mm school project, *Nocturne*, his first official collaboration with Tom Elling and Tómas Gislason, two fellow students he would go on to work with long after they all left the Film School. Elling, at the time in his mid-thirties, had been a painter (in the realistic style) since the early 1970s, and had also worked with video and conceptualist art forms. Gislason, at twenty years of age, was a student on the editing line.

Nocturne deals first and foremost with angst, already a rather well-worn theme for von Trier. A girl is awakened by a nightmare (a man comes crashing through her window) at three in the morning and turns on a lamp. There's something painfully wrong with her eyes … she can't bear the light. The room she lives in is always kept as dark as possible, and in fact the pet bird she used to keep in a cage died because of that. She is also apprehensive about a plane she should catch at six thirty that morning to South America. She can't bear the thought of travelling south into a climate of such bright sunlight. She rings a girlfriend who persuades her to take the flight as planned. It is stiflingly warm. She turns on a fan. At ten past six the first daylight breaks through. The girlfriend has promised to stand outside and watch as the plane passes overhead.

Here one can see hints of the visual style von Trier would utilise in his early feature films. Emphasis is placed almost wholly on the pictures, which are shot in a monochrome tint with colour appearing selectively. The theme was also, not surprisingly, one that von Trier connected to personally. He had a great fear of flying, a fear of travelling, a fear of many things.

Nocturne was selected to compete in the first European Film School Festival in Munich, in 1981, and won the award as the most interesting short film. This was the first prize a student from the Danish Film School had ever won and gave von Trier, Elling and Gislason more freedom to do what they wanted on their next project. To many, this was the proper start of von Trier's career. Unfortunately, the original positive print (there was no negative) is reported to be lost,[37] although a video copy exists.

The Last Detail

Von Trier's next School film, which Elling and Gislason also worked on, was *Den Sidste Detalje (The Last Detail*, 1981). A gangster film shot in 35mm, it came complete with rain, underground parking lots, bleak concrete landscapes and more rain. The doom-haunted atmosphere was further enhanced by the scoring of Alban Berg's *Lulu suite*. The film features the kind of bleak settings von Trier would re-create, albeit with more virtuosity and drama, in later films. In fact this film was not totally von Trier's, the script having being written by a student named Rumle Hammerich pursuant to, as noted, von Trier's refusal to shoot the script by Bente Clod. According to one of Denmark's leading Lars von Trier scholars, Peter Schepelern,[38] von Trier approached the film as an obligation, an exercise, and as such he shouldn't be held totally responsible for the results. As von Trier himself would recall, 'I never encountered a single viewer who didn't die of laughter after having seen it'.[39] 'A stiff-legged, pathetic, hyper-formulaic pastiche which had been laughed out by the school's invited audience,' noted Morten Piil of the film.[40] Like *Nocturne*, it appears to be lost.

Images of a Relief

Von Trier's final Film School production, *Befrielsesbilleder* (*Images of a Relief*),[41] shot in 1982, was his graduate project and was, on the contrary, not a film audiences would laugh at.

Tom Elling shot it and also co-wrote the script with von Trier, while Gislason was back on board as editor. Little noticed was a twenty-nine-year-old walk-on by the name of Niels Vørsel who was not a student at the Film School. Although only three years von Trier's senior, Vørsel had already made something of a name for himself in the avant-garde circles of Copenhagen as the author of three books and a radio play,[42] all of them of a conceptual, experimental nature. He would soon come to form a creative scriptwriting partnership with von Trier which has lasted to this day.

The film, shot in 35mm and running an almost feature-length fifty-seven minutes – highly unusual for a Film School production – was set in the chaotic final days of World War II, shortly after Denmark was liberated on 4 May 1945. To the film von Trier added previously unseen documentary footage of violent street scenes that transpired in Copenhagen in the wake of liberation. We see incidents of brutality and humiliation as citizens beat up stool pigeons and suspected collaborators. He managed to purloin this material from the archives of Danmarks Radio. ('If it happened, it should also be shown,'[43] was his motto.)

The first scene takes place in a ruined factory locale where collaborators and German soldiers have been interred by English troops. The claustrophobic atmosphere reeks of suffering and doom. Many commit suicide with their side-arms, which they have inexplicably been allowed to keep. The protagonist, a German officer by the name of Leo Mandel, attempts suicide but his pistol misfires.

He escapes from the ruined compound and makes his way through the city to the villa where his Danish lover, Esther, lives. She is in the process of hosting a garden party for the victorious Allied soldiers. Leo spies her in the embrace of a black soldier. He makes his presence known to her and she sends the soldier away. They talk. She accuses him of heinous crimes, of participating in the torture of a boy from the liberation movement who had his eyes gouged out. It seems he took no active role in the incident but was present and did nothing to stop it. Nonetheless she offers to hide him in the woods.

The third act takes place as they arrive in the woods. It is early morning and he is in a sentimental mood. He tries to talk with the birds, he recalls his childhood. But there are people in the woods and it quickly becomes clear this is an ambush arranged by Esther. Leo is bound fast, and Esther gouges out one of his eyes in an act of biblical 'eye for an eye' retribution. Now, quite literally, Leo rises to the sky, up over the sunrise. An ascension. A redemption. Esther's tear-stained face is seen reflected in the car's rear window.

Von Trier later claimed that many viewers fainted during the 18 June screening at the Film School, 'because', as he put it, 'I quite on purpose gave no release for the excitement which had been built up. ... I purposely increased the excitement by setting the characters in extreme situations.'[44]

To make a film set during World War II was in and of itself nothing special – there were many Danish films set in this period. But to show sympathy (as many saw it) for a Nazi officer seemed odd, not least in light of his parent's experiences during the War. He knew full well that the film would provoke discomfort in audiences who found themselves in sympathy with the German officer, but he rejected charges that the film had a fascistic viewpoint: 'I have not taken the side of the German officer because he is a Nazi but because he is the loser. ... I permit myself to be fascinated by that which has always fascinated people, among other things, death. War is always a good subject.'[45] As he elaborated in the film's press release, 'Precisely that form of moralising that says, "now we must not let ourselves be fascinated by the War, etc.", I believe is a prison. One must not lay limitations.'

The fact that von Trier's film pronounced no moral judgments on the Nazis was itself a provocative rejection of the accepted wisdom of the time that Nazi characters could only be portrayed in black and white, that they had to be condemned whenever they appeared. He took no moral stance on the issue. And if the film did take a stance, it was, from a Danish perspective, the wrong one. As Anders Bodelsen pointed out, the documentary

Niels Vørsel (far right) in a scene from *Images of a Relief*

footage he used of collaborators being publicly beaten and humiliated made Danes look as though they were 'hateful and thirsting for revenge. Conversely, von Trier seems very taken with the German's beautiful and desperate Götterdämmerung.'[46]

Just another provocation? Probably, but it was more complicated than that, even if von Trier's own brash utterances tended to stress the film's shock effect. Liberation Day in Denmark had really been Judgment Day: passive collaborators and fence-sitters became patriots overnight – old scores were settled and accusations, true and false, were levelled. Five years of pent-up emotions boiled to the surface in a blind frenzy of anger, joy, patriotism and lust for revenge. While today public debate about the sensitive issue of the Occupation in Denmark is wide ranging,[47] in 1982 perceptions of this complicated time conformed to a much more 'official' line: Germans were bad, Danes were good, and the Resistance had been heroic and widespread. Von Trier's attempts, however perhaps half-formed, to

investigate the ambiguous nature of good and evil and guilt and innocence
within the sensitive context of the War, was sure to offend many, particularly his elders.

Images of a Relief – reception

Images of a Relief was again accepted by the European Film School Festival in
Munich in November of 1982. It aroused heated debate among the Festival's
jury members. Opinion on it ran to extremes: some wanted it thrown out of
the Festival and others wanted to give it first prize. The pro camp eventually
carried the day and von Trier won the Festival's 'special award' which was
sponsored by Channel 4 Television, guaranteeing it broadcast in Britain.
And it got the previously mentioned theatrical opening at the Delta Bio in
Copenhagen on 30 June 1982 – the first time a Film School graduate project
had been given commercial exposure. Later it was also bought and broadcast
by Danish TV.

With the opening at Delta Bio, von Trier got his first reviews and they
were decidedly mixed. Many critics praised the film's visual power and
technical polish. 'A nightmare vision which seeks beauty in defeat and decay
and expresses itself with visual poetry,' went a typical review.[48] Yet many
found his message and motivation impossible to decipher amidst 'the abun-
dance of at once obtrusive yet completely hermetically sealed symbolism',[49]
as *Berlingske Tidende (B.T.)* critic, Ebbe Iversen, phrased it. Von Trier was
not the slightest bit interested in narrative clarity, he continued, and his
messages were fuzzily conveyed. He concluded that the film showed that he
could make spooky, surrealistic and extremely expressive pictures, which,
when taken one by one had a kind of magical, possessed intensity, but when
run in sequence become almost unbearably pretentious.

The film contained precious little dialogue or action. Single scenes went
on interminably – actors seemed little more than props in the carefully
composed visual set pieces. Pictures were to be sensed and indulged in, not
just looked at. Pure atmosphere. Aestheticism for aestheticism's sake.

It didn't work, concluded Per Calum in a review headed 'Film School
Pretensions', for *Jyllands-Posten*. To Calum, von Trier's aestheticism was a
goal in and of itself and not a means to convey any point of view, position or

humanity. Giving von Trier a theatrical opening with this film was a 'bjør-
netjeneste' (disservice) he opined. In other words it was nice but dangerous
and did the director himself no favour. He might in the future be encouraged to show more pictures like this to the public. God forbid.

To Anders Bodelsen, the film lacked plausibility, and was 'neither psychologically nor historically convincing ... The film in no way justifies the
bizarre final scene in the woods (where the officer is transported to heaven,
Ed).'[50] Yet he conceded that von Trier had managed to impress. The film
had been made with fantasy and diligence. This young film-maker had
many things to learn, but *Images of a Relief* presented clear evidence that he
possessed a certain talent in spades.

With this film, von Trier had established himself as the Film School's
most promising student, or at least the one getting most attention. He was
already being hailed by some as a genius, the future hope of Danish cinema
and a provocateur supreme. A genius he would still have to prove himself,
but a provocateur he undeniably was, taking, in one of the very first interviews with him (headlined 'Danish Film Is Totally Harmless'), the opportunity to slam the current state of Danish cinema.

> It's so dainty in its style that no one could ever be offended by it. They are
> harmless stories in a harmless style. Only topics which everyone can agree on
> are taken up. Like, for example, *Gummi Tarzan*. 'Ah ... that's a shame for the
> boy' we all say in unison. That is precisely the kind of preconditioned reaction I
> will go against.[51]

Gummi Tarzan (*Rubber Tarzan*), from 1981, was an 'endearing' tale about a
little boy who is teased at school for being a weakling but who eventually
finds strength in his friendship with a nice fellow who operates a construction crane. It won the Bodil, the 'Danish Oscar', and was roundly cheered by
critics and audiences alike. Such a collective outpouring of feel-good
humanism must have set von Trier's teeth on edge. Interestingly, *Gummi
Tarzan* was made by a film-maker he would later work very closely with:
Søren Kraugh-Jacobsen.

His own favourite themes ran to a darker shade: S&M, child-abuse,
autopsy trivia, mass-suicide, eyes being gouged out, and a Nazi officer cast

as a Christ-like figure in a supernatural redemption scene. He would say early in his career that 'a film should be like a stone in one's shoe'.[52] A stone indeed. At this point he was very much the typical young rebel looking to make life uncomfortable for his elders. The extreme subject matter he favoured was born from a desire to examine all the things that had been posted 'off limits' by bourgeois society, as well as to simply provoke and get a physical reaction from viewers. He saw the investigation of taboos as a sign of health, not of a sick mind.

*   *   *

When von Trier departed the Film School in 1982, he was asked what he thought about the place and replied, 'One can say that one never gets any-where because of something, but *in spite of ...* And in that sense the School has functioned brilliantly.'[53] His view of the School would soften somewhat over the years. It would become clear that it was here he honed his style and acquired the tools of the craft. And it was here that he connected with a small circle of collaborators and sympathisers who would contribute to his future film-making in very important ways.

Nocturne and *Images of a Relief* had given his budding career a boost and he entered into his next project, *The Element of Crime*, with diligence and energy. He would make the perfect film. At least he knew he was capable of it.

His core of Film School collaborators were back in their original capac-ities: Elling as cinematographer, Gislason as editor and Åke Sandgren as assistant director. Niels Vørsel was co-writer.

Two
From *The Element of Crime* to *Europa* and Zentropa

The Element of Crime – conception and filming

On 13 September 1982, a seven-page synopsis appeared with the working title, *Folie à deux* – a psychiatric term for a mutually infectious form of insanity which usually develops between two people who live together. The title was soon after changed to *The Last Tourist in Europe*, and finally to *The Element of Crime*.

The plot unfolds as a crime story with a mystical core: Detective Fisher, a European expatriate who has lived in Cairo for well over a decade, returns to a Europe 'sometime in the near future'. He has come back to help solve a difficult case – the sexual murder of a small girl. The Europe he finds is a decayed and rain-swept ruin, a place of gloom and perpetual night. In his quest to find the killer, he employs the radical psychological methods mapped out in the book *The Element of Crime*, which was penned by his old teacher, Osborne. Fisher must immerse himself totally in the psyche of the suspected serial killer, Harry Grey, in order to solve the crime, but he gets sucked in too deeply, with horrifying consequences and a horrifying revelation about who Harry Grey really is.

Von Trier counted *The Asphalt Jungle* (1950) among his favourite films and had a love of *film noir* in general. He described *The Element of Crime* as 'the first film noir shot in colour' – and run through the strainer of German Expressionism, he might have added. A kind of vague 'German-ness' informs the film: while the language is English, the last names and locations are German, the police are 'polizei', etc. For von Trier, Germany *is* Europe in many respects.

The Element of Crime had many similarities to *Images of a Relief*, most obviously its visual style which was conceived around a series of almost

Von Trier, about the
time he was working
on *The Element of
Crime*

freestanding, meticulously composed pictures. Elling and von Trier were
both painters and it showed in the look of the film. Additionally both films
displayed a precision and technical polish that was the result of thorough
storyboarding. This rigorous storyboarding and the meticulous planning of
every shot in advance was symptomatic of von Trier's almost maniacal desire
to control every last detail. Both films also evidenced his attraction to ruined,
nightmarish urban landscapes. Perhaps that was natural for a young man who
had grown up in such beautiful and well-ordered rural surroundings.

On the basis of a script treatment, *The Element of Crime* got manuscript
development support from the DFI upon the recommendation of consultant, Christian Clausen. But Clausen feared that the film was too violent and
extreme to get final funding approval and recommended to von Trier that

the murder of the little girl be changed to some other kind of criminal act, and that the final suicide scene be rewritten. Von Trier refused to change anything and the film still managed to get 3.2 million kroner in support from the DFI in the spring of 1983, although the fact that the film was in English almost caused them to withdraw their support. After all, according to the Film Law of 1972 to receive support, a film had to be shot in Danish and artistic and technical personnel had to be predominately Danish.

Another 1 million kroner was added to the budget by von Trier's producer, Per Holst, a bearded Dane in his mid-forties who had built a reputation for taking chances on daring and artistic films. In 1981 he gave Nils Malmros his proper start with *The Tree of Knowledge* and this same year, 1983, he was producing *Zappa* for Bille August. In 1987 he would go on to produce August's massive breakthrough hit, *Pelle the Conqueror*. However, in the early 1980s all three of these directors were risky investments.

With 4.2 million kroner now in place, another 0.3 million was thrown in by the DFI to cover an unexpectedly long shoot, as the budget topped out at 4.5 million kroner. Due to his meticulous pre-production work, von Trier was able to put 'every penny on the screen', as they say in Hollywood. It was hard for many to believe that he could make such a technically accomplished film for this relative pittance which also had to cover the wages of profesional actors.

He cast most of the main roles with actors he got from the UK, such as Michael Elphick (also known in Denmark for his TV series, *Private Schultz*), Jerold Wells, Me Me Lai and the blind Esmond Knight. Danes filled out the secondary roles.

The British actors made sense since the film was to be shot in English, but there was another reason: The 'professional pride' of the Danish actors, as von Trier sarcastically termed it, would be a hindrance during the shooting. They might demand to know their motivation. 'For me, it's an indication of professionalism that actors follow the director's instructions. It's *his* vision … Danish actors would demand to "understand" their roles. But what is there to understand if the director knows precisely what he must have?'[1]

That von Trier was obsessed with the technical mechanics of film-making and had no concern or affinity for the actors was a perception that would shadow him throughout his career, and it was born here. Several actors later said they felt like marionettes during the shooting. But von Trier also showed himself to be focused and professional, and had a talent for finding inventive solutions to problems that arose during production.

The shooting lasted seven weeks, stretching from September into early November 1983, and took place in all manner of odd locations that he had ferreted out to give the film the appropriate feel of ruin and decay. They shot in the ancient, subterranean dungeons and passageways of Kronborg Castle in Helsingør, in the sewers of Copenhagen, in chalk pits, in abandoned factories and in Trekronerfort, an old fortress out on an island in the Øresund Strait.

Scene from *The Element of Crime*: Fisher on the trail of mass-murderer Harry Grey

Most of the shooting was done at night without use of proper set lighting. The lights they used were long tube-type fluorescent lights, parking-lot lights, and according to von Trier, they exploded when it rained on them. And it rained practically the whole time, a cold autumn rain that made the shoots an ordeal. The use of these lights also contributed to the unique look of the film, which had a gold tint. To provide some atmosphere on the sets and inspire the cast and crew, Wagner music was played. The sets came to acquire the feel of an 'artistic happening',[2] what with Wagner music blasting, lamps exploding, rain pouring down, and all taking place in the middle of the night.

The Element of Crime – reception

It was a real coup when *The Element of Crime* was selected for inclusion 'in competition' at the 1984 Cannes Film Festival. In Danish (and European) film circles, Cannes was the ultimate stamp of approval, and this was the first time since 1975 that a Danish film had been thus selected.[3]

It had been chosen by Festival boss, Gilles Jacob, who ranged the world looking for worthy films. How did he ever hear about the unknown Danish film-maker? No doubt producer Per Holst buttonholed him on the issue, Holst having earlier had both *The Tree of Knowledge* and *Zappa* selected for inclusion in the 'Un Certain Regard' section of the Festival.

Von Trier, Vørsel, Elling and others connected with the film went down to Cannes in May. Von Trier, who would soon drop the 'von' for a while as another 'provocation', cut a rebellious figure in T-shirt, leather jacket and shaven skull. In 1984, before everyone got their head shaved, this was certifiably punk. Vørsel, clad in suit, bow-tie and dark glasses for the film's premiere, was Ying to von Trier's Yang.

Expectations were not originally high for the film, and public response after its premiere at Cannes 'was nothing to shout hurrah about', wrote Morten Piil.[4] 'The public is perplexed,' he noted. Nonetheless, it aroused a sensation in critical circles even if reviews were ultimately mixed.

But what *did* the film mean? The Danish public would by and large be asking the same question when it opened in two theatres in Copenhagen the day after its Cannes premiere. Was it all just an excuse to make some nice-looking pictures, as Trier and Vørsel hinted, or was it all vastly profound?

Von Trier wasn't saying. This was in jarring contrast to most film-makers who obligingly talked their films to death for the sake of good manners and good press, but it was probably a good move. For lack of explanations or even lack of a defence, people were left to wonder. It was perhaps a way of manipulating the press after all. And it was here that some would claim von Trier was creating meaning out of meaninglessness. Surely a director this brash, impolite and self-confident (or was it arrogant?) must be quite profound on some level, even if we didn't quite get it this time.

The evening of the awards came. *The Element of Crime* received the technical prize, while the jury, headed by actor, Dirk Bogarde, ended up giving the coveted Palme d'Or to Wim Wenders for *Paris, Texas* (1984).

In any case von Trier had made a name for himself. His press meetings were full, writers from all over the world wanted to interview him, people craned their necks to see him go by. He was something of a sensation, this odd, vaguely disrespectful fellow from that strange little country up north that had been a blind spot on the international film map for so long. That he didn't win what was arguably the world's top film award was hardly a surprise. He was just thrilled to be here, right?

Hardly.

He was incensed. To von Trier the technical prize was just a poor second-place finish, a shabby consolation given away by a cowardly jury that was afraid to give him the Palme d'Or he rightly deserved for making the best film. Period.

Such behaviour was so very 'un-Danish'. Who did he think he was? Somebody?

Yes, he did think he was somebody, according to at least one of his close collaborators, Tom Elling. 'Even though it was von Trier's film,' Elling would later recall, 'there was a lot of teamwork behind it. There were many of us who felt that the film was also a part of us. But we became completely swept to the side in Cannes.'[5]

Von Trier's suspicion that he had been swindled out of the Palme d'Or was confirmed in his mind several years later when he called up Bogarde to see if he would be interested in playing a part in his new film, *Europa* (1991). Of course he remembered von Trier. And no, he hadn't forgotten *The*

Element of Crime – he had hated it so much he would never forget it! According to von Trier, he thereafter learned that the rest of the jury was prepared to give him the Palme d'Or, but Bogarde despised the film so thoroughly that he threatened to walk out off the jury if they did.[6] And no, Bogarde wasn't interested in acting in any of von Trier's films.

'Unpleasant, Incomprehensible and Unforgettable' headed the review by *B.T.* scribe, Ebbe Iversen, fairly summing up the critical response – a mix of tempered fascination and confusion – that followed in the wake of its domestic premiere on 14 May. The film had its own 'decadent, jarring beauty', said Henning Jørgensen, writing for *Information*, while Bent Mohn of *Politiken* heaped on the adjectives calling the film 'a gift of stylised atmosphere, conjured-up apocalyptic poetry that is smartly obsessed. Delicious anarchy and gruesome splendour.'[7]

Most critics agreed that the film had a unique and compelling visual style, however 'difficult' many found its narrative structure. The fact that it was distinctly 'un-Danish', something very different from the 'black bread' social realism (akin to what might be termed 'kitchen sink' social realism in Britain) that had dominated Danish cinema throughout the 1970s, was cited as a positive. Something for punks and night owls, said reviewer Mogens Dangaard, who predicted a cult following for the film on some level.

If it was something new, that didn't hamper it from wearing its influences on its sleeve, and academically oriented critics had a field day pointing out its links to everything from *The Cabinet of Dr Caligari* (1962) and *The Third Man* (1949) to *Touch of Evil* (1958) and Tarkovsky's *Stalker* (1979), to name but a few. *Mad Max* (1979) and *Blade Runner* (1982) also seemed to have functioned as precursors to the desolate future world the film portrayed. Nonetheless, von Trier seemed to have created something new out of all this. Nobody accused him of theft.

Not that he would have minded. He would always willingly admit that he was influenced by other films and film-makers. He had a million influences floating around in his head, and because of this his films were very filmic. As he once responded to a writer who commented on his lack of experience in the 'real world', 'I have never had any desire to make films which are about reality. My films are very "film".'[8]

A dissenting view was expressed by Johs. H. Christensen of *Kristeligt Dagblad*, who called *The Element of Crime* pompous and posed. Its moral and aesthetic quality was well below that of pulp paperbacks, he continued, and the DFI had thrown its money straight down the drain. Von Trier probably didn't mind at all being slammed by the Christian paper.

The Element of Crime went on to win both of Denmark's top film prizes,[9] the Bodil and the Robert. On top of that, it had screened at a lot of film festivals and was still receiving invitations. It would eventually play seventy-six screening dates at festivals around the world, becoming the most 'festivalised' Danish film ever. Gislason, for his part, won a Robert for his editing work on the film and his career was launched. He soon acquired a reputation as an editing 'doctor', someone who could save a film.[10]

But its take at the box office was a real disappointment as only 37,000 Danes bought tickets. A lot of them were confused by the film and 'word of mouth' was less than overwhelming. *The Element of Crime* was a phenomenon created by the critics and the film festivals, not by the public, and to a degree one could say this of all of von Trier's early films.

Nonetheless, von Trier's reception in France outshone his welcome in Denmark, despite the fact he had won both the Bodil and the Robert prizes. In the land of foie gras (goose paté) and advanced lovemaking techniques he was treated like a rock star, invited to appear in person at the film's gala premiere in January of 1985 at the Cinémathèque française where he was surrounded by appreciative French film buffs. He was also invited to screen a 'director's choice' film and chose Dreyer's *Gertrud* (1964). It was the week's big media event, one in which the Danish embassy only belatedly agreed to participate. *The Element of Crime* would go on to sell 100,000 tickets in Paris alone.

Post-*The Element of Crime* period

Von Trier was quickly at work on his next film, which he hoped would have a German producer.[11] 'I want to make it in English,' he would say, 'The Danish language is too small.' In fact some Danes were already a bit offended that *The Element of Crime*, funded mostly by the DFI, was in English. It was hardly what anyone would call a 'Danish' film, whatever that might be. The DFI, as noted of course, had a remit to advance the production of *Danish* film. As it was, the Institute could make exceptions, or frame their interpretations as they wished, and von Trier would in fact always get special treatment.

The German producer he referred to was Bernd Eichinger from Neue Constantin Film in Munich. Following his success in Cannes, von Trier had been chosen to make the first film for them, yet he backed out on the well-paid but potentially creatively stifling deal. 'It would have transpired that if we could not reach agreement on how the film should look, I could risk to remain unemployed the rest of my life – naturally with pay. ... but I was fortunately wise and strong enough (ha ha) to say no!'[12]

The Element of Crime had been something of a minor hit in a few foreign countries, not least in France, but expectations that it would lead to a deal with a foreign producer never panned out and von Trier remained firmly ensconced in Denmark.

In the autumn of 1984 he and Vørsel mulled over the idea of making a TV adaptation of Henrik Pontoppidan's *De Dødes Rige* (*The Kingdom of the Dead*) but finally chose not to, instead launching into a film tentatively entitled *The Mesmer Organization*, to be set in Poland and Germany during World War II. A synopsis was written but the project was soon abandoned.

Following this, they worked on a film called *The Grand Mal*. Like *The Element of Crime*, it was to be another attempt to get at the spiritual heart of Europe, but was much less cryptic and much more of a melodrama, in the style of grand old family epics. Set in contemporary West Berlin, it involved the Mallett and O'Grandey families whose forefathers had moved to Germany from Ireland and had built a grand casino that was now a hangout for gangsters and drug-dealers. It would have been the second film in his 'Europa Trilogy'. Sometime after *The Element of Crime*, von Trier had begun to talk about this 'Europa Trilogy'.

Both von Trier and DFI film consultant Claes Kastholm Hansen (known as Claes Kastholm) sought financing for the project, primarily in Germany, but apparently without success, and it was abandoned when von Trier himself began to lose interest. He claimed he could get the financing[13] but that he had simply burned out on the project after dealing with it for so long. In any case, had *The Grand Mal* been made, it probably would have secured his reputation as a gifted film-maker much sooner than it happened. It was an obvious follow up to *The Element of Crime*, which had hinted at so much promise. And perhaps more importantly it would have been what people expected.

Instead, to stay busy and make some money, he produced an advertising film, *Gateway to Europe* (1985), for Copenhagen's airport. But it was a frustrating time for von Trier, a young, known, up-and-coming film-maker prevented from launching into his next film for purely financial reasons.

Epidemic – conception and filming
In the autumn of 1985 he visited Claes and they talked about his predicament. This led to a wager that would enshrine itself in Danish film lore: Lars bet Claes he could make a commercial feature film for just 1 million kroner if only Claes could come up with the money. It would be a true poverty-row production since a normal feature film cost seven or eight times as much to make.

Von Trier (r) and Niels Vørsel during the making of *Epidemic*

Claes took him up on the bet and actually found it easy to secure financing from the DFI since it was such a bargain. Nonetheless, the sum was so small that it aroused suspicion, and according to von Trier, 'I had to put up all sorts of absurd guarantees to prove I wouldn't abscond to South America with the money.[14]

Together with Vørsel he created Element Film to raise 200,000 kroner more in private funding, and in June of 1987 they got an additional 181,000 in completion funds.

With his new-found poverty, von Trier claimed he had also found freedom; freedom from the oppressive apparatus of commercial film-making, freedom to improvise, experiment and find spontaneity. While some claimed he was simply making a virtue out of necessity, he was by any measure now forced to tell and to make his film in a different way. As he expressed it, it was more important to challenge himself and grow and develop as an artist than to just give people what they expected.[15] Up to this point, though, nobody had accused him of pandering to the audience. The question rather seemed to be did he care anything at *all* about the audience?

Originally *Epidemic* was to be another collaboration between von Trier, Elling and Gislason, but they dropped out when it became apparent that this was no collective effort but would be very much a Lars von Trier film. Indeed, it would be the 'purest' Lars von Trier film. He was writing, directing, producing and partially filming a story that was about himself as he attempts to make a movie, and in which he plays two of the leading roles.

It opens with a film-making duo (played by the film-making duo of von Trier and Vørsel) in the process of completing a manuscript to a film entitled *The Cop and the Whore*. They are scheduled to present it to a DFI consultant, played by none other than DFI consultant, Claes Kastholm, in five days.

Suddenly their diskette accidentally gets erased and everything is gone – a year and a half of work! (Parallels to *The Grand Mal* here – a film simply abandoned.)

Rather than attempt to re-create that film from memory, they decide to write a manuscript to a completely new movie and hand that in to Claes instead. The new film will be about a plague and it will be called *Epidemic*.

They begin to research the subject. Von Trier visits a historian who describes frightful details about the Black Death that laid waste to fourteenth-century Europe. Over the course of the next five days, each constituting a chapter in the film, they struggle to finish the script.

Almost immediately now we observe the beginning of this fictional film, also entitled *Epidemic*. It takes place in a Europe of the near distant future that is on the cusp of a disastrous plague, though scenes of the horror transpiring take place off camera and we essentially see only barren rooms and empty fields. As the political order collapses, a group of doctors assemble in a crypt-like room to discuss the looming crisis. The idealistic doctor Mesmer,[16] played by von Trier, defies the advice of his colleagues and leaves the city in search of a cure for the people of the countryside. Suspended on a rope from a helicopter like an angel of mercy, he slowly glides over the fields, doctor bag in hand. Up in the helicopter a nurse, (played by the woman he would soon marry [in 1987]), fellow film school graduate, Cæcilia Holbek, watches over him from above. She will be the first victim of the plague.

Von Trier (l) looks on as the cab driver (Michael Simpson) discovers that his car can only drive backwards in a scene from *Epidemic*

This carefully staged, enacted and scored fictional narrative, filmed in 35mm mono-colour stock by Henning Bendtsen,[17] proceeds to interweave with the everyday reality of the two film-makers as they cast about for ideas. In this way the film's creative genesis becomes a part of the piece itself. At von Trier's behest, Vørsel lays out the film's plotline on a wall with a paint-brush. Put 'drama' two-thirds of the way through, Lars instructs him, because without any of that people will be about ready to walk out at that point. It is not only a film that reflects itself but also a film that mocks itself.

The fictional line, in English, is heavily stylised and the acting is under-played (a foreshadowing of the style he would employ in his next film, *Europa*). And the dialogue feels dubbed, magnifying the sense we get that we are watching a movie. Reality, on the other hand, transpires in Danish and in unstaged locations. It is shot in grainy black-and-white 16mm in a dead-pan documentary style complete with plenty of *non sequiturs* and what at least feels like a total absence of editing. In these 16mm sequences von Trier wears his hair (relatively) long and swept back and seems to be enjoying himself, while as an actor in the fictional line his head is shaven and he wears glasses, and says almost nothing.

The film functions as both a playful reflection on the film-making process itself and a sombre exploration of the psychology of plagues and the mythology they give birth to. On a kind of third level it gives viewers an opportunity to personally get to know von Trier in a way that none of his other films, before or since, have come close to permitting. The 'real' von Trier has a genuine presence, a sly, soft-spoken affability. He's relaxed yet mischievously conspiratorial. Niels Vørsel, on the other hand, appears edgy, as one might tend to be when placed in front of a camera without knowing what was about to happen. He's prone to inexplicable bursts of nervous laughter that can be a bit grating. His wife, Susanne Ottesen, who rounds out the central threesome, shares this tendency.

By intertwining disparate visual styles and technical and aesthetic approaches, *Epidemic* inevitably confuses and annoys many of those unpre-pared for what is very much an experimental film. On the other hand, many of those who can accept it on its own terms find it an audacious and enter-taining venture that, at least some of the time, is right on the mark. Von

Trier even has the nerve to show people in the process of *thinking* for extended stretches, an activity long deemed to be resolutely uncinematic. But of course people must think when writing a script.

'Reality' is full of apparent digressions, yet many of these go straight to the heart of the film-writing process itself. The chapter entitled 'The Girls From Atlantic City' is one of these. Here Vørsel talks about his correspondence with teenage girls from that town.

As he explains it, he wanted to acquire secondhand knowledge of a specific American locale and settled on Atlantic City after seeing *The King of Marvin Gardens* (1972). Posing as a sixteen year old, he got a local New Jersey columnist to publicise his desire for pen pals. And he got them, the overwelming majority being teenage girls who practically drove him mad with their trivial chatter. In any case, this was the same way that Kafka wrote 'Amerika', with impressions of the place supplied secondhand by his uncle, and this was the same way they were now attempting to write about the plague – secondhand.

Yet many viewers find the relevance of this prolonged digression doubtful, to say the least. In their heavily accented English, the two read letters

Udo Kier as 'Udo' in *Epidemic*

from the girls with mocking sarcasm and even play a cassette-tape communication one girl recorded. On a tour of Europe, one of the girls and her mother met Vørsel in a Copenhagen hotel lobby and he briefly restages that scene, donning a ludicrous wig in an attempt to appear sixteen while conversation stalls. It's the high point of this extended sketch and the only overtly staged moment of the reality line.

Another curious detour involves the drive the two take to Cologne, Germany. There is no apparent reason for this trip other than to take in the bleak industrial vistas of the Ruhr valley and visit old friend, Udo Kier. No sooner are they seated on Kier's couch when he tells them that his mother has just passed away. From her deathbed she told him about a horrible bombing attack she experienced during the War where she witnessed people burning alive, and he now relates that to his Danish guests, ending up in tears.

The trip is apparently just an excuse to get away from their work room in Copenhagen and get some fresh ideas for the script. As they drive, Vørsel types madly on a small portable typewriter propped on the dashboard. The purpose of visiting Kier, who never appears again, is unfathomable. Perhaps it's just an excuse to get entirely off the subject, or possibly an absurd attempt to give their movie star power.

The film is littered with other bizarre tangents and comic asides. Von Trier dissects a tube of toothpaste to find out how it is that the red and white stripes come out so perfectly – his interest piqued by the fact that buboes (inflammatory swellings of the lymph glands) caused by the plague contain liquids of two different colours, but when they are lanced the liquids don't mix. At one point he even breaks out into a 'you talkin' to *me*?!' routine in the mirror, and elsewhere there is a lecture on wine.

Up to this point he wasn't generally known as a humorous guy and these moments ran against the grain of how people perceived him, but however funny some of this was, his earlier prediction that lack of drama would prompt walkouts seems to be turning into a self-fulfilling prophecy.

As the days pass, a mysterious illness makes its presence felt. The two suffer headaches and stomach problems. Back in Copenhagen, Vørsel ends up in the hospital where he has a growth removed.

While von Trier is visiting him at the hospital he gets a chance to observe an autopsy. Clad in sterile gown and mask, he rides the little trolley that transports medical personnel along the vast subterranean corridors of Copenhagen's Rigshospital. In a scene that is tough to watch, he witnesses a doctor slice into the armpit of a cadaver to examine the lymph nodes. Apparently there are signs of the plague in the general population as well.

On the fifth day they prepare a formal dinner to receive Claes Kastholm, the consultant, and hand over the script – all twelve pages of it. He's shocked. A normal script usually runs 150 pages on average. And the plot, as they explain it, baffles him. Where's the action?

In an effort to demonstrate to him the dramatic potential of their film, they bring in a hypnotist (played by professional hypnotist, Svend Ali Hamann) and a medium, played by nineteen-year-old Gitte Lind whom Hamann had spotted at a youth club only weeks before.

He hypnotises her 'into the film' and back to the Middle Ages to experience the Black Death on the streets of 1340s London (or Paris – some uncertainty arises over which city he actually sent her back to – one of the tougher facts to check). She sees corpses – one of them a child's – swarmed by rats ... they begin to bite her as she sobs and screams.

Hamann recounted the scene years later.

> I said to her that she should try to go into a house. Lars stopped the camera, and while she was still under hypnosis, buboes were applied to her arms. Then we began to shoot again. I said to her – still under hypnosis – that she should try to look down at herself. When she saw the buboes she screamed. It wasn't that she *thought* she was infected – she *was* infected. She jumped on the table and the coffee cups flew all over. That was the longest and loudest scream in film history. I can still hear it. I have seen that scene many times since, and von Trier did not cut so much as a second of the sound. He was very happy with it as I remember.[18]

Hamann brings her out of hypnosis, but something is wrong – her eyes are now wide open but her cries of agony only increase. She leaps upon the table, suddenly revealing a cluster of buboes in her armpit which she stabs open as bile squirts out.

Von Trier studies historical documents pertaining to the black death in *Epidemic*

All in the room suddenly find themselves infected by the plague: Vørsel's wrist has black splotches, his wife vomits blood. Their fiction has turned into fact, and the reality of the horror they have been dabbling in in their dilettantish way now turns on them.

All involved in the film claimed that Lind wasn't acting, that this was real. This conformed with von Trier's stated goal that he didn't want actors playing parts but instead wanted real people experiencing real emotions. He wanted them to *be*, not to act, and this supposedly was more than any role-playing actor could deliver.

Lind herself claimed she remembered nothing after Hamann told her she was falling asleep. In fact she never even knew a movie had come out of it until she was back home in her little Jutland village and read in the local paper that it was playing in Cannes. (She did get paid.)

*   *   *

With *Epidemic*, von Trier was apparently seeking to shore up his own mental health as much as make a movie, and he pointedly addresses this issue in the booklet he published that contained the film's manifesto.[19]

I have employed techniques which I have not made use of in earlier films. First of all, cross-cutting, which was not used in *The Element of Crime*, and camera movements such as pan-and-tilt which in *The Element of Crime* were only used in conjunction with other parallel cinema movements.

I have approached these techniques with a great deal of skepticism! [Emphasis von Trier's own]

I use them in the present film only because of the need for a less restrictive aesthetic form – a form which reached its provisional culmination with *The Element of Crime*.

This 'new' technique is as inexpensive and effective as it is commonplace. It also tallies well with the idea of a more primitive film.

During much of the filming of *Epidemic*, no 'film techniques' were used. Thus, for almost one third of the film the camera rolled unmanned. This provided the film with its intimate atmosphere and most of all – *ease of mind!*'

'Ease of mind' is the key phrase here. He wanted more than anything else *relief*, not only from 'the apparatus' but from himself. Relief from the pressure he put upon himself to make a masterpiece, relief from the all-consuming, almost imprisoning aestheticism which had characterised *The Element of Crime*. It would become a mantra with von Trier that he couldn't bear to make the same film twice, and *Epidemic* was indeed different, 'a wild shot in the face of all these other nice films that resemble each other', as he put it.[20]

Nonetheless, despite his desire to create 'a more primitive film' shorn of technique, many of the shots, even in the 16mm segments, are evocative, stylish and meticulously composed. It seems he couldn't help himself.

Epidemic – reception

Epidemic was chosen for inclusion in the 'Un Certain Regard' section of the 1987 Cannes Film Festival, and von Trier and Vørsel once again made the trip down.

They were an odd couple, as reporter, Uffe Stormgaard, noted during his coverage of the Festival for *Ekstra Bladet*. Von Trier had dropped the leather jacket and close-cropped look and was posing as something of a dandy. 'All buttoned up with his tie pulled into a little knot, a freshly ironed shirt and a gigolo scarf, von Trier appears strange even in this bizarre crowd. Pale, polite, obliging.' Niels Vørsel was his diametric opposite, clad in punked-up leather jacket and with shaven skull. 'The warm smile, the fast reply, followed by the naughty grin. Poker face with charm.'

Von Trier had remained tight-lipped about the film in the run-up to its premiere, as if it contained some shocking surprise he couldn't reveal. The two images that comprised key ad art for *Epidemic* also gave little away: one was a picture of von Trier and Vørsel in tuxedos, raising wine glasses in a toast to something or other, and the second was an image of von Trier lounging in a bath tub.

The Cannes screening of *Epidemic*, on 17 May, left the near capacity audience largely bewildered. An energetic discussion went around among film writers as to whether Gitte Lind was the world's best actress or had been genuinely hypnotised.

At his press conference, von Trier refused to offer insight into his film and had precious little to say about anything. A fair number of journalists and film people found this to be offensive and it caused some chagrin back in Denmark. Ole Michelsen, host of the popular Danish TV film show *Bogart*, was particularly offended by von Trier's refusal to elaborate on his intentions and played the incident up as something of a scandal. Von Trier, many felt, was purposely playing the 'bad boy', or whatever one chose to call such behaviour. How awful! He gives us a totally incomprehensible movie and then refuses to talk about it or answer questions! How ungrateful of him after receiving the honour of being invited to Cannes. He was now Denmark's certified *enfant terrible*.

Nonetheless *Epidemic* got good reviews in the French dailies, *Le Monde* and *Libération*, the latter calling it 'an infectious enjoyment'. Several other foreign papers weighed in positively. The film was sold to a number of territories, and began its rounds of other film festivals where it would end up receiving sixty invitations. It would go on to become the most festivalised Danish film after *The Element of Crime*. As for its eventual Danish reception, von Trier, interviewed by *Aktuelt*'s Uffe Stormgaard at Cannes, displayed supreme indifference. 'The film is made for an international public, not least the French. When I shoot a film in Danish, that's only because the Film Law requires it.'[21]

Von Trier would later confide to *Weekendavisen*,

> It was an interesting experience to come home from Cannes and see how the Danish media treated events at the festival. We were somewhat surprised to see *Epidemic* described as a 'fiasco', while Gabriel Axel's *Babette's Feast* practically became launched as an international breakthrough. Purely, objectively seen, that is just wrong and distorted. *Babette's Feast* was hardly mentioned at all in the foreign press, and in any case the reaction to *Epidemic* was far more positive than the reaction to *The Element of Crime* in 1984.[22]

Von Trier had great difficulty finding a Danish distributor for *Epidemic*, but eventually found one who dared release it sight unseen. It opened in Denmark on 11 September at the Dagmar theatre in central Copenhagen, which Carl Th. Dreyer himself had programmed in the 1950s

Danish critical response was bad to indifferent with a few exceptions.

Ebbe Iversen, writing for *B.T.*, deemed the film neither a success nor a fiasco, it was simply a mirror held up in front of itself with nothing to reflect on. It had no story to tell. 'One must be a masochist to sit through *Epidemic*,' he concluded, calling von Trier a 'filmic terrorist'.[23]

A terrorist? A provocateur? Von Trier would no doubt have been satisfied with those kinds of reviews, but almost no one found it genuinely provocative. 'It cannot bother anyone,' concluded Bent Mohn in a piece headed 'Von Trier's Doomsday Puerility' in *Politiken*.[24] 'The film bites less than it thinks it does,' said Kim Schumacher from *B.T.*[25] 'A film should be like a stone in one's shoe,' von Trier had proclaimed, but Henning Jørgensen of *Information* found *Epidemic* only perhaps as irritating as a stone one had shaken out of one's shoe yesterday, and about as memorable.[26] 'A narcissistic little parade number,' said Piil writing for *Information*.[27]

One scene in the film that attracted particular criticism was Udo Kier's emotional reminiscence. Some, including critic Piil, thought it was real. But no, it was not real, von Trier and Vørsel had made it up. What appeared to be the one indisputably genuine kernel of emotion in the film was fake. This seemed cynical and was criticised, but von Trier countered that it was a scene he had written, just like all movies were full of scenes that were written.

Though they were in the minority, the film was not without its advocates. '*Epidemic* is a look down into the depths of the soul,' said Uffe Stormgaard, writing for *Aktuelt*.

> It is full of affectation and emptiness – and worth recommending. ... the last
> scene is brilliantly and artistically laid out ... shocking in its documentary
> immediacy. If one shall follow Lars von Trier's development, one mustn't miss
> *Epidemic*. The viewer will in any case experience twenty minutes of spooky,
> fascinating soul-strangulation at the end.[28]

Ib Monty, boss of the Film Museum, writing for *Jyllands-Posten*, called it 'a film full of likeable sarcasm, a desire to fantasise and an enthusiasm for the medium',[29] and Klaus Lynggaard, writing for *Kristeligt Dagblad*, called it 'a triviality which almost resembles a masterpiece'.[30]

Epidemic was many things: a challenge, an experiment, a provocation, a towering vanity, at least one great scene and a chance to follow the progress of Denmark's most enigmatic young director – but was it a *movie*?

While the world had not embraced it as a masterpiece, von Trier could at least console himself with the fact that Danmarks Radio[31] had agreed to buy the film sight unseen for broadcast. Nonetheless he insisted on giving their producers a screening so they wouldn't be buying a pig in a poke, so to speak.

According to von Trier, when the film ended and the lights came up, the producers, normally a contentious lot, found that this was the first time in their lives they were all in total agreement – this was the worst movie they'd ever seen! They would have no part of it!

Although it must have been a mortifying experience at the time, von Trier became very fond of that story and retold it often over the years. It seems he later felt a deep nostalgia for the days when he was truly on the outs with the establishment.

The Danish public didn't buy the film either, and only 5,000 tickets were sold during its theatrical run. A box-office fiasco.

As the years wore on, von Trier would distance himself from most of his early work. *The Element of Crime*, for example, he would call 'awful ... so pretentious',[32] but he claims to this day that *Epidemic* is his personal favourite, and in 1997 he rereleased it.[33]

Regarding the bet with Claes Kastholm on whether one could make a real movie for 1 million kroner ... no money ever changed hands.

Medea

After *Epidemic*, von Trier's next plunge into film-making was a TV project called *Medea* (1988).

Back in 1985 DR-TV had planned a production of Euripides' play *Medea*, which was based on the Greek myth of Medea, the princess with powers of sorcery who had helped Jason (of *Jason and the Argonauts*) get the golden fleece. Jason and Medea married and had children, but then he left her and she ended up killing the children in revenge.

After the original director, Søren Iversen, quit, von Trier was offered the project and a great deal of creative freedom. Instead of faithfully adapting Euripides' tragedy for the screen, he chose to use Carl Th. Dreyer's script of the same name which the director had written in 1965–6 but had never found financing for. Dreyer's script was not a straightforward adaptation of Euripides' play, but rather an attempt to re-create the original story which might have inspired Euripides. Von Trier's film, in turn, as he states in the prologue, was not an attempt to make Dreyer's film, but rather was his personal interpretation of the manuscript. In any case, *Medea* was not purely based on von Trier's own material, and this was exceptional.

Using two of Dreyer's old actors, Baard Owe and Preben Lerdorff Rye, he transplanted the story to a marsh in Jutland.

He shot the film on ¾-inch video tape, readjusted colour and light, transferred it to 35mm film and then copied it back to 1-inch video tape. The result of this laborious experimental process was a train of images that seemed on the verge of dissolving in murk and graininess. The classic dialogue, sounding a bit inappropriate in Danish, was then laid on post-sync.

Medea was broadcast over Easter of 1988 and critical response was overwhelmingly negative. 'An affected melodrama,'[34] wrote Randi K. Petersen for

Scene from *Medea* (1988): Kirsten Olesen (l) as Medea

B.T., 'very far removed from Dreyer.'[35] 'The striking visuals do not manage to hide the fact that von Trier has no sense for the deeper layers in the text,' wrote Dan Nissen of *Information*.[36] 'Comic rather than gripping,' according to Bettina Heltberg of *Politiken*.[37] This initial wave of condemnation was hotly disputed by two other critics, Christian Braad Thomsen and Jan Kornum Larsen, who maintained it was a masterful and innovative work. Yet again von Trier had managed to polarise, to put critics at each other's throats.

Post-*Epidemic/Medea* period

The post-*Epidemic/Medea* period was perhaps the most pivotal in von Trier's career. He no longer particularly seemed to be 'the-right-film-maker-at-the-right-time', or even 'the-new-voice-on-the-scene', that he had been, in the estimation of many, with *The Element of Crime*. *Babette's Feast* (1987), which had overshadowed him at Cannes, went on to win the Oscar for best foreign film in the spring of 1988, the first time a Danish film had won an

Oscar. The film did well abroad and sparked confidence and optimism in the Danish film industry. In 1988 Bille August's *Pelle the Conqueror* swept all the big awards, winning the Palme d'Or (the first Danish film to win one), the Robert, the Bodil and even the Oscar for best foreign film.

This was the beginning of the modern revival of Danish film and Lars von Trier had precious little to do with it; furthermore, the two films that started it were both historical costume dramas of the type he despised. They seemed to be the future of Danish film, not pictures like *Epidemic*.

The fact that the world ever heard again from Lars von Trier is something of a small miracle, not least in light of his box-office track record up to this point. *The Element of Crime* had been no great success, and its producer, Per Holst, had signed off his next film. *Epidemic* had been a disaster and *Medea* had been roundly savaged by the critics. Great momentum he did not seem to have at this point.

It is tempting to speculate whether Lars von Trier would have ever made another film if he had been working in a purely capitalistic film environment, such as America, where there were no chummy DFI consultants who had the luxury of believing in worthy films that had no public. One can also speculate as to whether he would ever have been heard from at all if he hadn't had the lifeline of the Cannes Film Festival, via the patronage of Gilles Jacob, to keep him afloat as he made films in English and searched for the public acceptance which he had not yet found in his native Denmark.

The popular conception of the man was that of a headstrong, temperamental, phobia-wracked artist driven to make films if only to find inner peace from his demons and to achieve the balance and harmony that for him was only obtainable by plunging into a creative new project – a man who could not be prevented from making more movies by any mere box-office bomb or savaging at the hands of critics.

So what did this temperamental artist do at this low point in his career to support his little family (Lars and Cæcilia had a daughter, Agnes, in 1987)? He stopped making movies and did what any sensible, well-adjusted young man would do and went out and got a 'real', steady, paying job – making commercials. This was the other more prosaic side of Lars von Trier that surfaces throughout the story: the very functional, very sensible person who can work with and get along with other people and who can make some very keen business decisions.

Commercials

After the commercial short he made for the Copenhagen airport in 1985, he made three more commercials in 1986. He preferred to just develop commercial concepts but also directed some. It should be noted that in Denmark commercials are first shown in movie theatres. They start the show and are followed by the preview trailers, then the curtains briefly close, reopen, and the feature film starts. Commercials are an expected part of the movie-going experience, and, shown and often shot on 35mm, they have the cachet of something a bit more classy than the made-for-TV variety. But for a director who would otherwise never dream of letting commercial considerations influence his film-making, it was a bit startling to hear he was now *making* commercials.

He even had a big hit with one of them: *Sauna – Take a Bath With* Ekstra Bladet, made in 1986 and photographed by Tom Elling. Ironically it was an advertisement for the daily tabloid that would go on to expose his private life with the most diligence. It takes place in a sauna complex with men and women in separate rooms. A young guy in the male sauna discovers that he can see into the women's section through a ventilation plate. The ladies sauna is, of course, full of gorgeous naked women, and the fellow ends up using a handy copy of *Ekstra Bladet* to drape over his erection. A matronly cleaning woman discovers his high jinx and reacts with stern disapproval. 'It's Good We Have *Ekstra Bladet*' concludes the text.

The commercial was wildly popular with Danish movie-goers, far more popular than any of his films to date, if valid comparisons can be drawn. With its full-frontal (female) nudity, it proved too cheeky for the TV station, TV2, which censored it. It went on to win the Silver Lion in the commercial competition at Cannes and even acquired a bit of a cult reputation outside Denmark.

And it caught the attention of a French actor-cum-producer by the name of Bernard Verley who saw it in Cannes and connected the dots: this was the same director who made *The Element of Crime*, which had done so well in

Paris. Verley at the time made his living by producing commercials that were not based on an idea or concept but on the name of the feature film director who made them. Now he would have von Trier make a commercial for the French transportation firm, Calberson.

This was a French – not Danish – approach: selling commercials on the strength of the director's name. 'There is a special aura in France,' von Trier would say in an interview with Arne Notkin of *Audio Visuelle Media*,

> a greatness, a grandiosity which we Danes don't know … yes, in France there is more snobbishness. There is all too little snobbishness in Denmark, or rather, Danes have a tendency to be snobby about the wrong things. In France people know that if you can provide something in one area, you can also lead yourself forward in another area. In Denmark, people have a very hard time with that idea.[38]

Commercial-making turned out to be perfectly suited to von Trier's approach; commercials were purely visual, non-narrative 'concepts' told in a limited series of finely composed pictures. He had definite ideas about them.

> I believe you should show the product as little as possible. *Ekstra Bladet* was only shown a few seconds during the sauna scene. A good commercial must leave an impression. It doesn't necessarily have to praise the product or even say what the product can do. It is not interesting that a soap washes something 'clean'. The interesting thing is what the soap represents. It is the *soul* of the soap which must be brought forward.[39]

'But in a commercial, shouldn't you also try to *sell* the product,' asked Notkin.

'I am convinced that if you manifest the product, you also sell it. Outside Denmark commercials are not always made to sell a product. They are made to maintain an exclusivity. They don't directly sell the product.'[40]

By the end of 1988, von Trier had directed or developed six commercials primarily for Danish newspapers. Following *Epidemic*, this was his bread and butter. He was a realist, saying that it is not possible to survive financially by making a feature film once every three years; indeed, especially when those feature films lose money. He would continue making commercials into the mid-90s, after which he was financially able – and happy enough – to give it up.

A change of style

By the start of 1988 a distinct change in Lars von Trier's ever-shifting sense of style was evident to the Danish public. Perceived through the 1980s as the punk provocateur of the Danish art underground, he had suddenly swapped his leather jacket and studied sneer for a suburban lifestyle. He was now flaunting his retooled bourgeois profile with a vengeance – and letting his hair grow.

'The Provocateur, Lars von Trier, has become bourgeois' ran a subhead in *Ekstra Bladet* on 31 January 1988. In the piece, von Trier boasted about all the totally un-hip things he liked to do, such as go on walks in the woods with his golden retriever and hunt and fish. To this point he had not been perceived as a rustic outdoorsman. He liked to tend his vegetable garden and mow his lawn, too. Stop the presses – Lars von Trier is a regular person! If he mowed his lawn as much as the press claimed that summer, he wouldn't have had any grass left! He also liked to potter around in the yard, play with his baby daughter in the sandbox, tend his tomatoes and, as he claimed, cry over really bad American films. 'The rebellious *enfant terrible* has developed gradually into the polar opposite,' speculated his old teacher Martin Drouzy, 'the sensitive man'.[41]

What was going on? Another provocation? Lars hinted as much in his round-about way. In any case, as he told *Ekstra Bladet*, 'Carl Th. Dreyer was also one of the most bourgeois people you could imagine, but at the same time he was really an avant-garde figure and a standard bearer inside the film world.' Von Trier was apparently taken with this kind of ambiguous duality, this recognition that strange or original thoughts could lurk behind a façade of normality (a theme also expressed in the David Lynch film from 1986, *Blue Velvet*, which was popular in Denmark).

Von Trier claimed that his seventy-three-year-old mother, committed left-wing cultural radical that she still was, always detested bourgeois mannerisms, and that his new-found passion for all things bourgeois caused her profound irritation.

There was a perception at this point that the old 'commie punk' had swapped ideologies and become a right-wing conservative, a perception that was addressed in an interview he did with *Alt For Damerne* (*Everything For the Ladies*) in their 19 May 1988 issue. He freely admitted he was no rebel in the political sense. To the contrary! He voted the political line of any bourgeois family man looking after his own interests, but denied he had become right wing. On the other hand, in a reflexive slam against left-wing political correctness, he maintained that interesting works of art could come from the right as well. 'Films with left-oriented messages are worn out and uninteresting.'

Von Trier would maintain periodically over the years that there was interest to be found even in fascistic or Nazi works of art, and, going further, that even neo-Nazis should have the right to demonstrate in Denmark. However 'un-Danish' he might have been in some ways, this position, that the state had no right to suppress or silence *any* group, was in fact very Danish.

Enter Peter Aalbæk Jensen

In February of 1988, while von Trier was making the commercial for Calberson, he was introduced to a little-known producer named Peter Aalbæk Jensen. They were about the same age and got on well together. They had a number of things in common: they were both stubborn individuals and they both had an over-developed sense of irony after the Danish fashion. Both had been Communist Party members (largely at the urging of their mothers), now badly lapsed, and both had attended the Danish Film School, Aalbæk Jensen having graduated from the producers' line in 1987. In fact they had had a glancing encounter back then when von Trier had visited the school to introduce a screening of Dreyer's *Gertrud*, though at the time he didn't make much of an impression on Aalbæk Jensen.

After graduating, he experienced a number of false starts trying to get his career off the ground, one of these as the producer of *Perfect World* which was Tom Elling's debut as a feature film director. The movie was very much in the same visually expressive style as *The Element of Crime* (which Aalbæk Jensen maintains he never managed to sit through).[42] Poet Peter Laugesen, who co-wrote the script with Elling, described the film as 'a collage of dreams – of bubbles or planets in the ocean or Universe'. It didn't open until April 1990, and proved to be a staggering commercial flop – reportedly seen by only sixty-nine people and leaving Aalbæk Jensen with a huge debt – but it was largely through Elling that he made von Trier's acquaintance.

Von Trier asked him if he would like to produce his next film, *Europa*. Neither of them had anything to lose: Aalbæk Jensen's production company had just gone bankrupt[43] and he needed the work; and after two commercial flops, 'von Trier was a hated man in Denmark,' as Aalbæk Jensen would later recall. 'Nobody would touch him after those two films.'[44] He agreed to produce *Europa*, and from this inglorious beginning sprang a partnership that would have incalculable value for European cinema in years to come.

Aalbæk Jensen had been raised in Osted, an unfashionable rural/industrial area far enough south of Copenhagen to be considered provincial. He was a shy and introverted boy, overshadowed by three rebellious sisters and a little brother. His father was Erik Aalbæk, a vicar who also happened to be one of Denmark's most respected postwar novelists. At home Erik was a tyrant, dominating and emotional, and it was through him that young Peter Aalbæk got his first taste of dealing with one possessed by an artistic temperament. After graduating from school he tried his hand at various things without great success. He enrolled at the Haslev Seminarian but was expelled due to 'laziness'.[45] For a while he taught troubled youngsters. He wanted to be a drummer but wasn't very good. Between 1980 and 1982 he worked as a roadie and sound-man for rock bands, living as much of a grubby on-the-road lifestyle as it is possible to live in little Denmark. Occasional stints as stage manager at rock concerts showed flashes of the organisational ability that would later stand him in good stead as a producer. He also made some music videos.

In 1984 he applied to the Danish Film School on the sound line and was accepted. He hadn't dreamed of applying to the producers' line, possessing at that point, as he later claimed, no affinity for numbers. Yet some time thereafter he received permission from school president, Henning Camre, to transfer to the producers' line. His graduate film *Island of the Blessed*, was made together with director-line fellow student, Susanne Bier, who would become one of the leading lights of Danish film in the late 1990s.

And now fate had led him into a relationship with Lars von Trier.

Europa – conception

But the task of producing *Europa* was too big and complicated for their little company (Element Film), and the DFI would not grant funds unless the project was taken on by a 'legitimate' studio; thus Nordisk came to produce (and own the rights to) *Europa*. Aalbæk Jensen ended up at Nordisk working together with producer, Bo Christensen. This was somewhat ironic since only a short time earlier he had been fired from Nordisk, allegedly due to laziness.[46]

In the meantime, throughout the course of 1988–9, von Trier and Vørsel worked on the script. Elements of the previously abandoned *Grand Mal* were incorporated. That film was to have been shot in CinemaScope, with gener-

Lars von Trier on the set of *Europa*

ous use of front and rear-screen projection as well as selective colourisation. This stylistic approach was now brought to bear on *Europa*. By such selective uses of colour and texture within the frame, it would be possible to emphasise specific areas or objects, to give the picture its own emotional geography, so to speak. This kind of thing might otherwise be attempted by camera movement, or with editing or split-screen processes. It was a very 'painterly' way to approach the challenge.

The revelation

Europa was set again in the immediate postwar period, and one of the characters was again to be Jewish. And again, this character would be played by von Trier himself. But this would be the last Jewish character he would play, both on-screen and in real life, so to speak, due to a startling revelation that awaited him one day in April of 1989, when he paid a visit to a room in Copenhagen's Rigshospital where his seventy-four-year-old mother lay dying. Here he would receive the biggest shock of his life.

Inger had a dramatic last confession to make. As she lay connected to all kinds of tubes, she called him close and in a faltering voice told him that Ulf Trier, who had died ten years before, was in fact not his real father – not his biological father, that is.

She had had an affair with a man who was, up until 1954, a colleague of hers at the Social Ministry, and who himself was married at the time. Inger explained that she went to bed with him because he came from an artistic family and she wanted a child with artistic genes. *He* was Lars' biological father, and he wasn't Jewish at all.

'Spooky' was the word Lars later used to characterise all of this. 'If this is a scene from Dallas,' he told her, 'it's a really bad one.'[47] But he repressed his shock and anger since she was obviously dying. On the other hand, she appeared to have retained either her sense of humour or an indefatigable sense of optimism, telling him that 'at least you can get some art out of it'. [48]

The anger would well up in him over the years to come, however, and no doubt contributed to the fact that subsequent descriptions of his youth were so relentlessly negative. Ulf had apparently known this dark secret, as had others in the family. All throughout his youth honesty and openness had been stressed: now he realised his life had been predicated on a lie.

That day in the hospital, Inger divulged to Lars the name of his real father: Fritz Michael Hartmann. Soon after his liaison with Inger, he had been appointed chief of a special court which handled disability claims, a position he had held for the next twenty-three years. And he was still alive, an eighty-year-old man living the life of a retired, upper-class gentleman in Charlottenlund, a town just north of Copenhagen in the heart of the well-heeled 'whiskey belt'. And while Hartmann himself had not been a creative sort, there were indeed artistic genes in his family: he was a descendant of J. P. E. Hartmann (1805–1900), one of the most famous Danish composers. Another famous composer, Niels Viggo Bentzon, was also in the family.

Von Trier's initial contact with Hartmann was very discouraging. 'He explained that he had never accepted "that child" – meaning me. It was his general perception that women should protect themselves against pregnancy ... He said any further contact should go through his lawyers.'[49] Already a famous director in Denmark at that point, von Trier promised Hartmann he would keep the information secret in light of the publicity that would undoubtedly result.

For an entire decade, through the 1990s, the secret held, despite the fact that among the small circle of people who knew the truth was at least one reporter, Jonna Gade, of *Ekstra Bladet*. But she kept quiet.

In February 2000, Fritz Michael Hartmann died at ninety-one years of age, and the secret was out. The story got fairly wide coverage in the press. *Ekstra Bladet* published side-by-side photos of father and son, and the resemblance was striking: the same prominent, somewhat sharp nose, the same mouth and similar facial contours. Von Trier himself had no comment upon Hartmann's death, but it seemed clear that his mother's project had succeeded.

Not long after his visit to her bedside, Inger died. Lars inherited the family house, and after fruitless attempts to sell it, he and Cæcilia decided to move in. In the summer of 1991 he began to renovate it with reckless abandon. 'There is something therapeutic about it. I rip down and throw out a lot. A couple of walls here and there. And the things that were most precious to my parents, I smash. This kind of thing I can recommend. Crystal objects shatter really good against a concrete floor.'[50]

Europa – story, casting and shooting

By the summer of 1990, *Europa* was rattling along the tracks: shooting was underway in both Denmark and Poland, where they had also previously planned to shoot *The Grand Mal*. All scenes involving the actors were shot in Copenhagen by Henning Bendtsen, while exteriors were shot in Poland with Polish crews and extras. It was considerably cheaper to shoot in Poland where, rather amazingly, some trains were still powered by steam. Since the end of World War II and through the subsequent communist era, time had seemed to stand still, and that was perfect for the film. The Eastern bloc still in large measure resembled 'Europe year zero'.

The meticulous pre-production work and detailed storyboarding that had characterised *The Element of Crime* was also employed with *Europa*. It figured as the final instalment of the 'Europa trilogy', but von Trier intended

A rear-screen image from *Europa*

this to be a more accessible and commercial film. In retrospect it seems that this was the film he should have made after *The Element of Crime*.

And it was, like all his films thus far – and all films period – a collaborative effort: Tómas Gislason wrote the shooting script, was second unit director and exerted considerable influence on how the film would look. As noted, extensive use was made of both front and back projection (which are indistinguishable to the viewer). These special projection processes were all done on the set, not afterwards in the lab, and contributed to the film's consciously old-fashioned, 'pure film' look. No modern digital effects here. This would be his most 'film' film.

Europa is set in the autumn of 1945, as Germany lies buried in the ruins of war and convulsed in social upheaval. As the film begins, we are hypnotised back to both this physical setting and the psychological state. In *Epidemic* von Trier attempted to hypnotise one girl … now he attempts to hypnotise the whole audience. Distinctions between what is reality and what is not are now frequently blurred.

The film's protagonist, a young, naïve, German-born fellow named Leo Kessler, has just returned from the US to secure employment with the long-established Zentropa Train Company. He is an idealist and believes that working a civilian job in Germany will go some way towards doing some good in the world. He is employed as a porter on a sleeping car, and with these train journeys through the land he comes to experience first hand the extent of the devastation.

Zentropa is owned by the powerful Max Hartmann, whose daughter, Katharina, Leo falls in love with. Hartmann is caught in the complex web of postwar politics: on the one hand he receives threats from the Werewolves, Nazi loyalists dedicated to continuing the struggle, and on the other hand he is obliged to play down his previous Nazi connections so that the Allies will allow him to continue to run a business in the new Germany. He is aided in the latter when a Jew falsely testifies that Hartmann helped him during the war. The American general, Harris, Max Hartmann's friend and handler, has arranged this charade to clear Hartmann who is of crucial importance to the Allies postwar reconstruction plans.

The fictional Max Hartmann has the same surname as von Trier's biological father, Fritz Michael Hartmann. This would appear to be much more than a mere greeting to or upbraiding of his real father as some suggest, for it is von Trier himself who plays the castaway Jew. It is von Trier who saves him with false testimony in a powerful scene fraught with painful and ambiguous emotion.

'Hartmann is my friend ... he hid me and gave me food,' says von Trier the Jew as he embraces him. Hartmann can hardly conceal his surprise and barely manages to return the embrace. But it is not gratitude that overwhelms him, it is shame: shame that he did not do the right thing before and acknowledge his forgotten children, the Jews and other outcasts sacrificed for the sake of 'doing business'; shame in recognition of the fact that he has been nothing but a tool employed by larger forces, playing the game he had to play to do business in Nazi Germany and now playing the game again under very different rules – perhaps the same way that Fritz Michael Hartmann, enmeshed in the codes of proper professional conduct and subject to family pressures, played the game that he was forced to play, and failed to acknowledge his lost child. Max Hartmann was no simple villain. Rather he was a man plagued by his conscience, plagued to death by it. Possibly von Trier did not see Fritz Michael Hartmann as a villain either, but as just a man who failed to do the right thing, who did the weak thing.

Following Max Hartmann's suicide, Leo is married to Katharina. She is, in fact, a member of the Werewolves, and the group's leader, Siggy, persuades Leo to cooperate in various ways. Finally Siggy convinces him to agree to a last job: placing a bomb on the train which will explode as it passes over a large bridge. Leo plants the bomb but then regrets it. He attempts to defuse it, but it nonetheless explodes and the train plunges into the river.

*   *   *

In its examination of issues of postwar complicity and guilt, *Europa* was very much an elaboration on *Images of a Relief*, but it was also much more – a trip back to Germany year zero. This country, in particular, had always fascinated von Trier. German culture contained, as he put it,

a great amount of both the dangerous and the beautiful ... They always tell us
that the extremes are found in America and that Europe is so boring. But I
would assert that at least the intellectual extremes have their origin in Europe.
Europe symbolises for me something incredibly dynamic.[51]

With a budget of 27 million kroner, of which the DFI contributed 7.8 million, *Europa* was von Trier's most expensive production yet. But, filmed in
German and English, was it a 'Danish' film? It was an open question to say
the least, but in any case it no longer needed to be filmed in Danish to get
support from the DFI, since the definition of a 'Danish film' had changed.
In 1972, as previously noted, the Film Law stipulated that a production must
be 'shot in Danish, and that an overwhelming majority of its artistic and
technical personnel be Danish'. But the Film Law had been liberally revised
in 1989, and the wording changed so that 'A film must be shot in Danish *or
possess a particular artistic or technical quality which contributes to the advance
ment of film art and film culture in Denmark*' [emphasis added]. Rather open-
ended, that last clause.

Nordisk Studio also funded the film, largely by bearing the brunt of costs
incurred when it ran considerably over-budget, but even more crucial was
the foreign investment von Trier and Aalbæk Jensen found: 4 million from
the EU media fund, Eurimages, and lesser sums from French TV and film
companies. Their ability to exploit new pan-European funding sources such
as Eurimages, founded in 1988, placed them at the forefront of a new wave
of producer/directors who would 'internationalise' and renew Danish film,
both financially and creatively. That, together with the recently liberalised
definition of what a Danish film was (or could be), laid the cornerstones for
the modern revival of Danish film. *Europa* was one of the first and best
examples of what was now possible.

Von Trier's casting approach was similarly international, with non-
Danes filling a majority of the leads. Jean-Marc Barr, a French actor who
had starred in the popular 1988 French film, *The Big Blue*, was cast as Leo
Kessler. He had spent time in the US as a student and spoke perfect English,
so he was ideal for the part. Barbara Sukowa, well known for her roles in
later-period Fassbinder films, played Katharina, while Ernst-Hugo

Jean-Marc Barr as Leo Kessler in *Europa*

Järegård, a Swede, played the role of Leo's uncle. All three of these actors would appear in subsequent von Trier films. Danish actors, Jørgen Reenberg, as Max Hartmann, Erik Mørk as the Catholic priest and Henning Jensen as Siggy, filled out the main roles. Old friend, Udo Kier, played Larry. Cæcilia Trier had a secondary role as a servant girl while her brother, Joachim Holbek, composed the music. The film's narration was dubbed by Max von Sydow with appropriate gravity.

Europa – reception

Europa was selected to participate 'in competition' at the 1991 Cannes Film Festival. No surprise there.

Von Trier took the train down to Cannes while Cæcilia and little Agnes arrived by plane about midway through the Festival.

Aalbæk Jensen was there too, and killed time before the premiere by bragging to the press about all the big deals that were in the works for von Trier, most sensationally an assignment to make Madonna's next music video. She was also at Cannes and had a meeting with von Trier on 16 May to discuss the creative and financial details of the project. She had been much taken with his video, *Bakerman*, one of three rock videos[52] he had made with Cæcilia's help in 1990 for the pop group, *Laidback-Highway of Love* (concept by von Trier and direction by Åke Sandgren) and *Bet It on You* being the other two. *Bakerman* had received heavy play in rotation on MTV and had generated considerable buzz.

But ultimately he never made the video for Madonna, possibly because the famously uncompromising von Trier refused to make any concessions on creative control, or possibly because rumours of the 3.5 million kroner deal were prematurely leaked to the press and scotched the deal. By 20 May Aalbæk Jensen was reporting that the video deal seemed to be on hold because of 'all the other exciting offers' they were getting, offers from 'three of the world's biggest production centres'. He 'let slip' that Brit Jeremy Thomas, who had produced Bernardo Bertolucci's *The Last Emperor* in 1988, was willing to give von Trier total artistic control on a project.[53]

While Aalbæk Jensen was busy pumping the press with rumours of deals that would never happen, von Trier was holding himself and his wife and daughter aloof from the circus of Cannes, at least as much as that was possible. And it proved impossible on at least one occasion where he found himself in a car surrounded by excited fans of Jean-Marc Barr. Of all his previous visits to Cannes, this one seemed the most discomforting. He was a family man this time, he wasn't posing as any kind of exotic character and he didn't need too, either, since *Europa* confirmed and solidified his reputation at Cannes all by itself.

Prior to the Cannes premiere he announced with a typical mix of bravado and irony that *Europa* was 'made as a masterpiece. I decided that in advance. It is conceived big and contains clarity of thought. That is typically un-Danish to gamble on making a masterpiece, and moreover, to admit that.'[54] As always, he was making the most of being 'un-Danish' and misunderstood back home. (Claiming to be 'un-Danish' is, in fact, a very Danish trait. It is rare, for example, to hear an American or Frenchman claim they are un-American or un-French.) Whether he actually was or not was a more complicated matter.

But for his 'masterpiece' he got no Palme d'Or, losing out to *Barton Fink* (1991) by Joel and Ethan Coen. He had to content himself with two lesser awards: the technical prize, again, and the Prix du Jury, which he had to share with Maroun Bagdadi's *'Hors la Vie'* (1991). As Claes Kastholm would comment in *Politiken*, '"*Hors la Vie*" dealt with – in contrast to von Trier's impressive if pretentious *Europa* – living people.'[55]

Simply put, he wasn't very content. In fact he threw his certificate away during the awards ceremony as if it was nothing but a worthless piece of paper. In fact it *was* nothing but a worthless piece of paper – a wholly symbolic blank piece of deckle-edged paper rolled up with a red ribbon around it. The real certificates would be sent on later, and the winners were all under strict orders not to open these in front of the cameras.

Von Trier wasn't the only temperamental film-maker Cannes had to deal with that year. Spike Lee, everyone's favourite to win the Palme d'Or for *Jungle Fever*, was also mightily disappointed when the film only won best supporting actor for Samuel Jackson's performance. Lee accepted the award on Jackson's behalf and later threw it into the sea.[56]

But von Trier wasn't finished yet and during his press conference he referred to the president of the jury, Roman Polanski, as a midget – a comment that immediately got wide coverage and even ended up on the wire reports. It turned out to be the scandal of the Festival. Von Trier explained that Polanski had called *himself* a midget in his own film, *Chinatown* (1974), hence it seemed OK to use the term as a casual witticism. But almost everyone else on earth took a different view, and Denmark was, as one, mightily embarrassed. 'Von Trier Amok in Cannes' screamed the front page of the tabloid *B.T.*, back home.

Von Trier seemed to have snatched defeat from the jaws of victory, and despite written and verbal apologies to both Gilles Jacob and Roman Polanski, this particular wise-crack would haunt him for years.

Polanski, for his part, seemed to take no offence from the remark and relations between the two, according to reports, remained friendly. Years later von Trier even had him over to his house for lunch. 'He *is* short, though,' mused von Trier after that occasion.

Danish reviews of *Europa*, which opened domestically on 16 August at the huge Imperial theatre, were mixed. Bent Mohn of *Politiken* called it a masterpiece. Palle Lauridsen of *Kristeligt Dagblad* called it a hypnotic masterpiece. Michael Blædel of *B.T.* called von Trier a 'great, expressionistic creator of pictures ... one of the few original, modern day film-makers and one of the most consistently self-assured'.[57]

On the other hand, Henning Jørgensen, writing for *Information*, thought it was a 'pompous parade (show off) number'. Ib Monty of *Jyllands-Posten*, who had liked *Epidemic*, didn't like *Europa*: he thought the film was a bunch of 'shabby clichés'.[58] Jan Kornum Larsen of *Weekendavisen*, who had reacted positively to von Trier's earlier films, found this one inaccessible and implausible, while others found the direction poor and the story less than impressive.[59]

Europa went on to win both the Robert and Bodil prizes, but the modest 31,000 tickets the film sold in Denmark had to be something of a disappointment. There still seemed to be a gap between what film professionals and average ticket-buyers thought about Lars von Trier.

The film sold well to foreign territories and played particularly well in Spain, France and even in Brazil where it was a hit in Rio de Janeiro. In the US (released as *Zentropa*), it was ranked the second best film of 1992 by Andy Warhol's *Interview* magazine, and von Trier was compared to the likes of Orson Welles and Alfred Hitchcock. (Not surprising since *Europa*, perhaps not so coincidently *looked* liked a film by Welles or Hitchcock.) Once again it was a case of a von Trier film receiving a better reception outside Denmark. This must have confirmed to his mind that Danes still didn't appreciate him.

Dimension

Von Trier considered himself as much of a 'concept man' or an 'idea man' as a film director, and back in March of 1991, with *Europa* in the final stages of post-production, he came up with his most ambitious concept yet, something called *Dimension*. The press unveiling on 1 March came complete with a photo of himself, co-writer Vørsel and Aalbæk Jensen standing beside a triangular black rock, inscribed with the words *Dimension 1991–2024*, and looking for all the world like a prop from an old *Star Trek* episode.

Dimension was loosely described as a thriller, but its *raison d'être* was the manner in which it was to be filmed: one three-minute scene was to be shot every year somewhere in Europe over the next thirty years, with the completed ninety-minute film to premiere on 30 April 2024, when von Trier would be sixty-eight years old. The idea was that the film would develop and grow along with the cast and crew, *and* the location – Europe. As yet unforeseen plot twists and the emergence of new themes were sure to lie ahead. For once, the component of *time* would be factored into the making of a film in a positive way. Time, so to speak, would be the star of the film. And unforeseen events, which most directors fear like the plague, would fuel the film.

The actors would consist of the young and the old, the unknown and the known, among them a contingent from *Europa*. All cast and crew were obliged to hand over a sealed envelope containing the name of the person who would replace them if death or some other unpredictable circumstance rendered their continued participation impossible. Von Trier himself had a replacement, but revealed only that it was a highly reputed European director.

In addition to von Trier, the people behind the project included Vørsel as co-writer, Aalbæk Jensen as producer, Tom Elling as cinematographer and Henning Bahs as set designer. Financial support for the first shoot in Berlin on 30 April had been secured from, among other sources, the DFI and Danmarks Radio. According to von Trier, a lot of European sponsors had shown a great interest in investing in the project.

The idea had come to him one day while he was in Berlin just as the Wall fell. 'When I saw all the Trabant and Skoda cars which putted over the border, something clicked in me. The powerlessness I saw in the eyes of the customs officials said something to me, and I got the idea to make a European film collage – a kind of monument to the future.'[60]

Later that year, in November, with his midget comment still fresh in everyone's mind, von Trier went to the Stockholm Film Festival and stayed long enough to win first prize for *Europa* – and comment to the Swedish press[61] that it would be just as well if Ingmar Bergman was dead.

A minor scandal ensued.

His remarks about the untouchable Swedish icon had been taken out of context, he felt, and he was more than happy to elaborate. He declared himself to be, in fact, a great fan of Bergman, especially *Persona* (1966) and *The Silence* (1963).

> But I cried when I saw *Fanny and Alexander*. I consider that film a mistake. It's like a rock video or something. Everything I had loved about Bergman, all my personal experiences, were ruined after seeing it. ... I feel full personal engagement in the films I see. In some cases I can feel myself completely betrayed.
>
> Bergman sits like a cork in Swedish film life, a power centre who hampers creativity ... It would have been better if he had died after those films. There are many directors for whom the same can be said – that they should have died after a certain film. Fassbinder did himself a service by dying at precisely the right time. Truffaut died too late. Now I'm talking about them more as film-makers than as people. Of course if they died it would be bad for their next-of-kin.

He added in subsequent clarifying remarks that it probably would have been best for his own artistic reputation if he had died directly after the premiere of *The Element of Crime*.[62]

Establishment of Zentropa A/S

The close of 1991 saw the partnership between von Trier and Aalbæk Jensen formalised with the founding of Zentropa Entertainment production company. The new company would earn money by making commercials, and it would be a 50:50 partnership between von Trier and Aalbæk Jensen, with an even split of all profits and an equal stake in all decisions.

In the first press that appeared on the company, on 24 December 1991, they laid out their goals. Zentropa would produce von Trier's upcoming film, described as an erotic melodrama called *Breaking the Waves*, and it would give him total artistic control over this and subsequent films. Additionally it would give them the opportunity to serve as executive producers for other worthy film-makers who would then be spared from the humiliating production conditions that passed as the norm in the film world. Bo Widerberg, Michelangelo Antonioni and Ken Loach were three directors named by von Trier who would be worth making films with in this capacity.

The thought of directing really bad B-films just to survive made von Trier's blood run cold. 'And with this company,' he proclaimed with a sense of irony intact, 'I now attempt to postpone the inevitable! ... People in the trade smile about it today, but in a few years our competitors will shake!'[63]

Zentropa soon found a home in a disused tobacco factory on Ryesgade in the mixed industrial/residential Copenhagen neighbourhood of Østerbro. Soon after that several other film companies joined them, including Peter Bech Films and Nimbus, a studio founded by ex-Film School students which now entered into a long-term equipment-sharing arrangement with Zentropa and became known as something of a little brother.

Von Trier and Aalbæk Jensen invested almost all their profits in film equipment, and by 1994 they owned 10 million kroner in equipment, all of it earned from von Trier's commercials, many made for German companies. By owning their own equipment, they were able to reduce costs on their own productions, at least in the future, and generate income by renting the stuff out. Furthermore the equipment could function as collateral in co-production arrangements. Zentropa was the only Danish film company besides Nordisk Film that owned their own pool of equipment.

Three
The Kingdom and Breaking the Waves

The Kingdom – conception

Still, in the beginning, the going was rough. 'It was impossible for Zentropa to get accepted in Denmark in the early years,' Aalbæk Jensen would later claim. 'The beginning of von Trier's career came at a point where there were more or less only two big companies here in Denmark, Metronome and Nordisk, who got permission to make films by the DFI. Nobody gave a shit about Zentropa at the start.'[1] In 1992, then, when von Trier was asked by Danmarks Radio if he wanted to make a TV mini-series for them, he agreed, primarily because they needed to do something so that Zentropa could survive.

Another enticement was the fact that DR agreed to let him make a ghost story. As a boy he had been a big fan of the French TV series *Belphégor*, directed by Claude Barmas. The series, which was very popular in Denmark and throughout Europe in the mid-60s, dealt with mysterious disappearances and murder in the subterranean passageways of the Louvre's Egyptology department. This show was in the back of his mind as he turned over the idea of making the mini-series. 'We wanted to "Dane-ify" *Belphégor*,' he would say.

Another major influence on von Trier at the time was *Twin Peaks*, the TV mini-series by David Lynch that aired from 1990 to 1991. While von Trier on at least one occasion described Lynch's feature films as 'rubbish',[2] he found *Twin Peaks* to be 'brilliant and different'. He found it inspiring both content-wise and as a working process. In his view, Lynch had made a 'left-hand' masterpiece that was infused with the spontaneous and unpredictable. TV had allowed him to escape from the pressures attached to making 'a great work of art' – a feature film – and it had liberated his whole creative process. Von Trier had a great desire to do the same, to escape the oppressive apparatus of the film industry, inclusive of the burdensome financial and artistic expectations.

In any case, there would be no *time* for perfection. This was TV and they had a mere fifty hours of shooting time to produce approximately five hours of fiction.

In the meantime von Trier hit upon the ideal setting for his modern-day ghost story, a place that frightened and horrified him for real – a hospital: the biggest one in Copenhagen, the giant Rigshospital which had in fact already figured as a location in *Epidemic*. In English the word means 'the

Morten Arnfred, Lars von Trier and Ernst-Hugo Järegård on the set of *The Kingdom*

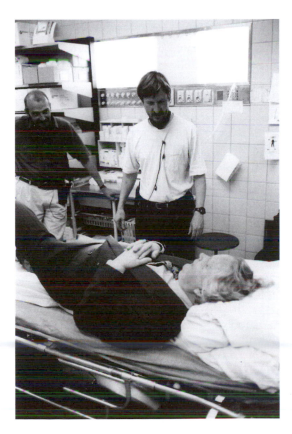

hospital of the Danish Kingdom'. Von Trier named his series, *Riget*, which in strict translation means, *The Kingdom*.

Founded in 1910, the 1,650-bed Rigshospital served 80,000 Copenhagen residents and also functioned as a training facility for medical students. The building had been completely rebuilt in 1963–72 but still possessed the kind of long underground hallways and mysterious chambers that approximated in some fashion the subterranean caverns of *Belphégor*'s Louvre. It was a place where the scientific merged with the occult, where the modern clashed with the ancient, and where, as in all hospitals, horrible things occasionally happened in the name of science and humanity. The Rigshospital itself was rich in a kind of morbid folklore: grotesque urban legends about diabolical goings-on between doctors and patients that had long circulated, and upon which von Trier claims he based the series.

By October of 1992 a synopsis had been completed. By February of 1993 the treatment was finished, and the final manuscript was ready by April. It was primarily funded by DR in cooperation with Swedish Television, but also received the thus far largest support grant – 2.2 million kroner – from the EU media programme, Greco, as well as funding from various Nordic media funds.

According to von Trier, who penned the script with the help of old mates, Niels Vørsel and Tómas Gislason, *The Kingdom* had been ridiculously easy to write, a joy, a lark, a totally 'left-handed' project that was a welcome break from the pressures of feature film-making. He got to break rules, ridicule authority figures and explore the dark side: supernatural phenomena and life-after-death experiences – the kind of things he had not been permitted to believe in as a child. It was a lot of fun. And it turned out to be very funny, which was not the kind of thing people expected from him.

As a working process, it is tempting to say that he got to rediscover the spirit of spontaneity and improvisation, but when did his films really ever have that, except possibly with *Epidemic*? The series might be described as one long escape act. First and foremost he was attempting to escape from himself, from the perfectionist, workaholic, control-freak Lars von Trier whose last film, *Europa*, had been a manifestation of all that. He needed to get away from that kind of film-making, just as he had needed to get away

from *The Element of Crime* by making *Epidemic*. He had always found it necessary to challenge and provoke himself, to move on, and this was just such
a provocation. It was as if each film was a trauma for him and the next film
was by necessity a rebellion against it. He not only didn't ever *want* to make
the same film twice, he physically couldn't.

The plot of *The Kingdom* had, in classic mini-series, soap-opera fashion,
several strands that played out simultaneously. Intrigues between doctors,
patients and staff in this microcosm of society were banal as well as mystical, comic as well as grotesque. Ominous portents and bizarre occurrences
were peppered in among the mundane trivialities of the daily work-a-day
world. Normal logic was turned upside down as idiots became the prophets
and the prophets – the bosses – were revealed to be the imbeciles. An
eccentric cast of characters and a story littered with absurd digressions and
bizarre red herrings spun around the main plot twist: a little girl called Mary
who had been brutally murdered by a doctor over half a century earlier and

Ernst Hugo Järegård (Stig Helmer) and Ghita Nørby (Rigmor) in *The Kingdom*

who now haunted the subterranean reaches of the hospital. The successful mix of drama, black humour and genuine spookiness was widely hailed as a unique achievement.

Casting

Von Trier took a radically different approach to casting. Not only did he seek out Danish actors – quite predictably since this was a domestic TV production to be filmed in Danish – but he sought out *well-known* Danish actors, many with classical theatre backgrounds. Six of the actors had starred in the late-70s TV series, *Matador*, a period costume drama set during World War II that might be described as a kind of Danish *Aston Family*, and which ranked as the most popular Danish TV series of all time. He also found a part for Jens Okking as Bulder. Since playing his father in *Secret Summer* back in 1968, Okking had gone on to fame in the 1970s as the lead in the popular police series *Strømer* (1976), reprised again in 1987. This revealed both the loyalty streak von Trier had when it came to such casting, and the fact that the pool of professional actors in Denmark was so small.

Udo Kier was back, playing Aage Krüger, with Erik Wedersøe's voice. Von Trier once tried to make his German pal learn Danish, but Kier found it to be a torment. Pop-star-cum-actor, Otto Brandenburg, who in his prime was something of a Danish James Dean, played porter Hansen, and the character Krogen was played by Søren Pilmark who had done everything from comedy to heavy drama to commercials.

The two leads, Kirsten Rolffes and Ernst-Hugo Järegård, both sixty-five, gave the show its darkly comic counterpoint. Rolffes, who began her career as a promising young star with the Danish Royal theatre and had also been in *Matador*, played the psychic Mrs Drusse[3] who comes into spiritual contact with Mary. Järegård, in addition to his role in *Europa*, had a long if sporadic career behind him as an extremely versatile character actor. Here he played the pompous and blustering Swedish head doctor, Stig Helmer, who spews hatred against all things Danish.

That von Trier got so many respected Danish actors to participate in such an off-the-wall series – when he himself was still an unproven commodity – is more than anything a tribute to the kind of freedom

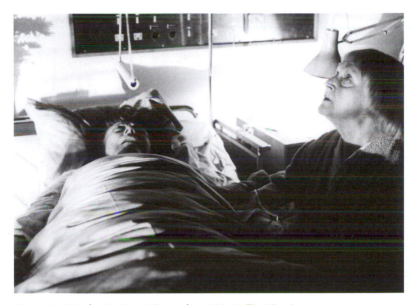

Kirsten Rolffes (as fru Sigrid Drusse) bedside in *The Kingdom*

established Danish actors have to take risks. It is hard to imagine their British or American counterparts doing – or being allowed to do by their agents – the same.

That he got such good performances out of them was, by all accounts, mostly down to the input of his assistant, Morten Arnfred, an established director in his own right whose strength was working with actors and who was often employed as a trouble-shooter on other productions. He was known primarily to the Danish public for his two features, *Me and Charley* (1978) and *Johnny Larsen* (1979), both good examples of the kind of 'black bread' social realism von Trier had rebelled against. As both people and film-makers, the two seemed to be polar opposites, but they had worked well together that spring on a commercial, and Arnfred was hired in the summer of 1993 when the original plan of having Cæcilia and Tómas Gislason take over directing chores on the second, third and fourth instalments was abandoned.

Their collaboration on *The Kingdom* went surprisingly well. Arnfred was considered essentially a co-director and an equal partner in the decision-making process, although in cases of dispute von Trier asserted himself, leaving no doubt that it was his film. Von Trier personally directed Järegård and Baard Owe, who played Bondo, while Arnfred directed the rest of the cast.

Shooting

Shooting lasted from September to December of 1993. During the shoots it was often Arnfred who seemed to be directing the film, as von Trier, with his phobia for elevators, heights (the upper floors of the hospital) and for hospitals in general, often secluded himself in a separate room, following the progress by monitors and staying in touch with Arnfred by a walkie-talkie. He was seen by cast and crew as somewhat of a odd, shy fellow.

Arnfred was in large part responsible for the unique comic tone of the film. 'I have always preferred underplayed comedy', he would later elaborate,

> 'to see characters behave normally in the most insane situations. In my conversations with Lars before the shootings, I remember emphasising that it was enormously important that we take all the characters seriously and that they be played with credibility – even though they were nutty. It was necessary to constantly maintain a naturalism in the acting style and not stress the farce-like elements which *also* existed in the script and could have easily been played up. We were both totally in agreement on this.'

In other words, to elicit the viewer's sympathy and engage them in what was such a far-out plot, the characters almost had to be twice as human.[4]

Stylistically, von Trier was very much influenced by two American TV cop shows, *N.Y.P.D. Blue* and particularly Barry Levinson's 1992 series, *Homicide*, which had taken the on-the-street reportage feel of the jostled, hand-held camera to its thus far furthest extreme. Von Trier would borrow this approach and embellish it, giving his supernatural ghost story the varnish of realism.

The Kingdom was shot in 16mm and digitally edited, while the colour was manipulated in the copying and colour-grading processes. This gave it the stylised look and feel of video. For long shots that had to be static, down

From the making of
The Kingdom: (l to r)
Niels Skovgaard
(special effects).
Morten Arnfred (co-
director) and Lars von
Trier

hallways, for example, a steadicam was used. A fixed camera was used for the special-effect shots where the film had to run twice through the camera, requiring perfect registration in what is known as a double-exposure process. This is the traditional way of depicting ghosts or shadow images, although in fact there were very few of these in *The Kingdom*.

Dialogue scenes in rooms were shot by cinematographer, Eric Kress, with a 'shaky' hand-held camera. He was aided by an assistant and a sound-man. In contrast to *Europa*, there was no storyboarding nor proper rehearsals. There were usually four or five takes of every scene, with the actors encouraged to improvise. They were taken from start to finish with no cuts, and no two were the same. Kress usually covered them from all four corners of the room, and, since there were no cables, he did so with full mobility, sometimes spinning 360 degrees and forcing the sound-man and assistant to dive to the floor. He was given little guidance by the directors and just told to proceed boldly and shoot what he found best. Shooting in this manner, some of it on-location in the hospital, went fast, as it had to. It also helped that they had dispensed with time-consuming lamp set-ups and used available light. The actors wore cordless mikes in their clothes and hair and the sound was transmitted to a control room where the directors could monitor it. Pictures from the camera were also similarly transmitted.

The actors responded well to this approach. Although the rapid pace of shooting – twelve to fifteen manuscript pages a day instead of the normal four to five – put pressure on them to know their lines, their performances were fluid and natural, full of apparently unmasked human moments and spontaneous reactions captured by an intrusive, probing camera.

On the other hand, the editing mitigated against or 'cheated' realism, at least as it is classically construed, as von Trier attempted to 'dismantle psychological continuity'.

> Each scene is filmed with as many different expressions and atmospheres as possible, allowing the actors to approach the material afresh each and every time. Then we edit our way to a more rapid psychological development, switching from tears to smiles in the course of a few seconds, for example – a task which is beyond most actors. The remarkable thing about this cut-and-paste method is that the viewers can't see the joints. They see a totality, the whole scene.[5]

The apparently haphazard way the pictures were composed and edited flew in the face of the time-honoured wisdom that the camera shouldn't cross the optical axis, or centre-line, along which the action progresses. To violate this precept means that the same piece of action is presented from two different directions, and that is supposed to disorient the viewer. It has long been considered proof of poor film-making, usually evidenced in cheap B-movies. But what to make of *The Kingdom*, where the rule was broken so aggressively and consistently?

Von Trier figured that modern viewers had a sophisticated enough relationship with pictures to maintain their orientation. This old rule was a millstone around a film-maker's neck, he said, and would disappear in a couple of years. In fact he proved prophetic on this point as viewers adjusted with surprising ease to the new visual language of *The Kingdom*, and before long this shooting and editing method became a (perhaps over-used) means of expression in and of itself.

But at the time no one could have predicted that viewers would happily pay to sit in a theatre and watch five hours of shaky, grainy, digitalised images (blown up to 35mm, no less), that they would be able to follow all the frenetic motion, and that they would like it!

Reception

But like it they did. All over the world.

The theatrical version premiered on 6 September 1994, out of competition in the 'A Window to Fantasy' sidebar at the Venice Film Festival. The screening came complete with a lunch break. The next day it received glowing praise in the Italian press. *L'Unita* called it an event … better than *Twin Peaks*. *The Kingdom* evidenced the personal stamp of its director, noted *La Republica*, which was something one didn't often see in television work. *La Nuova* praised the show's unique mixture of *Hamlet*, *Belphégor*, *Twin Peaks* and *General Hospital*. All in all this was characteristic of the kind of praise that would be repeated around the world.

The Kingdom had its gala premiere in Denmark on 11 November at Copenhagen's Imperial cinema. Von Trier didn't show up (nor had he been in Venice).

Two weeks later, on 24 November, the first of the four episodes aired on Danish TV and was an instant hit. Sky-high ratings, favourable reviews and plenty of buzz greeted each new episode, which aired weekly into mid-December and attracted viewers across the age spectrum. Many who had pointedly disliked von Trier's feature films loved *The Kingdom*. The streets of Copenhagen were almost deserted when *The Kingdom* was broadcast, and workplaces and cafés were abuzz with chat about it the next day.

The Danish critics were also finally, virtually without exception, on von Trier's side. In January 1995 he won the Bodil for the series, beating the other big hit of the year, Ole Bornedal's *Nightwatch*, and creating something of a scandal into the bargain. A few days previous to the ceremony, von Trier had pressed the selection committee to divulge the results beforehand, stating that he would only show up if there was something to show up for.[6] Bornedal found out about it and boycotted the ceremony in protest. Von Trier showed up, collected his trophies and left in haste, pausing long enough at the microphone to deliver a parting remark: he had to hurry home to relieve his babysitter, he said. He was called Ole Bornedal and he hadn't had anything better to do that evening. It was a crack that many thought went too far.

In March he rubbed salt into Bornedal's wounds by winning the Robert prize as well.[7]

The Kingdom worked its way into the collective Danish consciousness and created a few new myths of its own, helped along by a layout in *Ekstra Bladet* which probed reports from cast and crew who claimed the Rigshospital was haunted for real. The film's technical director, Tove Jystrup, told of how her cat seemed to be possessed by the devil – wailing, screeching and dragging itself strangely across the floor – when she had played a working copy tape of the film at home. Other technicians had been contacted by spirits, she reported. 'In the beginning we all laughed when people talked about strange noises, shadows and happenings, but no one's laughing anymore.'[8]

Additionally it was reported that an old elevator in Zentropa's building on Ryesgade, only about a ten-minute walk from the Rigshospital, had begun to operate by itself late at night, and that some employees refused to be alone in the building after nine o'clock.

Kirsten Rolffes willingly confessed to past encounters with spirits. One night, as she recalled, she had awoken to discover an assembly of spirits gathered in her bedroom, observing her. 'Disappear!' she screamed. On another occasion after that she was contacted by a spirit while she stood washing children's clothes. She said that she became so irritated by the spirit that she slammed the table and screamed 'stay away!'

But if all the hocus-pocus swirling around *The Kingdom* seemed to be farfetched, reality was proving to be even more so, as it came to light that a night watchman at the hospital had been charging people admission to take them down into the cellar under the pathology labs to view the corpses, and directly before the premiere a pair of frozen legs were found in a nearby park.[9]

Although its length and the fact that it was made for TV generally disqualified it from inclusion in festival competition slots, it did become an unexpected hit on the festival circuit, playing to huge crowds at the Rotterdam and Berlin film festivals at the start of 1995 and going on from there. A big splash was planned at the Berlin Film Festival: a midnight screening with special food, drinks, music and atmosphere – and von Trier in person – in one of the city's biggest theatres. But once again, von Trier pulled out. He was getting to be one of the most dependable 'no-shows' on the international festival circuit.

Post–*The Kingdom* period

Looking back, 1994 had been, from all appearances, a good year for the von Trier family. Lars had finally broken through to both public and critical acclaim with *The Kingdom*, and in mid-December had received an Ingmar Bergman travel grant for 50,000 kroner.[10] Cæcilia herself had made a well-received documentary that year entitled *The Invisible Art*, about the functioning and traditions of the Danish Music Conservatory, established in 1867, and in November she had received an Edith Allers memorial grant of 30,000 kroner.

Furthermore, on 23 December, they had their second child, a daughter they named Selma.

They were perceived at this point as proof that people could stay focused and have a down-to-earth and stable family life in the film-making profession, a world of glitz, glamour and big egos. A sensible Opel Ascona parked outside their cosy half-timbered house completed the picture of normality. Nothing particularly exciting or scandalous about all this, but somehow to the average tabloid reader there was a certain satisfaction in knowing that von Trier had grown up and was starting to act responsibly. He always thought he was somebody. Now he was just like everybody else. He even took a two-month leave-of-absence from work to look after his family. And next summer they would all travel to Scotland where he would shoot his next film, *Breaking the Waves*. After that, Cæcilia would start work on her next project, *Nonnebørn* (Agnus Dei), about a young girl's coming-of-age experiences.

Seemingly all was well.

Unfortunately Cæcilia's pregnancy had been a difficult one. She had been wheelchair bound during its later stages, and also after the delivery. In early February 1995, *Ekstra Bladet* reported that she was seriously ill.

Von Trier was livid. Through his lawyer he 'protested unconditionally' to the paper about this intrusion into his private life, and attempted to forbid all such future publicity unless prior written permission was obtained in advance from himself. The letter containing these demands was sent out to other papers as well.[11]

Danish media people were greatly surprised, then, when just a few days later, on 6 February, startling reports filtered out of Göteborg, Sweden, where he and other film notables, such as Ben Kingsley and Wim Wenders, had been invited to participate in a seminar on the future of European film. When it came his turn to speak, von Trier couldn't resist confiding in the audience about the new love of his life, going on to confess that he had left his wife just four days previously. His new companion, Bente, was there with him. He declared that through his eight years of marriage, he had always been faithful to his wife. And every time he thought of his little daughter, he cried. The audience, according to a Swedish journalist, was stunned and embarrassed.[12]

Since von Trier had broken his own prohibition in such dramatic fashion, *Ekstra Bladet* hardly felt compelled to muzzle itself and ran the story with bold front page headlines: 'Von Trier Leaves His Wife'. The tabloid went on to disclose how he had ditched his ill, forty-one-year-old wife for a 'newer model', Bente Frøge. The ferry back to Copenhagen was jammed with Danish reporters. The statuesque Bente, sitting apart from Lars and still fairly unknown, managed to give them the slip. At this point they moved into an editing suite in Zentropa which had a bed in it. There they lived for half a year. Following Göteborg, though, no one was saying anything more to the press, in part out of consideration for Cæcilia and Bente's jilted husband.

While von Trier offered no further public comment on the situation, the apparently considerable pressures he had faced throughout the last half of 1994 had no doubt contributed to the split. He had been obliged to put his career on hold to tend his sick wife and look after the family, all of it in the glare of the publicity *The Kingdom* had suddenly wrought. He was, as previously noted, somebody who needed work, who needed creative challenges to find harmony and balance. Instead he was obliged to become a house-husband and a full-time nurse, and to care for little Agnes. All of this he had

Scene from *The Element of Crime* (1984): (l to r) Michael Elphick as Fisher, Me Me Lai as Kim and Lars von Trier as the receptionist referred to as 'Schmuck of the Ages' (courtesy of DFI)

The pathologist (played by János Herskó) performs an autopsy on a murder victim while Fisher contemplates the killer's next move (courtesy of DFI)

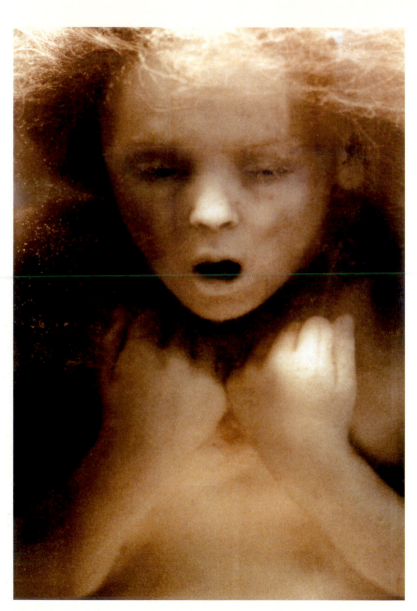

The body of little Mary preserved in a glass jar in *The Kingdom* (1994)

Bess (Emily Watson) and Dodo (Katrin Cartlidge) share a quiet moment in *Breaking the Waves* (1996)

Bess comforts paralysed husband Jan (Stellan Skarsgård) (courtesy of DFI)

Happier times: Bess and Jan before Jan's accident (courtesy of DFI)

Bess as the literal personification of the 'fallen woman' (courtesy of DFI)

Frau Drusse (Kirsten Rolffes) and Bulder (Jens Okking) in scenes from *The Kingdom II*

Spazzers go for a nude romp in the yard in *The Idiots* (1998) (courtesy of DFI)

Lars von Trier shooting a scene from *The Idiots*

Björk gazes up at policeman Bill in *Dancer in the Dark* (2000)

Björk (centre) in a courtroom fantasy sequence from *Dancer in the Dark*

Björk in a fantasy sequence from *Dancer in the Dark*

Lost in the desert: a scene from *The King is Alive* (2000), Dogma film number four by Kristian Levring (courtesy of DFI)

Bodil Jørgensen, who played Karen in *The Idiots*, is seen here as Bente True in *The Lady of Hamre* (2000), directed by Katrine Wiedemann (courtesy of DFI)

reportedly done with diligence. 'I believe he is the only director I know who leaves work early to pick up his daughter from play-school (Kindergarten),' testified Aalbæk Jensen in the press. The fact that von Trier had fallen in love with Agnes' play-school teacher (Bente Frøge) was no doubt added incentive.

Bente later recalled the moment Lars proposed to her in an interview with the Danish weekly magazine, *Sunday*: one day as she stood in the school's garden, surrounded by little children, the world-famous film director came up to her and in deepest seriousness, proposed to her. She said yes.

> I cannot explain it. I just knew at that moment that I did the right thing, and that I would have regretted it the rest of my life if I hadn't said yes. ... I thought he was insane, but I have since come to understand that he's just like that. He has a goal and even if it seems totally unrealistic, he still manages to reach it.[13]

The Kindergarten, however, saw things differently and fired her, apparently on the grounds that she had broken some rule by falling in love with a kid's parent.

Breaking the Waves – conception

Von Trier had been working on *Breaking the Waves* ever since the immediate post-*Europa* period in 1991, and his desire to make an erotic film had gone back even further, to his school days, when he would tell anyone who would listen that he wanted to make a porn film, an erotic film. This desire of his to explore the ambiguities of power relationships in a sexual context would turn out to be every bit as controversial as his previous explorations of guilt and innocence in the context of World War II; but first things first.

The origins of the film were two seemingly disparate literary sources: the novel *Justine* by the Marquis de Sade, and a lost children's picture book he remembered from his youth called *Guld Hjerte* (*Golden Hearted*). But upon closer inspection, they bore an underlying similarity.

Golden Hearted was, as he recalled it, about 'a little girl who went out into the woods with some crumbs in her apron and ended up giving all her possessions away to needy passers-by. When the rabbit or the squirrel said, "now she has no dress ..." she replied, "I'll be all right." In the end she was naked and had no more bread, because she was so good.'[14] But the last pages of the book had fallen out, he said, so he had no idea how the story ended.

Justine is about, as many readers are no doubt aware, a pure and innocent young girl who goes through life encountering one degradation after another at the hands of her fellow man, but never loses her trust and goodness. After surviving incredible villainy and suffering, most of it of a sexual nature, she is reunited with her sister and lodged in her home, apparently a safe haven. 'And finally all turns out to be well!' recounted von Trier enthusiastically. 'As she lays in her soft bed she says "Thank you, God. You have shown that if one is just good the whole way through, then one will receive one's reward" – whereupon she was immediately hit by a bolt of lightning and died! Split right in half!'[15] Hilarious, he thought.

Both stories dealt with the inextinguishable and almost inhuman extremes of purity and goodness harboured in a woman's heart. These two female characters are much more than simply naïve. Their willingness to sacrifice all for a belief that seems irrational, and which leads to a humiliating fate, recalls more than anything else the Christian saints and martyrs.

Script evolution

As early as August 1991, von Trier was describing the as yet untitled project as a straight adaptation of *Justine*. It would be an erotic film, a sex film, but it wouldn't be pornographic, he said, as those kinds of films would be impossible to get financed. It would take place in France and be in English. He wasn't worried about the incongruities in setting and language. People were used to this kind of thing, he said, and English was a good universal language for the movies.

Thanks to Peter Schepelern's diligent examination of various script drafts,[16] the development of the film can be charted through its various incarnations.

In the first synopsis, dated 10 October 1991, the setting has been moved up to the early 1960s and the story now involves a language professor named John who is happily married to a former student, Caroline. They live in a large European city and have a baby son. Suddenly John suffers a stroke and thereafter his condition steadily worsens. He knows now he will never be able to live a normal life, and asks Caroline to take a lover and tell him about her experiences. This she does as his condition continues to decline, and then goes even further and presses him to divulge his innermost fantasies, which become increasingly debauched, so she can act them out. Their acquaintances are shocked. The baby is removed at the behest of Caroline's mother, but she persists in her scandalous behaviour. John is about to die. Caroline seeks out a notorious man who dwells in a house down by the harbour and their sexually abusive excesses result in her death – as John simultaneously and miraculously recovers. Doctors reckon she has committed suicide in a fit of insanity. In the end John stands by her grave with their son in his arms.

In the next draft, two weeks later (24 October 1991), the title, *Breaking the Waves*, is in place. The setting is changed to the Belgian coastal town of Ostende, and John becomes a virile sailor by the name of Jan. He and Caroline, who now comes from a very religious Catholic family, are married. Their first sexual encounters have an overwhelming, almost addictive effect on her. When Jan is called back to work on the ship, she flies into a fit and prays to the virgin Mary to bring him home by any means. Soon after he has a stroke and is brought home unconscious, though by degrees he partially recovers. Knowing he will never be well again, he asks her to take a lover and tell him about it. After initial opposition, she agrees to the idea. When he seems to improve, she continues, even in the face of the warnings and condemnation from her neighbours and friends. But then he suffers a relapse. As he lies dying, Caroline searches out a spooky building down by the harbour where depraved and debauched sex flourishes. Here she meets her death. At the same time Jan miraculously improves. He steals her body and buries her from his ship at sea. The next morning the crew is aroused by the heavy clanging of bronze church bells – 'The sound comes from high up and all over,' von Trier noted.

By now the script had all the basic elements and much of the plot construction in place. The final 'miracle scene' with the heavenly church bells clanging in the sky, was not, so to speak (no pun intended), pulled from out of the blue. Von Trier had placed 'miraculous' scenes in other films, notably the redemption scene of the Nazi officer in *Images of a Relief*. As corny as it sounds, he believed in miracles, at least in the movies. And he wanted the film to be corny, to be both brutally realistic and to be a children's fable at the same time.

In a later treatment dated 16 July 1992, Schepelern finds that 'the sex scenes become more elaborate and take on the character of pornography. Here Caroline has sex first with the doctor, thereafter with the man in the bus, with a man in a rowboat, and participates in an orgy with a woman and many men in a cottage in the woods, which is followed by a rape in a stream where she is about to drown. ... The scenes often have a perverted and violent character':

> Caroline caresses her vagina with her mouth. The woman lays a while with closed eyes. Then she opens her eyes and looks at Caroline. 'You well know that you must also have a kiss ...?' Caroline looks at her. 'Yes', says she quietly. The woman opens Caroline's pants, pulls them down and proceeds with enthusiasm. The three men look silently on.

The rape scene was particularly violent:

> He knocked her down. She screamed in terror. He ripped her clothes into pieces. She splashed out into shallow water. He beat her to get her to stop screaming. Now he grabbed her by the hair while he fucked her. She struggled to hold her head above water. Then he finished. He rolled away from her and lay quietly on his back in the water with closed eyes.

Caroline's response to this new world of depraved and promiscuous sex is, through all the various drafts, ambiguous. Does she herself derive any pleasure from what she is subjected to, as did the captive female in one of von Trier's favourite films, *The Night Porter* (1974), or is she exclusively motivated by a martyr's willingness to sacrifice all, including her last shred of dignity and even her life, for the man she loves? The answer to this seemed to change from draft to draft, but there can be no doubt that in the final script version (March of 1995), Caroline, who is changed to Bess, is only repelled and nauseated by these encounters. This seems to be a clear departure from von Trier's original idea, but also one that perhaps not so coincidently would make the film more commercially palatable. Audiences can understand and digest victimhood and humiliation, no matter how extreme, but if Bess had in some way derived enjoyment from the sex – that would have been far more controversial and would have led many to label the film pornography.

Equally ambiguous through the draft phases was John/Jan's response. Did he force her into this exclusively to free her, or did he also derive some voyeuristic pleasure? That is less clear in the final film. Other changes were made as the script evolved: Bess acquired a close friend, Dodo, who became a central character. The stroke changed to an accident, and Jan works on an oil rig instead of a ship.

As the film changed from an 'erotic melodrama' to a 'religious melodrama with erotic overtones', religion became a more crucial element in the story, and a credible setting was sought. French locales and Ostende, proposed for the most part in hopes of getting a French co-producer on board, were out when that didn't happen. Locations in Norway and Denmark were also considered. Norway did not have the kind of close-knit, religious community needed. Denmark did – the puritanical church of the Inner Mission, which held sway in certain areas of the west coast of Jutland – and for a while the film was to be set in an isolated fishing village there, but the Western Islands of the Scottish Outer Hebrides were finally chosen. Here villagers had subscribed to the dogma of the strict Presbyterian Free Church for generations. The geography, both desolate and dramatic, was far more evocative than anything that could be found in Denmark, and the harsh, changeable weather suited the mood of the story. It was easy to imagine how important faith was to those who lived in these rugged, isolated valleys and dales, and how, living in such isolation, they could naturally grow suspicious of outsiders.

Funding, casting and shooting

Funding for the film, which would be shot in English, was difficult to put together as potential backers didn't buy the idea of Lars von Trier making a love story, but thanks to the success of *The Kingdom*, the 42.6 million-kroner budget belatedly fell into place. Von Trier had producer Vibeke

Windeløv, who worked in tandem with Aalbæk Jensen, to thank for that. Her first involvement in film had been as a scriptwriter on *Normannerne* (*The Normans*) in 1976, which her husband, the famous artist, Per Kirkeby, had co-directed. Some years later von Trier asked her to produce *Epidemic* but she declined because she was working on something else at the time, and in any case didn't want to. At that point 'I only knew Lars second-hand,' she later remembered, 'and thought he was spoiled rotten – he was always arguing with people.'[17] Armed with degrees in psychology and business management, she went on to produce Susan Bier's first film, *Det Bliver i Familien* (*Family Matters*) in 1993, and that brought her to Zentropa. While her production experience stretched back to the mid-70s, this – a complicated package that involved twenty-six different financing deals with investors all over Europe – would be her baptism by fire.

The absence of any American funding, which usually came with final-cut and casting strings attached, allowed von Trier relative freedom in choosing the actors. Many of the roles were filled by native-born Brits, which gave the film a certain authenticity.

The twenty-eight-year-old English actress, Helena Bonham Carter, who had come to prominence in such films as *A Room With a View* (1986) and *Howard's End* (1992) was cast as Bess. Versatile Swedish actor, Stellan Skarsgård, who had played in art-house hits like *The Unbearable Lightness of Being* (1987) as well as commercial thrillers like *The Hunt for Red October* (1990), was cast as Jan, while Dodo, Bess' confidante and protector, was played by Katrin Cartlidge, best known at that point for her role in Mike Leigh's *Naked* (1993).

Other British actors included Jonathan Hackett who played the minister, Sandra Voe, a Scot, who was cast as Bess' mother, and Adrian Rawlins who would play Doctor Richardson. Small roles were given to actors who had been in previous von Trier films such as Jean-Marc Barr, Barbara Sukowa and Udo Kier, who portrayed the sexual degenerate, now living on a trawler anchored off-shore rather than in a house, with conviction. Morten Arnfred was hired as assistant director again, and a dialect specialist, Elspeth MacNaughton, was employed to help give the film linguistic authenticity.

But by the start of May the picture was on the brink of crisis when Bonham Carter broke her contract and left the production, reportedly after giving the manuscript a closer look and rethinking her participation in the sexual scenes. London-born actress, Emily Watson, whose only experience up to that point had been stage work, was hired as her replacement and the production lurched on as Windeløv desperately searched for the last 15 per cent of the budget.

*   *   *

Von Trier had definite ideas about how he wanted to shoot the film, and had discussed the project a few years earlier with the Dutch cinematographer, Robby Müller, whose previous work for directors like Wim Wenders and Jim Jarmusch he admired. Müller was eventually hired as cinematographer.

The hyperactive and fluid shooting style used on *The Kingdom* would again be employed on *Breaking the Waves*, but this time with a hand-held 35mm CinemaScope camera. Some static long shots were used to give the bleak Scottish landscape a prominent presence in the film, but these fixed shots were few. Von Trier wanted as much as possible shot with hand-held cameras, at one point growing annoyed with the professional cameraman they hired who seemed to place more value on shooting a perfect pan than on *what* he was shooting. And in any event the presence of nature was to be largely conveyed by eight digitally created panoramas illuminated by artificial light sources. These were created by Kirkeby. They would serve as title plates to the seven chapters and the epilogue of the film, as if it were an old-fashioned, picture-book fable. These panoramas were scored with period pop songs like 'Goodbye Yellow Brick Road' and 'Suzanne' in a rather futile attempt to give the film's early 70s setting some credence.

The 35mm film material was later transferred to video, digitally edited and then transferred back to 35mm for release-print production. The shaky, hand-held quality of the camera work and digitalised grain imbued the pictures with a documentary quality that lent realistic counterpoint to a story that would be sentimental in the extreme.

Von Trier wanted to make a modern, sentimental film that was free from the Disney-like iconography associated with traditional melodrama.

If one is going to make such a basic or clichéd story, you get a better effect if you do it very realistically. When you see a film with this traditional fantasy-like feel today, it's quite obvious that the world is not like that. Here we've done the opposite and made the world as it looks.[18]

As with *The Kingdom*, von Trier wanted spontaneous and realistic acting, and encouraged the actors to improvise in movement, intonation and expression with each new take, no two of which would be the same. It would be the cameraman's challenge to seek out and capture the best of it. And the old rule that an actor should never look into the camera was broken by Watson. Her glances directly into the camera made the viewers active accomplices and confidantes, and drew them into the story — willingly or not.

Interior scenes were shot in various studios and locations in Denmark through the summer of 1995, while exterior shooting on location in Scotland took place that autumn in biting winds and frequent heavy downpours. A raw edit was made in November.

With its focus on the story and the acting, *Breaking the Waves* gave birth to the popular conception that von Trier had been transformed from a director obsessed by control and technical mastery to a director who could now work with living flesh-and-blood people. His new working methods liberated the actors and liberated the crew as well, went the accepted wisdom. Morten Arnfred hailed his rebirth as an 'actor's director' while Katrin Cartlidge called his transformation a 'personal perestroika'.

To a large part this was probably true, although it wasn't quite so cut-and-dried. Von Trier would have plenty of trouble working with certain actors in the future, and if Cartlidge apparently found him easy and pleasant to work with, perhaps that was due in large measure to the fact that he had fallen madly in love with her, as he later confessed in print.

Regarding the technical aspects of the film, there was still plenty of illusion at play in spite of its realistic style, much of that the result of digital manipulation which von Trier and company exploited to the fullest. While much was made of the rugged Scottish nature, a good portion of it was implanted from elsewhere: clouds from Norway, waves from Denmark, and so forth. And what there was didn't last long: viewers only got six minutes of actual exposure to the beautiful Scottish landscape, as Aalbæk Jensen boasted. He viewed digitalised effects as an economic god-send and a force for the democratisation of cinema. So much could be done so much cheaper.

Nonetheless the film had a jagged immediacy and energy about it which derived from the camera work and was further accentuated in the cut-and-paste editing process, which, à la *The Kingdom*, sought out the most genuine and spontaneous moments. A hyper-realistic style was used to tell a very melodramatic story. This was a novel approach and gave audiences the feeling that they were seeing and experiencing something new. The traditional glossy style of melodrama had always allowed viewers the luxury of maintaining a comfortable distance from the pain the characters felt. Not here. Melodrama was spacious and epic and entertaining, but *Breaking the Waves* was claustrophobic and uncomfortable and unavoidably engaging. There was no safety zone here. This was not a comfortable movie.

Reception

Breaking the Waves was chosen to participate 'in competition' at Cannes. And as von Trier stated in the Zentropa company bulletin (issue 4), this time anything other than the Palme d'Or would be a shock for him.

But the shock for Lars came early, on the morning he and Bente arrived at Copenhagen's main station to board the train. There at the platform awaited a Danish IC-3 train, not the expected German inter-city train which tended to be a bit older and more 'user active', meaning, among other things, they had windows one could open. The IC trains were hermetically sealed capsules of carpeted, air-conditioned luxury, with automatic doors and suchlike. To von Trier it was claustrophobic hell. He was appalled that the windows couldn't even be opened. He refused to board the train and they went back home.[19]

How to get to Cannes? Flying was out of the question. They did attempt to go by car, but that too came to naught when for some reason they turned around and came back after reaching Puttgarden, the first town in Germany off the ferry.

So he simply never went down to Cannes.

Von Trier was already known in Denmark as a man of a million phobias, but the press couldn't buy this and saw his absence as a sign of arrogance. Danish columnist, Camilla Kjærsgaard, for example, wondered if it wasn't 'festival phobia' rather than 'travel phobia' that kept him in Denmark, while Christel Skousen patiently explained how his behaviour was evidence of agoraphobia.[20] In any case, his absence in Cannes reaped him a bonanza of almost exclusively negative publicity, and according to some in the Zentropa camp, worked against his chances for a Palme d'Or.

As Cannes kicked off, *Breaking the Waves* and Mike Leigh's *Secrets and Lies* soon emerged as the two favourites, with the Coen brothers' *Fargo* and Jacques Audiard's *Un héros très discret* also given an outside chance. After the screening of *Breaking the Waves* on 13 May, it was widely hailed as the clear favourite, with Emily Watson also tipped to win best actress. It received accolades across the board as major papers in America, Germany, Italy, Spain and England sang its praises.

On 19 May, two days before the awards ceremony, Bente flew down to Cannes. If Lars won the Palme d'Or, she, Aalbæk Jensen and Vibeke Windeløv would be ready to ascend the stage and accept it on his behalf. The day before the awards, all winners were told that they had won a prize, but not which one. They were now among those thusly informed and expectations grew.

Tuesday, 21 May – the night of the awards – finally arrived. Von Trier sat at home with Christel Hammer, his press agent for the last fifteen years. While she sat and watched the ceremony on TV, he went into the next room and played a computer game. *Breaking the Waves* won – but 'only' the Prix du Jury, while *Secrets and Lies* went on to take the Palme d'Or. 'He was sad he didn't get the Gold Palm,' Hammer would later recall, 'but he shrugged it off. He does that often. But it wasn't funny.'[21]

Emily Watson, who lost out to *Fargo*'s Frances McDormand for best female lead, read a brief telegram of thanks on von Trier's behalf.

The next day he met up with fifty members of the press at the Zentropa cafeteria in Ryesgade. 'All these people give me claustrophobia,' he cracked. 'While I'm happy now to get the next-best prize in Cannes, when I was younger I would otherwise have preferred to finish dead last. I have softened up a bit over the years. ... Bille August has won the Gold Palm twice,' he added jokingly (for *Pelle the Conqeror* in 1988 and *The Best Intentions* in 1992), although it clearly grated on him.[22]

Breaking the Waves opened in Denmark on 5 July, for all those Danes who hadn't managed to sneak their way into the almost 'sold out' press screening. Danish critical response was almost wholly rendered in superlatives, with one of the most moving tributes penned by Christen Braad Thomsen, the writer whose first impression of von Trier was that of the disrespectful student who wore the Walkman during his lecture at the Film School fourteen years earlier.

The film went on to win both the Bodil and Robert awards in 1997, a considerable vindication for Zentropa in light of the fact that the troubled production had almost brought the company down. At the ceremony von Trier was his customary no-show self and Emily Watson accepted the statue on his behalf. He had, however, sent a tape of himself, and it was played. With a sarcastic glint in his eye, he 'forgave' all the members of the press and film industry who at one time or another had put obstacles in his way or treated him badly.[23]

Outside Denmark, the film was sold widely to foreign territories and proved both a popular and critical hit. *Breaking the Waves* was the clear turning point in von Trier's career, proof that he had learned how to tell a human story on a broad emotional register. He seemed to have mastered his craft and to have matured as a film-maker as well as a person.

The majority of critics praised the film to the skies. Since the death of Kieslowski, von Trier ranked as the most outstanding film-maker in northern Europe, wrote Nigel Andrews for the British *Financial Times* in early October, 1996. He was the only film-maker in Andrews' view who would dare attempt such a rich mixture of symbolism, melodrama, psychodrama and black comedy. On the front page of the *New York Times* cultural section, lead critic Janet Maslin heaped on similar praise of the kind that would echo around the film world.

Interestingly, American prints of the film had been censored, however briefly. 'We had to cut Stellan Skarsgård's limp wiener out,' Aalbæk Jensen would later report. 'That was simply too strong for the Americans.'[24] That scene, where the disrobed couple get physically acquainted and make love, was not just another one of von Trier's provocations: it was practically all that had survived of his original intention to make this an erotic film, a sex film. The physical lust that Jan and Bess felt for each other had been the core of the original idea, now reduced to practically a single scene – and that scene handily cut out (at least in part) by the prudish Americans.

The general public, at least in Denmark, wasn't quite as unanimous in their praise of *Breaking the Waves* as the critics were. Evidence of this could be seen in the leftist-intellectual paper *Information*, where numerous letters to the editor disparaged the film throughout the course of that summer.

Some criticised what they saw as von Trier's one-dimensional depiction of a religion he had no first-hand experience of. These were not deeply religious people (who in fact very rarely seem to go to the movies), but average viewers who questioned his sincerity and motivation, his handling of the subject. Was the religious aspect in the film intended as reality or metaphor? Were these just scenes that were written, like all movies are full of scenes that were written? The style of the film suggested to the viewers that they were getting 'the real stuff', but realism was not his goal. Rather it was an aesthetic choice, a technical means of conveying a story. He was after all a *storyteller*. He had even arranged the film like a picture book. It could get confusing.

Substantially more criticism was directed at the character, Bess, particularly by a female segment of the audience. Here was a childlike, naïve, vulnerable, superstitious (a.k.a. super-religious) woman who had no control over her own life, caught as she was between the patriarchal forces of the community elders and her 'outsider' husband. In the end she sacrifices all for the man she loves and is rewarded with 'suffering, damnation and nothingness', as Johannes Fibiger and Gerd Lütken put it in an editorial headed 'The Profane (Female) Saint'[25] which weighed in critically on von Trier's female characters. Her degradation transpired, according to some critics, under a lurid pall of voyeurism and sadism. Maybe von Trier was a bit of a sadist himself, some speculated.

Bess didn't even get the 'happy ending' the story-book character Golden Hearted got: the children's book had been found after Schepelern had publicised his search for it on 11 April 1997. It turned out that a little boy Golden

Hearted had helped was really a prince. The last thing she would give him was her heart, and they would marry and live happily ever after in his castle. Bess, on the other hand, was caught in a limbo, denied the happy endings of innocent children but also deprived of any scrap of wisdom or experience that most adults have, if only by default – given an adult body and the soul of a child. To critics, she was the ultimate victim. A problematic character to say the least. To others she was the heart and soul of the film, just about the greatest piece of casting in film history.

In any case, Bess would have company, as von Trier announced that *Breaking the Waves* was the first part of a new trilogy, the 'Golden Hearted Trilogy', which would explore the nature of female goodness in different settings.

For his part, von Trier acceded that a hard-core 10 per cent of the audience couldn't 'buy' the story. 'These are people who have problems going along with the film on an emotional level ... for them it is a horrible film.' In other words you had to buy it before you could be touched by it. He claimed he cried every time he saw it. Another one of his rebellions against an upbringing of emotional suppression.

He was convinced his family would *hate* the film. The only surviving member of his family, Ole, did hate it in fact, calling up Lars after a preview screening to tell him it was awful. Nonetheless it was important for him to get tickets to the gala premiere, which Lars arranged. After the gala he called Lars again and told him it was no better the second time![26]

Breaking the Waves went on to sell 300,000 tickets in Denmark. A healthy success if no blockbuster.

Four
The Birth of Dogma and *The Idiots*

The birth of Dogma

Back at the start of 1995 as *Breaking the Waves* entered the final post-production phase, von Trier accepted an invitation to attend an international directors' symposium in Paris that would focus on the future of film. It was timed to coincide with the centennial of motion pictures.[1]

He usually hated this sort of thing and routinely turned down such invitations. What was different about this? That question was answered beforehand, on 13 March, when he announced to the Danish media the establishment of something called Dogma 95. By 18 March the Danish press started picking up on it. Von Trier was always good copy. 'Lars Von Trier Goes into Artistic Cloister – The Director Will Start a New Wave With Chaste and Naked Films', read a headline in that day's edition of *Politiken*. Debate was already starting to ferment in Danish film circles as he left for the symposium.

On the afternoon of 20 March, a panel discussion was held at the Odéon theatre in the centre of Paris. When it came von Trier's turn to speak, he asked permission to depart from the agenda and then stood up and announced to his esteemed colleagues and the audience that he represented the group, Dogma 95. He proceeded to read the group's manifesto and threw a handful of red leaflets containing the text off the stage, after which he promptly departed the theatre.

Such was the dramatic birth of Dogma 95, a radical film 'movement' which at this point only contained two people, von Trier and his young colleague and fellow Film School graduate, Thomas Vinterberg.

Von Trier was already very much conscious of the importance of a good wave. Back in the summer of 1987 he had ruminated about the nature of 'waves'.

It is clear that during great periods, such as The New Wave in France, or new German film, with Fassbinder, Wenders, etc., a lot of people can suddenly become incredibly inspired and a great amount of exciting films can get made. And a wave is formed. But at present the wave has washed over and we find ourselves up on the beach where a little wave laps up once in a while. It leaves some mucky, scummy water and then slowly recedes back to the sea. That is where we are just now. And the only thing one can do as a film-maker in such a situation is to attempt to reach forward to a new and fruitful period. One must experiment.[2]

The situation had changed little since then: all the old waves had broken long ago. The French New Wave was the stuff of history books, the surviving founders a bunch of very old men from a different time. The German new wave of the 1970s was clearly past: Fassbinder – dead, Wenders and Herzog, no longer relevant. And America – it didn't matter at all. Despite its much-hyped independent scene, in America there could be no such thing as a proper wave with the requisite political/revolutionary overtones. America was apolitical and apathetic, the embodiment and engine of the status quo. America was counter-revolutionary.

By 1995, with special-effects laden Hollywood blockbusters like *Jurassic Park* and the endless *Die Hard* franchise gobbling up movie screens around the world, enough was enough – it was time to invent another wave. Why not? What the hell? So he called up Thomas Vinterberg one day out of the blue and asked him if he wanted to make a 'new wave?' Sure, came the reply.

With his blond hair and classically chiselled features, Vinterberg was the proverbial 'fair-haired boy'. Raised in the enlightened intellectual/progressive environment of the Nordkrog commune north of Copenhagen, he seemed destined for a successful career in the arts, music being his original passion. Relatives and friends of the family were well placed in cultural circles. His father was the famous critic and editor, Søren Vinterberg, while the musician, Henrik Strube, and the physicist and philosopher, Tor Nørretranders, were also part of his 'alternative' family. His uncle, Dan Nissen, was second-in-command at the Danish Film Museum. Vinterberg would go on to great success in the film world, but a rags-to-riches story it was not. And rarely is in Denmark where it often seems that within the close-knit cultural circles everyone knows – or is related to – each other, and where the film community is often referred to as a family.[3]

The Dogma declaration, signed by the two on 13 March, had purportedly been drawn up amid continuous laughter in only twenty-five minutes. It contained a manifesto and ten strict 'vows of chastity'[4] that spelled out in technical specifics how a film should be made. Dogma would bring purity back to a medium that had been corrupted by money, creative dishonesty and laziness. Dogma would save the bodies and souls of film-makers who had sold out to the false gods of special effects and easy solutions, film-makers who had become addicted to the medium's grab-bag of slick tricks and had lost their ability to tell a good basic story that dealt with genuine human emotions. They needed to go cold-turkey. That's why Dogma was severe, almost like a detoxification programme or the radical 'deprogramming' of someone who has been brainwashed.

The rules were ultimately intended as a means to liberate film-makers, not punish them; to liberate them from the oppressive apparatus of 'major motion picture' film-making with its big money, big crews, big pressures and big temptations. They needed to get grounded, to find themselves, to find their stories again. They needed to try it 'un-plugged'. Simplicity, spontaneity and honesty would once again flourish, and it was good. Von Trier had experienced the joy of this type of freedom in *The Kingdom*, only to once again feel the weight of the apparatus pressing down on him in *Breaking the Waves*.

He had always been intrigued by manifestos. He had studied *The Surrealist Manifesto* as a mere adolescent, and he himself had issued manifestos before, for *The Element of Crime*, *Epidemic* and *Europa*. These were ironic piss-takes on his own once fervent communist past as well as manifestations of a genuine urge to change the (film) world. They tended to be characterised by a consciously overheated and somewhat obtuse rhetoric. He was an angry, if not always serious, young man.

But Dogma 95 was perhaps something a bit more serious, something more than just an excuse to provoke his esteemed colleagues in Paris and leave a dull panel discussion early. The future of cinema? If things didn't change radically, the future wouldn't be worth thinking about.

Dogma 95 declared that it would produce five feature films in 1996 for a total cost of 20 million kroner. With comrade Vinterberg on board, von Trier had someone to do interviews, press functions and other such dirty work he disliked. The twenty-six-year-old Vinterberg, two years out of the Film School in the directors' line, was good for that, but thus far he had only one short-film to his credit, *The Boy Who Walked Backwards*. If Dogma 95 was first and foremost a means of liberating directors from the oppressive apparatus of major motion-picture film-making, Vinterberg had little to be liberated from. His first feature film, *The Greatest Heroes*, was still a year away.

Søren Kraugh-Jacobsen, the next film-maker to join Dogma 95, was by contrast a well-established director in Denmark. At forty-eight, he was also,

On the road in Sweden: scene from Thomas Vinterberg's first feature film *The Greatest Heroes* (1996)

thus far, the senior member, and he would be the one to most actively question its rules. Originally trained as an appliance repairman back in the
1960s, he went on to attend the famous Prague film school, FAMU, in 1969,
but in 1971 was thrown out.[5] Back in Denmark, he found employment in
DR's children and youth department. Beginning in 1977, he made a string of
generally well-received 'children-friendly' feature films, including von
Trier's behated *Gummi Tarzan*, but he was equally well known to the Danish
public as a musician – a guitar player and folk singer in the troubadour style.
His 70s hit, 'Kender Du Det?' ('You Know the Feeling?') about a boy's first
love, is a golden-oldie for every Dane.

Other directors were considered for inclusion as the concept of Dogma
was playfully bandied about over the course of a 'night of red wine' which
took place at a secluded summer house that spring. 'We sat around a table
drinking a lot of wine,' Kraugh-Jacobsen recalled.[6] 'We didn't agree on a lot
of things. So we screamed and shouted – Danes being like Italians – and we
questioned each other: "How do you want to deal with rule 5" – or whatever.
I found it very funny ...'

Soon after, two more directors joined up, Kristian Levring, who was living in Paris at the time, and Anne Wivel.

The thirty-eight-year-old Levring had also graduated from the
Film School, in the editing line. He had thus far made one feature
film, *A Shot From the Heart*, in 1986. It was a low-budget futuristic action
film which was a flop with the critics and sold only 3,354 tickets, even less
than *Epidemic*. He went on to work as an editor on documentary and feature
films, and in 1988 began to make commercials, many of them for foreign
companies. He lived for long stretches in London, Paris and elsewhere.

Anne Wivel was the daughter of well-known author, Ole W. Wivel, and at
forty-nine she was now the senior member of the group. She had been making social-realistic documentaries since her graduation from the Film
School in 1980, where, as previously noted, she had been a student repre-
sentative on the selection committee that had accepted von Trier into the
School. Approximately two years after the foundation of Dogma 95, however, she quit, and it became a true 'brotherhood'. 'I think', said Aalbæk
Jensen later, 'her attitude was "stupid boys!", or "stupid games!", or some-

thing ...'[7], while Levring was of the opinion that she favoured the documentary genre and didn't care to make fiction.

Other directors that von Trier and Vinterberg invited to join weren't interested, among them the Finnish film-maker, Aki Kaurismaki, who, as the Danish tabloid *Ekstra Bladet* reported, 'gave Dogma the finger',[8] dismissing the idea as stupid and childish. And others that they *didn't* ask to join also refused, such as Ole Bornedal, who weighed in with his opinions in a big 25 March spread on Dogma that appeared in *Politiken*. 'It's a *concept*, and one can always waste time on concepts if one has nothing else to do. ... I would rather fuck than become celibate,' he opined in reference to the 'vows of chastity'.

Von Trier and Aalbæk Jensen claim that the initial reaction to Dogma was overwhelmingly dismissive, but this was hardly the case. In the same comprehensive 25 March piece that contained Bornedal's comments, Mogens Rukov, von Trier and Vinterberg's old manuscript teacher from the Film School, got lots of space to praise the idea to the skies. Even Aalbæk Jensen himself got room in the article to sing the praises of Dogma, albeit with his usual sense of irony: 'If shit comes out of it, at least it's cheap shit.' Others, such as director Niels Gråbøl, had mixed opinions about it but saw it as a healthy challenge. And, as many pointed out from the very start, film history was already littered with antecedents to Dogma 95.

But the review von Trier remembered best was delivered by his colleagues down in Paris. 'Why do you come here when you hate film so much?' he remembered them asking him.[9]

The (first) death and rebirth of Dogma

Meanwhile the buzz of Dogma 95 continued to percolate in the press. The idea so intrigued the Danish cultural minister, Jytte Hilden, that in 1995 she gave von Trier a verbal promise that the government would support the Dogma project with 15 million kroner. He assumed he could supplement that 15 million with 3.75 million from his own company and could raise the rest from the DFI through the normal consultant channels.

On 14 August he wrote to Hilden to remind her about the deal, commenting that the 15 million kroner she had mentioned 'outside the normal DFI channels' sounded fine.

He got no reply to this letter, but in any case the project continued with 'the gang of five' (still inclusive of Wivel at this point) giving each other a handshake, valid in Danish law, and agreeing that they would set the plan back a year and reserve 1997 for their Dogma films.

On 14 February 1996, Aalbæk Jensen wrote to Hilden, referring to von Trier's earlier letter and asking about the status of the money.

He got his answer four months later, not from Hilden but from the DFI who announced that they had just received a new pool of money from the Culture Ministry – 15 million kroner – earmarked for the support of so-called 'low-budget films' and to be distributed over the next three years. Hilden wrote back to Aalbæk Jensen explaining that the DFI would administer the funds through the normal channels, and that he should contact them directly to get the low-down on the concrete possibilities, signing off with 'good luck'.

Von Trier was furious to discover that there was no special grant for Dogma 95, and that now all five Dogma films would have to apply for grants individually, in competition with anyone else who wanted to apply for the money. He had no doubts he could get his own Dogma film funded, but the whole idea was to do this as a group, in solidarity. This was supposed to be a 'wave' after all. Aalbæk Jensen claimed that they could have easily secured funding from foreign investors, but that that wasn't the point: this was 'a Danish thing' as the T-shirt might have read. Von Trier was also angry that his Dogma concept had been used to stimulate production of 'low-budget film', but that he himself was not getting anything out of it.

And what was all this 'low-budget film' talk, anyway? Dogma had nothing specifically to do with budget but rather specified a technical process that was just a means to an end – the end being the liberation of creativity. Von Trier wrote back to Hilden

> That Dogma films, in highest probability, can be produced cheaply has nothing to do with the original idea ... Dogma 95 is an artistic concept, not an economic

concept ... If I should make more films, as I hope to, the stupidest thing I could do would be to denigrate the relative commercial success I've achieved by throwing myself into a Danish-spoken low-budget film project ... and that was also not the intention.[10]

Hilden suggested they meet at the start of 1997 to discuss it, but in the meantime the DFI held its ground, refusing to grant a lump sum of money for a package of films, sight unseen, to any production company. That would surely draw charges of favouritism from other companies. First and foremost, the films had to exist as individual entities, to have titles and scripts, etc. Then they would have to be submitted for evaluation on their respective merits before funding could be approved. This was the basis of the consultant system that had underpinned film production in Denmark for many years. 'Dogma's proposal would have been a radical way of erasing that system,' commented DFI consultant, Mikael Olsen, several years later.[11]

It was also highly unusual for the cultural minister to meddle directly in the DFI's business, usurping the consultant's role and violating the 'arms-length principle'. She was a politician, not an expert in film production. The whole affair smelled of a private arrangement between Jytte Hilden and Lars von Trier, conducted through the press, with the DFI relegated to the role of bank clerk.

The meeting between Hilden and von Trier never took place: she had stirred up considerable controversy above and beyond this imbroglio with von Trier and was relieved of her post before the meeting could happen. Now he had only the DFI to direct his angry letters to, and that was cold comfort indeed.

While *The Kingdom* and *Breaking the Waves* were being hailed by critics around the world, von Trier found himself ensnared in a dreary political feud in little old Denmark.

At the start of 1997, he declared he would not appear in public or give any more interviews, leaving it up to Aalbæk Jensen to clarify things. In an 11 February interview with *Ekstra Bladet*, his partner clarified that Dogma 95 was now dead.

But by 9 April Dogma was alive again, thanks to Danmarks Radio which had cobbled together the 15 million kroner with the help of other Scandinavian TV stations and the Norwegian Film and TV Fund. They now would fund the films (which still had no scripts), and this would be the first time since the establishment of the DFI in 1972 that a Danish feature film was produced without any state support. In return DR got permission to broadcast the films only three months after their theatrical premieres, an unusual circumvention of the standard twenty-four-month 'hold back' period normally respected by TV to allow films to exploit second-run theatrical situations, video rental and 'sell-through'. In fact, Zentropa would dispute this after the first two films were finished, claiming a new deal for a six-month hold back had been renegotiated with DR.

In any case, Dogma was back on track.

Psykomobile #1: The World Clock (and other conceptual experiments)

While the Dogma drama dragged on through 1996 and 1997, von Trier stayed busy on a variety of other projects, one of which, *Psykomobile #1: The World Clock*, had nothing whatsoever to do with film. Rather, it was a conceptual happening, a performance piece with touches of avant-garde theatre about it.

It had been suggested to von Trier back in 1992 that he create an exhibit for the Association of Art in Copenhagen. The Association's leader, Helle Behrndt, had been inspired by Peter Greenaway's exhibition in Paris (1992–3), *Le Bruit des nuages*, and was interested in having a similar multimedia exhibition take place in Copenhagen. Von Trier, however, didn't show much interest until 1994 when the first plans for Copenhagen's hosting of Culture Capital of Europe 1996 began to take shape.

By May 1995, he had created a concept with the help of Niels Vørsel. On 18 July the call went out for (unpaid) actors – fifty-three of them. The result: fifty-three different characters with personalities scripted by Vørsel and von Trier. They would inhabit nineteen different rooms in the Association's cavernous building on Gammel Strand, typical living environments such as a hospital room, a young girl's bedroom, and so forth. But von Trier had never wanted to 'direct' the thing himself, and eventually Morten Arnfred took on the job.

The 'exhibit' opened on 7 September and ran for fifty days. During the three hours a day that it was functioning, the actors would improvise basic scenarios alone or with each other. Their ever-shifting moods were dictated by the changing of four coloured lights installed in the rooms. Which light was lit depended upon the collective mood of ants dwelling in an ant hill in New Mexico, USA, which was monitored by video cameras. The video images were transmitted live to Copenhagen and fed into a computer where a program processed the signals into different modes of behaviour, which in turn activated different lights that signalled aggression, contentment or panic, for example.

Hence ants in New Mexico would be controlling a miniature society halfway around the world in Denmark. 'The ants have taken power,' began a review of the exhibit in *Information* 'as they will do when people have been bombed out of the world.'[12]

Psykomobile was a sensation, playing to full houses throughout its run and figuring as one of the biggest hits in the Association's 171-year history. Not bad for a guy who had previously been rejected by the Art Academy. Jesper Jargil covered the action with two small video cameras and that eventually resulted in a documentary entitled *The Humiliated*, released in 2000.

In his role as 'idea man', von Trier would in this way frequently depart from the film medium to engage in a host of other projects, everything from directing live theatre to creating stage design for opera to innumerable Internet conspiracies, and even at one point inventing a new ride for Copenhagen's Tivoli amusement park. He received lots of offers. His participation in a project guaranteed buzz, and whether or not it failed or succeeded, or even came to fruition, it was sure to be something new.

These conceptual experiments had and would continue to include the medium of TV.

In 1994, von Trier had conceived and directed six episodes of *Lærerværelset* (*The Teacher's Room*), what might be described as an experimental talk-show. Here well-known Danish celebrities were confronted, interrogated and chewed out by other well-known personalities posing as headteachers. It was supposed to be tough, sharp and funny, but despite respectable ratings, the show's premise never really worked and it was cancelled.

In 1996, he took another stab at the experimental talk-show concept with *Marathon*. The idea here was to put a well-known Danish personality and a journalist together in an isolated location for twenty-four hours. They would have no choice but to talk to each other. Assumedly defences would drop, masks would fall away and they would reveal their true selves in conversations that became increasingly more honest and poignant. Eight episodes were shot and edited down to one hour each, with a little clock in the corner of the screen to show what point in the twenty-four-hour period the viewer was presently observing. This show also proved to be a disappointment. One thing seemed certain, though: poor, sensitive, phobia-ridden Lars von Trier wasn't afraid of exposing *other* people to psychological stress!

The Kingdom II

While *Psykomobile* spun on through the autumn, von Trier was busy putting the finishing touches to *Riget 2* (*The Kingdom II*).

The delayed sequel to his hit TV series had kicked off with a press launch back on 11 June. Eighty to a hundred journalists had packed into a room that day in Danmark Radio's TV City, many coming all the way from Sweden. But von Trier never showed. He had actually been in the building but refused to attend the festivities due to a feud with DR over who controlled the rights to the show. He had even threatened to move out of Denmark because of it, although, according to a 12 June 1996 report in *Ekstra Bladet*, most reckoned this was just a ploy to put pressure on DR. His surliness could also have been interpreted as a lack of enthusiasm for the task ahead, making what looked as if it would be the same film twice. Behind the scenes there was real worry right up to the last minute that he would just walk away from the project. Morten Arnfred was back as assistant director, but Ernst-Hugo Järegård, again playing Stig Helmer, stated that if von Trier left the show, he would leave the very same second. Things were finally resolved and shooting began that same month and proceeded through to the end of August.

According to von Trier, *The Kingdom II* contained more fireworks than the first series, and the tempo was twice as fast this time around. And there was more going on. 'In the original *Kingdom* there were approximately five parallel stories that developed at the same time. Now there are 11 or 12 ... in the new episodes things become a bit more satirical. There is satire on many different levels.'[13]

The presence of evil was also more pronounced this time. Von Trier claimed he had no interest in the psychology of evil *per se*, but rather that his interest lay in exploring a person's dark side. And as a film-maker it was much more satisfying to deal in visual terms with evil.

> Evil is, to a higher degree than good, based on the visual. Trying to depict goodness does not make for good pictures. The visibly good becomes easily banal. You let a ray of sunlight fall across a person or a situation and all you achieve is that the picture becomes pathetic and banal.[14]

The new series premiered on 5 September again at the Venice Film Festival, where expectations ran high. Kirsten Rolffes attended, and at a press conference following the screening took the opportunity to thank Morten Arnfred for his good direction. 'Lars von Trier', she flatly stated, 'cannot direct actors.' Not true, countered the ever diplomatic and loyal Arnfred.

A press launch was held in Copenhagen on 22 September. Neither von Trier nor Ernst-Hugo attended. Nobody seemed to know where von Trier's head was at at this point. The actors had been told to reserve May of 1998 in their schedules for the shooting of *The Kingdom III*, but von Trier had just sent them letters telling them to forget it, that he could never have a script ready that fast. This had sparked rumours that he was on the brink of collapse and DR was in panic;[15] his no-show at the press launch did nothing to quell the rumours.

But what on earth did the public expect of him? Bente had given birth to twins on 18 September. The birth had been premature and both Bente and the boys, Ludvig and Benjamin, would remain in hospital for some time to come.[16] His mind wasn't on press launches.

In early October Lars and Bente were finally married amid considerable secrecy, Bente now becoming Bente Trier.

The gala premiere of the theatrical version of *The Kingdom II* was held on 26 October. Von Trier, no doubt moved by his new state of paternity, had arranged for the surplus from the ticket money (expected to be 100,000 kroner) to go to his newly created fund for 'victims of law number 460, Chapter 2, paragraph 3'. This was a law that had just been passed by the parliament on 1 October which made it illegal for single women or lesbians to be artificially inseminated, and even stipulated punishment if they were. This was perceived by von Trier, among others, as a fascist pro-family political move, a violation of basic human rights and the criminalisation of a minority. 'When politicians forbid a small group of women to become artificially inseminated, I don't perceive this law as a desire to save money but rather as a punishment action against women who choose not to live in the traditional nuclear family.'[17] It was a rare glimpse of the political von Trier.

The first episode of *The Kingdom II* aired on Danish TV on 10 October to great expectations. This was due in part to press reports that *The Kingdom II* had already been sold to more foreign countries than any other Danish TV series. Condensations of rave reviews by foreign scribes had also been published in the dailies. Stephen Holden of the *New York Times*, for example, compared it to *Twin Peaks* and found it superior. '*The Kingdom II* has greater mysteries to solve.'[18] (This kind of glowing review from America, or reports that a Danish film had been sold to America, could even occasionally make the *front* page of Danish papers.)

As for David Lynch, von Trier had somewhat triumphantly asserted at the start of *The Kingdom II* that he, as opposed to Lynch, knew how and when to end his series.[19] Not everyone agreed with that, now that the goods were on the table. Even though this was not the end of the series, some thought it had already derailed. In contrast to the overwhelming praise the first *Kingdom* series had received, many Danish critics were now decidedly negative. Anders Jensen, writing for *Politiken*, felt that the story and character development fell apart. That made it hard to interest or involve oneself in the series as a whole. It wasn't the sum of its parts, but just the parts, single scenes and exchanges that had a sketch-like quality about them and featured the kind of easy jokes found in situation comedy. *Information* called it chaotic, pretentious and trivial, and wondered if just being ground-breaking and new — von Trier's calling cards — was the same thing as being good.[20]

Ratings for the first episode were clearly disappointing, with *Ekstra Bladet* daring to call it an out-and-out flop.[21]

As for von Trier, work on *The Kingdom II* had not been particularly fun or satisfying. If the first *Kingdom* had been a 'left-handed work', this had been a no-hands-on-the-wheel endeavour. *The Kingdom III*, then, he predicted, would have to be done with both hands tied behind his back if there should be any freshness in the process.

In regards to *The Kingdom III*, DR now expected to see a finished manuscript by the middle of 1998 with shooting pencilled in for May of 1999, and broadcast slated for October/November of 2000.

But those deadlines too would go by the board, and the fate of the series was cast further into doubt when the two main leads both died. It had been known for some time that Ernst-Hugo Järegård was ill with cancer, and therefore his death on 6 September 1998 was a sad occasion but not a shock. The death of Kirsten Rolffes, on 10 April 2000, at seventy-one years of age, was however quite unexpected, her age notwithstanding. Many wondered how the series could possibly continue without its two principal characters.

It could and it would, explained Aalbæk Jensen to *B.T.* two days after Rolffes' death.

> It's a lucky thing we're making a ghost story. When Ernst-Hugo fell ill, we made a model which enabled the personalities in the story to slide in and out in a natural way that does not necessitate them to be on location when *The Kingdom III* begins shooting. Before Ernst-Hugo died, Lars made a deal with him that would allow us to use him as a ghost in the rest of the series. He himself thought that was great that several years after his death he would be seen again in a film. In fact that was a great comfort to him after he was informed he had a terminal illness. Now we shall confer directly with Kirsten Rolffes' husband to see if it is OK that we also use her in *The Kingdom III*.[22]

(In addition to eternal life on film, Ernst-Hugo would also get a Danish train named after him.)

This final instalment, which Vørsel expected to get written over the summer of 2000, would be just a single concluding episode of 110 minutes that would tie up all the loose ends. As of publication, however, nothing further has been heard of *The Kingdom III*.

The long-rumoured American version was finally set in motion in late July 2001 with the announcement that none other than Stephen King would write the script for at least the first episode, and perhaps all fourteen of them. It would be his first major assignment after surviving a near fatal car accident two years before. But while King was reported to be a huge fan of the first two *Kingdom* series, this would be a completely new Americanised version, not a remake. Possibly it would draw on his own near-death experience and his subsequent encounters with the world of hospitals. Aalbæk Jensen claimed they couldn't care less about this new version as long as they got paid.[23]

The Idiots – conception

Von Trier's public silence at the start of 1997 lasted through most of the year, and even compelled him to dodge a public audience with the Queen to be knighted.[24] He still got knighted, but opinion remained split as to whether his disappearing act was a sign of courage or cowardice, and there was some debate in the media about it that included the by now routine charges of arrogance.

It was again left to Aalbæk Jensen to explain:

> He hates to say anything standard and be a party to the hypocrisy that is part and parcel of making a film ... but for me as a producer, it's not funny to have your director take this position, and the American distributors are furious that he won't talk. After all, a director is supposed to promote his films. The bigger the budget, the bigger the press. But the man is an artist and wants to communicate through his work – and he has taken the economic consequences of his phobias and made cheaper films. Therefore he is now working on a Dogma film with a budget of 5 million Kr.[25]

That film was *Idioterne* (*The Idiots*).

Von Trier sat down to write the script for it in mid-May of 1997. He wanted to do an ensemble piece with plenty of improvisation. Two films that

Scene from *Weekend* (1962), the first Danish 'new wave' film and a source of inspiration for *The Idiots*. The script for *Weekend* was written by Klaus Rifbjerg, a friend and collaborator of von Trier

served as sources of inspiration were the 1973 Italian film, *La Grande Bouffe*, about four men who shut themselves into a villa and eat themselves to death, and a Danish film, *Weekend*, from 1962. *Weekend*, scripted by Klaus Rifbjerg, was a study of two couples who spend an awkward and emotionally painful weekend together at a summer house. It was the first real attempt to make a New Wave film in Denmark, and one of the first Danish films to deal with sexuality in an adult manner.

After just four days of writing, von Trier was finished. Further discussions with Mogens Rukov, who was also co-writing Vinterberg's Dogma film, *Festen* (*The Celebration*), helped shake out the wrinkles. Aalbæk Jensen and Windeløv read the script but showed no great enthusiasm for it.[26]

Von Trier has said that whenever he needs inspiration, he gazes across the tracks to the Ravneholm woods where he played as a kid. It was here he literally found his setting for *The Idiots*, in the leafy environs of the neighbouring town, Søllerød, a bastion of old money and wealthy villas just five minutes' walk from his house.

Here in an old, vacant villa inhabited by a collective of ten young Danes, *The Idiots* unfolds. The group, led by a malcontent named Stoffer, is engaged in the social experiment of separating themselves from the society in which they are otherwise productive members. They do this by passing themselves off as mentally handicapped. They attempt to find their 'inner idiots' by pretending to be retarded and openly 'spazzing'. It's part obnoxious fun, part mobile group-therapy session and part journey into self.

They keep up the façade among themselves as well as with the public. They take trips into town where they visit a swimming hall and a factory and stop in at a bar and a restaurant, evoking embarrassment, confusion and/or misplaced sympathy in onlookers. They are each on their own mission, so to speak, and they provoke themselves as much as the townsfolk. In the end the whole charade begins to wear thin as they find their inner doubts instead of their inner idiots, and are revealed to be just as hung up as the 'normals' — or so we are helpfully informed by neatly packaged promotional synopsis.

Once again von Trier was grappling with the theme of individuals who are outsiders in their own society. He had always felt himself an outsider as a child, and all his success as a famous film director had really not changed things at all.

Shooting

On 21 May, as he was assembling and preparing his actors, he began to record his thoughts and impressions on a dictaphone, often when he couldn't sleep. This would be his diary on the making of the film. He had long expressed a desire to see this kind of thing from other directors, and this was also in line with his goal to demystify the film-making process, to make it visible.

Into the microphone he confided a host of thoughts and anxieties as the shooting wore on through the summer, and as he himself crashed through various peaks and valleys of enthusiasm and self-doubt. He also ruminated on topics that had nothing directly to do with the film. He talked about his fear of getting cancer of the oesophagus, he mused about how his vegetables were doing and he reported on the therapeutic value of paddling in his kayak. There was some thought given to it being published.[27]

After some amount of preparation with the cast, which included trips to hospitals and institutions, shooting began on 16 June. He was in high spirits, he had great hopes. The actors started getting into their roles, the film was becoming important to them. Von Trier reckoned this would be a great masterpiece, better than *Breaking the Waves*. One night after watching a documentary on TV about what would happen if the earth collided with an asteroid, he had a dream that it was about to happen, and that *The Idiots* was to be fired into space in a capsule and saved – 'this bizarre cocktail of a film', as he termed it.

But more immediate problems soon came to the fore, particularly with the improvised approach to the acting. At one point everything ground to a halt.[28] The improvised scenes weren't working. The actors lacked a frame or a model to play off, they needed 'building blocks', he came to realise. Most of what would end up in the final film was what had been in the script or was inserted in rewrites done on the run, contrary to the popular perception that the film was, by and large, improvised.[29]

The 'halfway party' was held on 5 July, and von Trier was still in fine fettle. He danced for the first time in many years, doing all his old John Travolta routines that he had learned at dancing school in the 1970s. There was a general sense that something new and good was coming out of it all, and there was a sense of solidarity between Lars and the cast, particularly on the 'all naked days' which transpired in a relaxed and asexual atmosphere.

But conflicts with the actors, which had existed from the start, soon became more and more frequent. By attempting to make a film which required him to work so intimately with a troop of actors, he was provoking himself, directly challenging his own abilities or lack thereof to direct actors – challenging his ability to simply just get along over a period of months with a group of people engaged in a process that he well knew would be psychologically exhausting.

Many in the cast were apprehensive about the nudity and sex scenes. 'Risky' moments lay ahead and they wanted to get their contracts drawn up. But when they raised the subject, von Trier 'became furious', according to

Knud Romer Jørgensen, who played Alex. 'He said that if we insisted on acting like a bunch of wimps then he wouldn't bother further with us.'

His relationship with the individual actors was also problematic, especially with Romer Jørgensen, whom he called 'Tosse-Knud' (Knud the sim-
pleton). The 3 July entry of the diary reads at one point that he used the day
to, among other things, humiliate Knud. Romer Jørgensen in turn called
von Trier 'Lorte Lars' (Shit Lars), until they agreed to a truce. 'He humili-
ates, exposes and makes fun of people, but he can be incredibly polite and
sweet to those he has just humiliated,' remembered the actor. 'He is an
eccentric voyeur, a sadist ... I felt like I was in a porno film for *adult babies*.'
Von Trier, he recalled, could be brutally sarcastic. 'When a scene didn't
work, he would say, "Thanks, that couldn't be worse."'[30]

No false praise there. But that was a good thing, according to Anne-
Grethe Bjarup Riis (Katrine). At one point von Trier told her, 'You quiver
your lower-lip as if you were in a fucking Bergman film.' She responded:

> I knew he was right. I had over-played the scene. Other directors might say,
> 'That was excellent, but we'll just try it one more time.' But the actor knows that
> is a lie and grows more insecure by receiving false praise all the time. His
> honesty ensures that you are completely secure ... but you are forced to have a
> sense of humour to be together with him. You are forced to have a sense of self-
> irony.[31]

On the other hand, as all conceded, von Trier was also capable of praising a
good performance in lavish terms.

Von Trier admitted to the dictaphone that he had feelings for both Bodil
Jørgensen and Anne Louise Hassing, the actresses who played Karen and
Susanne respectively. He ruminated about his past, apparently platonic,
relationships with actresses in his films. At the start of his career it was an
almost constant state of war – actresses didn't have confidence in him and
believed he was just trying to take them to bed. With *Breaking the Waves* all
that changed when he fell properly in love with Katrin Cartlidge.

There wasn't much of the 'proper' about his relationship with Hassing.
He fell desperately in love with her, at one point arranging a private meeting and then inventing some pretext to connect it with the film. Hassing

reciprocated his feelings to some degree, later stating that her work with von Trier came at great emotional expense which it took her some time to get over. He, for his part, confessed in the diary that his restless nights included, on average, five bouts of masturbation.[32] He tried home-spun therapeutical methods to work through his feelings for the comely blonde and managed to cut down to twice a night and get more sleep in the process. Bente was at this point in the hospital, pregnant with twins.

But as the shooting entered the final stage, the relationship between von Trier and Hassing – and all the others – cooled. He began to feel more and more like an outsider himself, excluded by the actors who had formed their own bonds. 'Von Trier was omnipotent,' Romer Jørgensen would say, 'and therefore he was lonely.' There were clashes, von Trier admitted, 'because they were allowed to show their inner idiots, and they were so unpleasant to me.'[33] They, in return, accused him of being impossibly sarcastic. Ironically von Trier was not only making a movie about outsiders, but becoming one himself and experiencing the issues first hand.

At various points the film seemed to be on the brink of collapse. Several times he left the set entirely and nobody knew where he was. A feeling of frustration and anticlimax settled over the production as it came to a close. Suffice it to say, everyone was burned out and ready to move on, one bold experiment in film *and* life behind them.

Dogma aesthetics

In line with Dogma precepts, the technical specifics of the making of the film had a direct bearing on its content and the formation of its aesthetic.

For example, no fake blood or tears. Emotions and the physical by-products of such had to be real – no props in any sense (Vow of Chastity number 1: No props) – Nikolaj Lie Kaas (Jeppe) got a genuine nose-bleed, and Bodil Jørgensen got her eyebrow gashed after being hit by a plate in the closing scene. 'Dogma blood!' shouted von Trier in the last instance, sticking the camera in her face. 'She was already on the way to the emergency room,' he would enthusiastically recall, 'before I stopped her to get a picture in the can.'[34]

Techniques of psychotherapy were used to get Anne Louise Hassing and Bodil Jørgensen to cry, the latter using at one point emotional recall –

the recollection of a sad old funeral hymn from childhood – to produce tears.

Erections also had to be real. This became an issue when Jens Albinus (Stoffer) had difficulty achieving one during the shower scene at the swimming pool. This led to some soul searching as von Trier mulled over the ethics of employing a stand-in.[35] What if the stand-in's skin tone was different? Could he colour-correct that in post-production? No, according to the fifth law of the 'vows of chastity', optical work and filters were forbidden. Blast.

On the other hand, stand-ins – professional porn actors – were brought in for the party scene which develops into an orgy. Hence were produced the few seconds of actual penetration footage that in large part gave the film its scandalous reputation and forced censorship boards around the world to clock in on overtime.

The actors could not deal with it, having porn models going at it in the corner while they played the scene in the foreground.[36] Some had to leave the room. But von Trier felt it was necessary that actual penetration be part of the film.

> It is important for me because it gives the film a roughness that it needs and maybe also a dangerousness that it needs since it is so superficial or lightweight in some scenes. And because a consultant who worked at an institution for the mentally handicapped said that our portrayal of the handicapped was very much on target, but that there was something lacking in the sexual sphere. I am certain that sexuality is a very big part of many of the characters, or ought to be. Especially exaggerated and uninhibited sexuality is an important part. It is therefore also important for me to get that facet right. To make a film on the mentally handicapped without taking that fact into consideration, is, after all, just like ... yeah, evangelical literature on sexuality.[37]

But for all the talk about hard-core sex, everyone on the set agreed that the spitting up of cake during the spazzing sequences was the most transgressive and shocking thing in the film. For von Trier personally, the most sobering moment was the food-play scene when the idiots spazzed out 6,000 kroners of genuine Iranian caviar.

On the road to Cannes

Shooting finished towards the end of August, and soon after a wooden trailer with avid editing equipment was installed in von Trier's back yard on Islandsvej. In early September editor Molly Stensgaard began the arduous task of panning through the 110–20 hours of footage that von Trier, Kristoffer Nyholm and Jesper Jargil had shot with small Sony cameras. It was so much footage that von Trier himself felt it was 'almost impossible to re-see'. Of the footage used, 80–90 per cent ended up being what von Trier had shot. Jargil used some of the collective footage in his documentary about the making of *The Idiots*, entitled *The Humiliated*.

Editing went on around the clock. Stensgaard edited during the day, and then von Trier went in at night and further edited what she had done, and then she later edited that further. He thought that worked out well. Eventually he had some rough-cut scenes to show to different people. They didn't dismiss it outright but seemed rather indifferent to the whole thing. 'It might well be a boring film,' he told himself in one of his last diary entries, 'but I do think it's wonderful.'

At the start of 1998 a print of the film was ready to run through a projector, and on 26 January a test screening was held at the Reprise cinema in Holte where the audience was duly requested to fill out questionnaires at the end. (In spite of their distaste for all things Hollywood, test-screenings didn't seem to be out.)

The Idiots and Vinterberg's *The Celebration* were completed in time for Cannes 1998 where they had both been selected in 'competition'. The inclusion of *The Idiots* was reportedly contingent upon von Trier showing up in person this time.

Once again began the ritual of von Trier's journey – or attempt thereof – down to Cannes. Would he make it this time? An entire nation held its collective breath as he set out on 13 May in his camper-van, armed with a stack of Country and Western CDs and a co-driver named Carsten.

On day one of what was dubbed 'Tour von Trier', *B.T.* published a map with a dotted line tracing his progress. He'd crashed through the Puttgarden barrier this time and struck into the heart of Germany – Hanover. By day two, chewing handfuls of Fontex (Prozac), he plunged south to Frankfurt.

Christian (Ulrich Thomsen) is violently ejected from the party in Thomas Vinterberg's *The Celebration* (1998)

From there it was all the way down to Avignon, and the next day just a short hop over to Cannes. 'Miden (the maggot) has landed,' reported Aalbæk Jensen, using the nickname von Trier had been tagged with because, as his partner explained, he was 'so little and pale'. 'Trier Wins Over Phobias' ran the headlines in *B.T.*[38]

Von Trier was installed in the exclusive Hotel du Cap, but the manager immediately insisted that he move his *déclassé* van out of their parking lot lest someone mistake it for a trailer camp. It was soon re-parked on a side street.

He began his bouts with the press, thanking Gilles Jacob for bringing him and Thomas Vinterberg down to Cannes to unveil Dogma 95 to the world. He claimed *The Idiots* had no chance of winning, 'It's not that kind of film,' he said. Anders Lange and Sten Wrem, covering Cannes for *Jyllands-Posten*, found him to be accommodating, 'but one never knows what is going on with him. His hands shake, he appears to be a man in disharmony. But also a sharp analyst – some call him a manipulator. But no one ever calls him uninteresting.'[39]

Most of 'the idiots' arrived in Cannes soon afterwards in a handicapped bus that had been driven for twenty-eight hours, straight down from Denmark. Von Trier's diary was to be published in French on the same day as the film's Cannes premiere, together with the manuscript, *Les Idiots – Journal Intime and Scenario*.

'Intime' indeed. Some of the actors were reported to be furious. It went beyond the pale for many, even by von Trier's standards. Bente had read the book in advance and approved it. That was good enough for some, including Trine Michelsen (Nana), who now poked through it to find her name and then tried to decode the French and figure out what was being said about her. The actors could always wait for the Danish publication in July, timed to coincide with the film's domestic premiere, or they could read the juicy excerpts that would fill the Danish papers over the course of the next few days.

As for the shapely, blonde, green-eyed Michelsen, she was right at home in the sun and sand of Cannes, pulling off her bikini top on various occasions for the benefit of the paparazzi ... getting half-serious offers from American porno producers promising to make her a star.[40] Actually she was already a porn star when von Trier had cast her, having posed for *Penthouse* magazine and acted in Italian soft-core porn films. She was also the daughter of the previously mentioned TV movie-show host, Ole 'Bogart' Michelsen. Her participation had given the film buzz from day one: provocative nude shots of her in *Ekstra Bladet*, where she had previously appeared as a 'page nine girl', had been used back at the start of filming to attract volunteer walk-ons. She had been the only non-actor in the cast and never spazzed, but had provided much of the film's nudity. At one point she had left the set in tears, accusing von Trier of using her as a clothes horse without clothes. All that was now apparently well behind them.

On 20 May, *The Idiots* screened at 8.30am for the press. The film was met with salvos of applause as well as boos. Von Trier was a no-show at the official press conference that followed the screening, leaving Aalbæk Jensen, Windeløv and the assembled idiots to fill in the gaps. He explained, via a note read by Windeløv, that he had to concentrate all his mental energy on the gala screening that evening. 'I apologise that I can't be here now, but I promise that it is no great loss for you, for I myself find that the film is full of moot points.'

That night, after the gala premiere, he claimed total indifference. He felt old, he said. He used to care about winning, but no longer.[41] The whole thing appeared to be a tremendous strain on him.

The Idiots party followed that night. Anne Louise Hassing was there. With the publication of the diary that day, his feelings about her were made public, but it all seemed like so long ago for both of them. It had been one of those weird psychological things that happens during the shooting of a film and means nothing in relation to one's marriage, von Trier would say. When the film is finished, that kind of thing is over and done with and it's back to 'real life'. It was just that kind of crazy business.

Dreyer knew all about that. He was often away from his family for many months at a time when he was shooting a film, and during those periods he led 'an independent life'.[42] The making of a film was an all-absorbing experience, a new reality, and that applied to the emotional side of it too. To simply put it out of your mind when you went home at night was a luxury that didn't exist.

The Danish public found it a bit harder to understand, and von Trier was obliged to reaffirm his love for his wife on more than one occasion, even faxing a statement stating as much to *Ekstra Bladet* from his camper-van as he headed back to Denmark where the tabloids were breaking the story. 'The book is meant as a description of a working process, and ought to be read as such,' he said. 'It contains my thoughts from that time – I have not reread it or corrected anything. For me it is a finished chapter which must stand as it is.' Taken in its entirety, the diary was in fact hardly the outrage it was portrayed as in the popular press.

The Palme d'Or ended up going to Theo Angelopoulos for *Eternity and a Day*, while *The Celebration* won the Prix du Jury to great fanfare. *The Idiots* won nothing. Although he had claimed he had no expectations for it, he seemed crushed. But Dogma had made its mark, and like a stone cast into a pond, the ripples were already widening.

The festival that launched Dogma, ironically enough closed with a fearsomely hyped premiere screening of exactly the kind of film von Trier and company had declared war on, *Godzilla*.

Critical reaction

While *The Idiots* did get some very positive reviews, it was a flop with the majority of critics and audiences in many foreign countries. Von Trier was regarded by some as something of a spoiled brat who was just seeing how much he could get away with, just breaking rules for the sake of breaking rules. He was a film-maker with an over-inflated reputation, wrote the *New York Free Press* reviewer, 'who attempts to make fun of the fact that he doesn't believe in anything'. Others found the film's message trite, like Xan Brooks of *Sight and Sound* who opined that 'The film's inner child message is a banal and well worn one.' Still others couldn't abide the film's primitivism and experimental narrative structure.

Particularly in America, *The Idiots* looked like a case of premeditated 'careericide', a confusing film that yielded up only one certainty: after this von Trier would never make movies in Hollywood. He had come to personify the industry's stereotype of the arrogant, self-absorbed European 'film artist'[43] who only made movies for himself and didn't care a lick about the audience. These kind of director were responsible for the fact, went the popular wisdom, that European films could hardly hold onto 20 per cent of their own markets! Annoyingly enough, von Trier had proved he *could* make big hits. Apparently he just didn't care to. That it had always been more important for him to experiment, change and express himself than have a proper career was something the Hollywood boys would never understand.

That many foreign viewers didn't 'get' *The Idiots* was no surprise. It was by far von Trier's most Danish film, acted out by an ensemble of Danish archetypal characters and with a very Danish subtext to much of it. In one scene, for example, a bureaucrat from Søllerød city hall visits Stoffer's phoney halfway house to inform him that if they chose to relocate to Hvidovre commune (county) there will be a substantial amount of money in it for them. Here was a reference to the practice of rich communes like Søllerød 'selling off' unwanted social services that they were otherwise obligated to provide to poorer communes, like Hvidovre, that needed the money. The rich communes would thus be rid of the visible manifestation of the problem and rid of the unfortunates that came with it. 'Fascists!' shouts a naked and raging Stoffer after the bureaucrat as he makes a fast getaway. Bureaucrats who, like better-known fascists from history, could also make such problems 'disappear'.

On the other hand, there were aspects of the film that resonated with, or rather, provoked, foreign viewers and critics more than Danes. All the nakedness, for example. This kind of thing isn't that provocative to Danes who have a more easy-going attitude to issues such as public nudity. Ditto the several seconds of explicit sex. Naughty, yes, but in a country where hard-core pornography is shown on public TV and where movie censorship for adults over eighteen was abolished back in the 1960s, scandalous it was not.

The Group

Many critics, even in Denmark, assumed that von Trier's motivation in making the film was the same as that of the character, Stoffer: to attack the bourgeoisie. Had this been true it would have made for an unoriginal film. As it was, several Danish critics called his portrayal of the bourgeoisie stereotypical and his attack on them flat and toothless. But it was hardly his objective to re-fight an old battle from the early 1970s, or even, as some critics and Zentropa's own blurb writers saw it, to show how futile that battle was.

He had set himself a much more difficult challenge: to explore the concept of 'The Group' which is instilled in Danes almost from birth and which stands as the cornerstone of modern Danish identity – and which really has nothing to do with the bourgeoisie *per se*.

In Denmark 'The Group' is what is called 'velfærdsdanskere', which literally translates into 'members of the Danish welfare state'. (In Denmark the term 'welfare state' has positive connotations, while in America it is something akin to a swear word.) 'Velfærdsdanskere' are, simply put, the vast majority of Danes. They pay their taxes and they vote. They are plugged into the system and they believe in the system. The system is right and good and just, perhaps the best in the world, but if it has flaws they will fix it by consensus.

'The Group' in a Danish context does not mean the Establishment. The people *are* the Establishment and hence the term has no meaning. It does not mean the rich or the powerful or the petite-bourgeoisie or the middle class or the working class. It means *everyone* – except the obvious outsiders. In this respect, Denmark stands in sharp contrast to Britain and America, for example, where identity is bound up in class, race and regional differences – visible differences – and where The Group has fractured into many groups.

Since The Group in Denmark is all-encompassing, it is also by its very nature invisible. The outsiders, be they foreigners or Danes, are the ones who are identified, categorised, counselled, debated over and dealt with ad infinitum while The Group itself remains an anonymous, monolithic and disembodied presence – just a state of mind, really. But to Stoffer and other real-life dissenters, like the autonomes[44] and the immigrant no-hopers, it is more like a conspiracy.

Søllerød was the perfect setting for the film/experiment not because it was a wealthy, upper-class area, but because by primarily economic mechanisms it has been cleansed of outsiders. It is pure 'velfærdsdanskere' territory, pure state of mind.

Not that outsiders, on the surface, are treated badly in Denmark. To the contrary, they get full admission to the generous welfare-state benefits. No expense is spared, as the dim view would have it, to keep them institutionalised in a kind of eternal limbo. They are kept in the system but out of The Group. In return for spending money and seeking solutions to help them, The Group gets absolution from charges of racism, prejudice and indifference – important for a people who consider their society to be an exceptionally human one.

That the spazzers themselves were 'velfærdsdanskere' was no great irony. This was no ill-fated rebellion by naïve idealists against an entrenched elite. It cannot be said they were discontented drop-outs, just as it cannot be said that living in a commune in Denmark, as many prominent Danes did, meant one was 'dropping out' in the way that it did in America or Britain. To the contrary, it was a sign of dropping *in*, of seeking to improve society by finding different ways to make it work. The trip these people were on was as much of an inner journey as any kind of outward rebellion. The same can be said of Stoffer's spazzers. The invisible wall that they were striking out at and trying to make visible was also the wall within themselves. How far could they go? Could they ever really leave The Group?

On the surface of it, von Trier had made a film spiritually rooted in the early 1970s, concerned as it seemed to be with a reprise of the dated 'total theatre' antics of the 68'ers. But in fact, with his explorations of The Group, he was dealing with one of the central dynamics at the heart of present-day Denmark's wrenching transformation into a true multi-cultural society, despite the fact that nowhere in the film does he tackle the obvious issues like racism or immigration. The Outsiders had already been over-defined, over-counselled and over-debated. Now it was time to find out who the Danes were.

Despite the overwhelmingly positive response the film got from Danish critics, it was too close to the bone for many Danish viewers who hated it or just didn't want to deal with it. The film was a masterpiece of awkward pauses and embarrassed silences, and reached people in different and not always pleasant ways.

The use of real mongoloids[45] in one scene bothered some. Bad and tasteless enough that von Trier's troop of fools *pretended* to be retarded, but to bring in the genuine item was beyond the pale for many. 'One must be Lars von Trier to escape serious charges of mocking the handicapped,' wrote Johs. Christensen for *Jyllands-Posten*, speaking for many.[46]

The segment of the feminist community that hated *Breaking the Waves* also hated this second instalment of the 'Gold Hearted Trilogy'. Ida Nilsson, writing in *Politiken* on 8 August, in a review headed 'Trier's Fascist Propaganda', found the film offensive in the extreme. She deemed von Trier's central female characters to be throwbacks to the idealised depictions of docile, self-sacrificing women found in fascist propaganda of the 1930s. (In *The Idiots*, Bodil Jørgensen [Karen] was the 'golden-hearted' character).

And not all Danes got the message. Aalbæk Jensen, for one, maintained he never understood the film,[47] but was still proud of von Trier for making

it. A lot of people couldn't get past all the talk about pornography and
provocation, and he appeared to be one of them, crediting von Trier for
'kicking the audience in the face'[48] by following up an acclaimed masterpiece like *Breaking the Waves* with a film like *The Idiots*. Yet that was never
von Trier's goal, to kick the audience in the face, or to see how much he
could get away with. He had often sought to provoke in the past, but ironically now that he had finally made a totally sincere film, everybody was
taking it for a provocation.

Theatrical censorship

As expected, *The Idiots* caused censorship problems. In Ireland the film was
simply banned, while in Norway censors sat and debated over seven seconds
of erection footage before deciding to release it uncut. This not only made
the censors look ridiculous but reaped the film lots of free press and gave it
the allure of the forbidden. In Sweden and Norway, for example (where the
Danish social issues also had resonance), *The Idiots* was only rivalled at the
box office by *The Celebration* and *Saving Private Ryan* (1998).

In the UK, *The Idiots* premiered in early November 1998 in an uncen-
sored version at the London Film Festival – festivals not being bound by the
BBFC's censorship dictates – and drew a full house. Thereafter it seemed
certain to get tagged with an R18 rating and end up confined to Soho sex
shops, but in a highly publicised decision it escaped uncut with a mere 'over
18' classification, and in so doing set a British censorship precedent. Von
Trier's *Breaking the Waves* had been a hit in the UK with public and critics
alike, and he was considered an artist, not a pornographer. Indeed, save for
a few seconds in total, *The Idiots* was as far from a porn film as could be. One
can only imagine the disappointment of the punters down in Soho had it
ended up there.

In South Korea the film also set censorship precedents. In Japan it was
shown in a censored version. In America, where it was released after a two-
year delay, prints came complete with black censorship bars over certain
body parts. News of the American censorship was announced in the 12 May
2000 issue of *Politiken* that came complete with a sample picture of the
naked, capering idiots sporting black bars over their bare behinds, drawing

ridicule from Danes. 'Americans must not see naked body parts in *The Idiots*, but they may freely observe the most barbaric and brutally violent scenes in films,' ran the caption. Writer, Karen Durbin from the *New York Times*, interviewed von Trier in Denmark and, according to the article, 'bought' the idea that the black bars were Aalbæk Jensen's idea.[49]

Filterisation scandal

On 20 August 1999, while *The Idiots* was out in the wider world splitting critics and public alike, von Trier got what was for him some disturbing news from a couple of the other Dogma brothers. They had heard from a couple of 'loose lips' at Zentropa's film lab that Aalbæk Jensen and Vibeke Windeløv had instructed them to use a post-production filtering process to lighten the film when they struck the release prints.

Von Trier was furious and fired off press releases damning this breech of the Vows of Chastity (vow 5: Optical work and filters are forbidden). Windeløv was in the US when she recieved von Trier's 'completely hysterical, completely insane' phone call.[50] He demanded that all prints be recalled, which was of course impossible.

Aalbæk Jensen and Windeløv apologised but countered that they felt themselves economically pressed to lighten the film, otherwise it would be too dark to see anything. Reportedly von Trier had actually already seen a print of the lightened version and hadn't noticed (which raises the question of why they needed to make a lightened version). Von Trier felt patronised, that people were telling him it was 'for his own good', and that's what infuriated him the most.[51]

A meeting was arranged between von Trier and Aalbæk Jensen. There was much shouting and yelling before von Trier stormed out four minutes later. The fate of the studio seemed to hang in the balance. Since the formation of the company back at the start of 1992, they had more or less gone their own ways and pursued their own agendas, yet they had worked surprisingly well together over the years. For his part, Aalbæk Jensen had always been grateful to von Trier for turning down big offers from foreign producers and staying in Denmark and working with him. This was the first really serious, or at least first really public, blow-up between them.

It seemed that Zentropa might be finished.

'When we started this company,' said Aalbæk Jensen 'we gave each other a handshake that the whole thing could be dissolved in ten minutes.'[52] Whether it would come to that, he didn't know. If it did, he claimed he would get out of the film business altogether and buy a hog farm. He apparently had a softer place in his heart for farm animals than for employees or competitors, as practically the only photo this writer ever saw of him without his cigar was one of him lovingly holding a chicken.

The four-month shoot of von Trier's current film, *Dancer in the Dark* (2000), had just wrapped. It was at that point the most expensive film ever made in Scandinavia and it was rumoured to have been a troubled production, plagued by fights between the film's star, the Icelandic pop singer, Björk, and von Trier. If true, that must have added immensely to the mental strain he was feeling at the time.

Aalbæk Jensen was asked by *Ekstra Bladet* whether *Dancer in the Dark* would be affected by their feud. 'I don't know,' he replied, 'but Lars is contractually obligated to finish it. If he refuses, our insurance company will come after him.'[53]

There was a press meeting the next day with the Dogma brothers to announce something called 'The Millennium Project', and it was doubted that von Trier would show up in light of all the bad blood.

The blow-up eventually blew over. It was agreed that all copies of the film in the future would be released as '100% controlled Lars von Trier versions', and von Trier himself later played down the incident, chalking it up to a communication problem.

Some wondered why he was being such a purist about the fifth Dogma rule when there were, in fact, other violations in the film. Couldn't the porn actors be considered 'props' brought in from outside? And the wheelchair that ended up in the tree. Lars had told Windeløv he needed one. 'I brought it to the house,' she remembers, 'and told Lars it was outside. He became totally hysterical and said it couldn't happen like that, that we should leave it elsewhere and one of the actors would fetch it.'[54] Hence she assumed it was also like that with lightening the film, that if she asked him straight out he would have to object, but that maybe it was OK if it just happened. In any case, how strictly the Vows of Chastity were to be interpreted was an issue of considerable debate. 'Dogma 95,' von Trier himself had stated, 'contains certain impossible and paradoxical rules,'[55] and as the Dogma website put it, 'There is an implicit duplicity in the Dogma manifesto. On one hand it contains a deep irony, and on the other hand is seriously meant.'

Dogma goes to Hollywood

While von Trier occupied himself with his new and in many ways very un-Dogma-like film, *Dancer in the Dark*, the ripples from Dogma were continuing to widen beyond anyone's initial expectations.

Thomas Vinterberg was in Los Angeles in January of 1999 to attend the Golden Globe Awards, for which *The Celebration* had received a nomination, and while there had lunch with Steven Spielberg, a declared fan of the film, and attempted to convince him to make a Dogma film. The Dogma boys had challenged lots of established directors to make Dogma films, from Kubrick to Kurosawa, but the creator of *Star Wars* (1978) figured as nothing less than the anti-Christ, and his conversion would have been the greatest coup. Failing that, at least the attempt was good publicity for Dogma. And fail it did. Despite Spielberg's surprising announcement in an October issue of *Time* magazine that he would make a Dogma film, nothing ever came of it. More Dogma smoke.

The Celebration was also nominated for an Oscar that year, and while it won neither a Golden Globe nor an Oscar, it was clearly a much bigger hit, if a much less daring film, than *The Idiots*. In Europe *The Celebration* was perceived as the kind of pan-European success that was needed to break the grip Hollywood had on their theatre-going public.

At that year's Rotterdam Film Festival, about the same time Vinterberg was lunching with Spielberg, former Warhol cameraman, Paul Morrissey, was presenting his new Dogma project at the Festival's market sidebar, Cinemart, in hopes of attracting funding. Entitled *The House of Klang*, it was to be a comedy about the fashion industry and would be produced by Vibeke Windeløv. It would be Dogma film number five, as Anne Wivel had never been replaced, and it would star Udo Kier, who Morrissey had directed back in the early 1970s in *Flesh for Frankenstein* and

Blood for Dracula (a.k.a *Warhol's Frankenstein* and *Warhol's Dracula* in the US).

'I was already making dogma films thirty years ago,' noted Morrissey.[56] 'Back then they were called something else, and were "dogma" out of pure necessity. But I am probably thus far the only director who has adhered to the manifesto's point number 10: that the director must never be credited.'

Following Rotterdam by only a few days was the Berlin Film Festival, where on Saturday, 13 February, Søren Kraugh-Jacobsen's *Mifune* – Dogma film number three – was to screen 'in competition'.

The film was not considered a contender, but after its screening senti-ment swung in its favour. The buzz became so substantial that Aalbæk Jensen refused to sign any of the foreign sales rights that he had already negotiated, hoping a Silver or Golden Bear would drive up the price. The tactic didn't win him any friends among the distributors. 'I don't dare go out alone in the evenings,' he commented to *Ekstra Bladet*,[57] 'People are about ready to beat us to death. ... Last year in Cannes no one really cared about

Søren Kraugh-Jacobsen on the set of *Mifune* (1999)

Dogma, but here in Berlin it's become a label, just like Coca-Cola.' Zentropa had now signed deals for no fewer than sixteen new Dogma films.

Mifune did win a Silver Bear, and raised the bidding to higher levels than anyone had expected for a Dogma film.[58]

Kraugh-Jacobsen went on to dutiously promote *Mifune* in America where it did relatively well in limited release on the art-house circuit. Vinterberg had also gone to great efforts to promote *The Celebration* in America. Not so with von Trier. Let other directors flog their films through the land of McDonalds, the death penalty and the death penalty of creativity — Hollywood — but he would not and could not and just couldn't be bothered, it seemed. And anyway, they didn't let old communists into America, did they? He no doubt would have been happy had that been the case.

Dogma had become an international phenomenon. It had been given the blessings of all the right people. There were Dogma cells and cadres all over the world, there was a Dogma website and there were Dogma film festivals. Dogma was a shining inspiration to film-makers everywhere, particularly in the American independent scene which had always been in opposition to the tendencies of commercial film-making. The feminist group, STIGMA, was one of several organisations to embrace the Dogma approach there, issuing their own 'Vows of Chastity' which included 'no shopping montages', 'no male fantasy lesbian make-out scenes' and 'no glamorous naked female corpses'.

And as fodder for mindless cocktail chatter in film circles, Dogma was inexhaustible. One could mention just about any forgotten old film director and ask what he was doing now, and inevitably someone would say he was making a Dogma film. Then somebody else would chime in that said director had made Dogma films long before the term had been coined. But a backlash was already starting to form. Some people were sick of Dogma. Dogma was cliché, Dogma was counter-revolutionary. Anti-Dogma groups were springing up, issuing their own anti-Dogma manifestos.[59] All of which was just fine with Aalbæk Jensen and the brotherhood. Dogma, they maintained, was never intended to become the norm. Bring on the new rebellions!

But as a profitable cottage industry for Zentropa and Nimbus, the goods had never been fresher. Though they had never copyrighted the term, its unexpected success as a sellable commodity, and the potential for others to unfairly exploit it, suggested that some kind of certification process was necessary. By May of 1999, any official Dogma film had to be certified and approved by the Dogma brothers.

Later that same year, in October, a Dogma secretary was employed to answer enquiries and update the Dogma website, and an honour system was instituted. Would-be Dogma directors would sign a pledge stating they would honour the Vows of Chastity and, after paying a fee, their Dogma certificate would arrive in the mail. The Dogma brothers were now relieved of the impossible task of looking at every home-video somebody sent them and then discussing it ad infinitum. They'd never get another thing done in their lives if that continued. Applicants could easily cheat, admitted von Trier, but first and foremost they would be cheating themselves.

Five
Projects and Provocations

Quiet Waters

Back on the brink of his memorable no-show in Cannes (not) to accompany *Breaking the Waves*, von Trier had pulled another prank on the Danish public – or so it had seemed at first glance when on 30 April 1996, he had purchased the film rights to the books of the popular author, Morten Korch (1876–1954). It was hailed in the press as the Danish film deal of the century. Von Trier and the author's son sealed the deal with a handshake as flashbulbs popped.

As a Zentropa promotional blurb expressed it,

> Korch's writing rested on invariable [*sic*], permanent pillars – the will for
> financial, social and individual independence, true harmony in a patriarchal
> family life between husband and wife in the home, and Our Lord as the guiding
> Light. Korch strongly emphasised man's ties with his kin, land and country, and
> always assured his readers that things would work out in the end.

If Korch meant this to Zentropa, he meant something quite different to most cultured Danes: pure kitsch. To von Trier's culturally progressive parents, for example, 'Morten Korch was the worst swear word one could utter.'[1] Here, then, was another rebellion against his upbringing. Except that he also agreed – Korch was totally *beyond* sentimental.

Nevertheless, the author's old films seemed to be enjoying a revival in the 1990s, even with young viewers. Above and beyond that, the pairing of Lars von Trier and Morten Korch aroused interest. How could this be true, wondered the average Dane? Von Trier had done everything under the sun to break with Danish film traditions, while the countless adaptations of Korch's rustic folk melodramas were the essence of that film tradition in its most inert form.

Could a post-modern wise guy tame his fiendishly clever sense of irony and do 'straight up' Morten Korch? He claimed that was his mission: to bypass the film adaptations and go straight to the literary source material, to film the books as literature without irony.

In any case, with his distaste for shooting other people's stories, he had no intention of directing any of the films himself. Rather, he intended to act as a kind of creative producer and shape the projects. To this end he drafted in a cadre of other directors who included most of the usual suspects: Susanne Bier, Thomas Vinterberg, Anders Refn and Morten Arnfred. If he wanted to commit careericide, fine, but now it seemed he was trying to drag a good chunk of Danish directorial talent over the cliff with him. According to von Trier, they all screamed with laughter when he first told them about the idea. Arnfred, after having caught his breath, cautioned von Trier that one would ruin the material if one distanced oneself from it.

It wasn't certain which director would be the first to film a Korch novel. In fact none of them would as they all pulled out of the project on one pretext or another.

The first return on the film deal of the century was no movie at all but a twenty-six-part TV series entitled *Quiet Waters*. Von Trier was the series' very 'hands on' executive producer and promoter, and had spent considerable time on the manuscript through the spring of 1998. The relatively unknown Henrik Sartou directed the first part of the series with Lone Scherfig directing some of the later episodes.

Set in rural Denmark in the 1950s, *Quiet Waters* was the story of a close-knit farm village and the passions that flare and the triumphs and tragedies that play out among the unsophisticated cast of characters who don't experience a single dream sequence or bizarre cameo by Udo Kier. The first episode aired on 25 February 1999.

If *The Kingdom* had been a new invention of some sort, this seemed to be a rebellion against new inventions, a shockingly straightforward period costume drama that was as far from anything that could be called hip as possible. 'It's my belief that we will achieve something lasting with all this,' von Trier stated in a promotional blurb. 'More than mere entertainment for the television screen, it will be a jab in the side of all that is pretentious and laboured.'[2] And with some viewers, at least, he succeeded. Fans of the series found it to contain real substance and a modern relevance. To them it was not just a nostalgia trip or secondhand tribute to Korch.

The trouble was that there weren't many of them: *Quiet Waters* was only a modest success, if that, and lacked the buzz of previous von Trier projects.

Only a single feature film ever came out of the Morten Korch project: *Fruen På Hamre (The Lady of Hamre)*. It told the story of Bente True, who, after inheriting the family farm, Hamre, promises her dying father she will marry Gorm Trolle from the larger neighbouring farm, even though she really loves the poor smallholder, Mogens. A sensible marriage with the coarse Gorm turns into a power struggle over who shall control the farm. (One had to wonder what Monty Python would have done with the material. Or even a young von Trier, who in the past had expressed a fondness for the English satirists.)

Originally the film was to have been directed by Susanne Bier but was later assigned to Katrine Wiedemann. Bodil Jørgensen (Karen, of *The Idiots*) had a part. Vinca Wiedemann wrote the script and found von Trier to be positive and constructive in their constant give-and-take, although he had her under strict orders not to talk to Susanne Bier, at that time still the director, since the intention was that the manuscript should have *his* fingerprints on it.[3]

Released in early 2000, the film was a flop with the public, ranking thirteenth at the box office out of the sixteen Danish features released that year. After that nothing more was heard about the Danish film deal of the century.

Project D-Day

The new millennium was fast approaching, and so was a new collective Dogma endeavour called *Project D-Day*, the final incarnation of 'The Millennium Project' that the brothers had announced back on the heels of *The Idiots* filterisation scandal.

The idea had originated at Nimbus Film where Thomas Vinterberg was resident director. It wasn't originally intended to be a Dogma project as such, but came to be perceived as one after Vinterberg talked his Dogma brethren into participating.

The concept was intriguing: on new year's eve four professional actors would be fitted with discreet earphones and shadowed by one cameraman each as they were put into motion on the streets of deliriously chaotic Copenhagen. Armed with only a vague story outline, each actor would be directed by a specific Dogma brother via the earphones. Over the course of the seventy-minute 'movie' the four plotlines would be brought together in a single ending. As for rehearsals, only one general test was held and it was a disaster. It was a gamble to be sure, but few Danish actors could turn down a chance to make history with the country's hottest crop of directors. And anyway, it was a time for risk-taking. After all, on new year's eve of 1999 nobody even knew what was going to happen to the *world*.

If the concept seemed new and novel, the advance promotion was old-fashioned overkill of the kind any old show-business pro could admire. To some, like writer Hans Jørgen Møller, who dubbed it 'The Dogma Brothers' Flying Circus', it had the feel of a media stunt.

The next evening, on 1 January 2000, at 7.30pm – the prime TV slot of the year – the result was broadcast over seven Danish TV channels (the four major stations and three affiliates) in an unheard of act of corporate cooperation that would be hard to envision in any other country. (Originally the intention was to broadcast it globally.) Viewers had six options to choose from and could zap between the channels to edit and create their own films, or so went the idea. One could follow any of the four individual storylines develop or watch all four stories unfold on a four-panelled screen. Two other stations offered a behind-the-scenes peek at the directors at work in their communications bunker in the Tivoli amusement park, excepting von Trier who, in deference to his legendary shyness, was allowed to operate from the secretive confines of Zentropa's new studio in Avedøre. The intense media glare must have begun to wear on the three directors left to face the music, as the advance hype was staggering.

The greatest show on Earth, as the media would have it, to mark the biggest global celebration in living memory.

How could it *not* fail?

And fail it did. The story of a bungled bank robbery was less than compelling (or coherent), and for lack of a good old-fashioned script, the actors were often left with nothing specific to do except run through streets and alleys and up and down stairways, yelling hysterically. Perhaps the high point was when one of the actors improvised and handcuffed another to a filing cabinet in the bank, shutting down one of the storylines until desperate threats and pleadings from all concerned persuaded him to un-cuff her.

'The idea was better than the result', headed a piece by Helle Hellman in the 4 January issue of *Politiken* which surveyed the reactions of Danish scribes. A worthy experiment, said some, including most of the TV executives involved. A con-job and a farce, said others.

Average Danes, less apt to indulge conceptual experiments, thought it a flat-out fiasco judging by the general feedback in the media and this writer's own extensive if informal poll. They were confused, mystified, frustrated. 'It departed too much from fundamental principles,' Vinterberg would later comment. 'We didn't create a common story but ended up fiddling with our own stories ... people didn't get the connecting information, the sense that a common story was taking place. ... People felt the four characters, each controlled by a different director, were not able to react to each other.'[4]

Nonetheless, *Project D-Day* raised some interesting issues about interaction between director, actor and audience. Viewers, for one, were encouraged to be active and participate in the process in a medium that usually demands only passivity. Moreover, here was a film broadcast twenty-four hours after it was shot – not the usual twenty-four *months* it takes the normal commercial feature film to reach the screens. Consider the revolutionary concept of a film (or whatever it was) received simultaneously by the press and public, enabling the audience to form their own opinions and experience a sense of discovery. Normally one doesn't get a chance to see a film until it has been reviewed, promoted and discussed to death. With *Project D-Day*, results notwithstanding, the sense of discovery was back, and the sense of immediacy was nigh-on revolutionary. It was, if nothing else, a radical experiment. Nobody knew what was going to happen, not the actors, producers or the big TV company executives.

It was announced that *Project D-Day* would be conformed into a regular feature film and released in 35mm prints to Danish theatres in March, and thereafter rolled out to the international market.

Nothing further was heard about this for many months, not surprising considering its flop with the public. On 4 December it was reported in *Politiken* that the film version had in fact been delivered as arranged but that von Trier wanted to make changes. It hadn't been until October that the final version had received the approval of all the Dogma brothers.

And it wasn't until another year after that – almost two years after its inception – that the hour-long *Project D-Day, the finished version* aired on Danish TV (28 December 2001), this time without all the hoopla. Opening with a pastiche of scenes of the four Dogma brothers directing their actors over headsets, it quickly cut to the chase and a real plot emerged.

A woman named Lise has got the phobia-ridden Niels Henning, the portly Carl and the well-dressed Boris involved in a plan to blow up a bank safe which, she promises, contains 10 million kroner. As they each make their way to the rendezvous point they must overcome bizarre distractions. Boris encounters by chance an insane comrade from his school days named Jørgen whom he can't shake, while Niels Henning and Carl meet a man about to commit suicide up on a roof top where they have gone to reconnoitre the area. (They talk him into postponing his jump for fifteen minutes in exchange for procuring him some female company.)

Finally they blow the safe at the stroke of twelve, and – pausing to toast with champagne – find no money at all, only papers. Panic ensues. Lise has set them up: her husband runs the bank and she merely wanted to obtain his private notes to find out if he was having an affair. In the chaos, everybody flees back into the streets.

Double-crossed and despondent, Carl and Niels Henning end up breaking into Tivoli where they steal a bottle of champagne and take a ride on the Ferris wheel. Boris, still trailed by Jørgen, has a change of heart and invites his old classmate up to his flat for a toast. There Jørgen shows Boris the wad of bills he found while wandering through the bank looking for a match to light his fireworks. Lise corners her husband at a party. He denies having an affair, only to have his mistress – Lise's sister – make an awkward entrance, quickly followed by the police who tell him his bank safe has been blown up. Touched by Lise's perseverance, they reconcile.

While some of the characters' idiosyncrasies were perhaps played too broadly for laughs, *Project D-Day* was now an entertaining mixture of pathos and dark comedy, an engaging and well-paced film which set to advantage what had all along been some pretty good performances. Editor Valdis Oscarsdottir, whose name loomed large in the opening credits, had managed to make a good film out of a mountain of largely aimless footage. And she hadn't used any new footage, everything in this finished version had been culled from what had previously aired.

In the final analysis *Project D-Day* shows how important editing is. It shows how hard it is to make a movie, and it proves perhaps that it's too tough a job to be left to amateurs – the viewers. And that, seemingly, is the opposite of what the project was attempting to demonstrate.

Project D Day was intended to collapse the element of time in film production. What was happening with that other risky conceptual experiment, *Dimension*, that had been intended to do the opposite, to turn it around and take it through the wrong end of the telescope?

Nothing much, according to von Trier.

> I thought it was a good idea at the time. At the moment it seems like a really bad idea. It's insanely hard to make. … There are some big dramatic problems in it. It's completely impossible to get any emotion or drama going when you only make two minutes of film every year. You don't know which actors you can continue to use, for one thing. It was a very funny idea, but it demands so much energy, and I don't have so much energy to give it at the moment. I'm tempted to lay the material I have out on the Internet for free use so people can take it further if they want to. I don't know what will happen with it.[5]

Dogumentary

At some point in April of 2000, von Trier and Aalbæk Jensen met with Zentropa colleagues, Carsten Holst and Maria Gade, to discuss how to go about putting the focus back on the documentary genre, which they felt was under-prioritised in relation to commercial feature film-making. Von

Trier, for his part, had toyed with the documentary form before in both *Epidemic* and *The Idiots*, and he continued to believe that the worst approach was to take the conventions of the genre as holy writ.

This get-together resulted in the formation of a new production company called Zentropa Real, with Gade as administrative director and Holst as creative director. The company would dedicate itself to the production and broadcast of documentary film and non-fiction TV.

They were already on the hunt for ideas and a number of projects lay in various stages of development, most notably a documentary on the making of *Dancer in the Dark*, entitled *The 100 Eyes of Lars von Trier*. Another project in the works was *Living Miracles*, a documentary about the phenomenon of Madonna figures that weep blood and people who exhibit stigmata, while a third project was called *Pølsesnak* (translated into either *Sausage Chat* or *Sausage Nonsense*). It would star Zentropa's own irrepressible Peter Aalbæk Jensen who, together with two other 'fat guys', would tour the country's *pølse vogns* to exchange witticisms and sample the greasy goods.[6] His two compatriots would be stand-up comic, Amin Jensen, and a character known as Master Fatman who had previously made his mark as a (Caucasian) Danish Barry White imitator.

Two other Zentropa Real projects involved von Trier himself. *Big Klaus and Little Lars* was a series of brutally frank discussions between von Trier and his good friend, the author, Klaus Rifbjerg, who had written scripts for some of the more influential Danish films of the 1960s, including *Weekend*, and who had previously played the dominating headteacher in von Trier's less than successful 1994 TV series *The Teacher's Room*. The conversations would be filmed over a two-year period, with the first show finally airing on 17 December 2001. The second project, *The Five Obstructions* was a face-off between von Trier and another one of his good friends, the esteemed documentarian, Jørgen Leth.[7] Here the two would exchange ideas and challenges as they attempted to hinder each other in the process of making films. They would force each other to improvise, economise and cut their ideas and technical execution down to the bone, using limitations as creative inspiration.

Von Trier was his own company's biggest star and they weren't shy about exploiting that, but would the general public be interested in the verbal jousting and witty exchanges fired off among these film milieu insiders? Perhaps, but as von Trier commented, 'Whether anybody wants to watch it, we really don't care.'[8]

The launch of Zentropa Real had been a perfect opportunity to issue a new manifesto – or four, in this case, all contained in the 6 May 2000 issue of *B.T.*. Four new manifestos by a quartet dubbed 'The Documentary Dogma Brothers'. Besides von Trier, they included Leth, his uncle, Børge Høst, and Tøger Seidenfaden, the editor of *Politiken*, who would bring a journalistic sensibility to the project.

Von Trier's manifesto stated:

> We are searching for something that is neither fiction nor fact ... that which cannot be contained by a 'story' or grasped by an angle.
>
> ... The material we are searching for is to be found in reality, the same reality where creators of fiction find their inspiration, the same reality which journalists believe they are describing but in fact cannot see because they are blinded by their techniques – techniques which have become the goal in and of itself.
>
> To seek a story ... is to suppress it. By emphasising a single pattern, genuine or artificial, by presenting the world as a puzzle picture with solutions chosen in advance (is to suppress it).
>
> In their search for the Story, the Point, the Disclosure and the Sensation, they have taken this subject matter from us – this; the rest of the world which is not nearly as easy to relate to or depict as that, but which we cannot live without!
>
> The story is the villain. ... That which one calls the wealth of real life has vanished under our feet, squandered by journalists who worship clarity and focus above all else, draining the life out of it in the process.
>
> How do we find it again? And how do we communicate it or describe it? That is the challenge of the future – to search without searching, to defocus! The defocusers will be the communicators of the day, no more, no less!

A year later, in the spring of 2001, Danish documentarians Michael Klint, Klaus Birch, Bente Milton and Sami Saif formed the first working 'Dogumentary' group of film-makers. Later Swedish and Norwegian directors would be added, with each of the six slated to make a film aimed at the Scandinavian TV market.

In October of 2001, the practical dimensions of Dogumentary became clear when von Trier issued nine 'Vows of Chastity' for Dogumentary along with a manifesto.[9] Zentropa, for its part, announced plans to challenge foreign broadcasters to choose a director from their own country to make a film that conforms to the new rules. As to whether this new 'revolution' will have as much impact as Dogma remains to be seen, but in any case the battle will be waged for the most part on the TV screen.

Von Trier's role in all this was perhaps best characterised by Birch: 'Dogumentary is like an experiment involving a bunch of people, with von Trier poised above us like a wizard waving his wand to see what happens. Will we fly at each other's throats or will we make a few interesting films?'[10]

Six
Dancer in the Dark

Conception and shooting

Dancer in the Dark, which had been in the planning stages since 1996 was the story of a Czechoslovakian immigrant by the name of Selma who comes to America in the mid-60s to get her son, Gene, an eye operation. The two of them end up in a small town in the state of Washington where Selma finds a factory job making kitchen sinks – tough work as her own eyesight is fading due to genetic causes. Her bleak existence is made bearable only by escape into a fantasy world full of music. They live in a backyard cottage owned by the policeman, Bill, who is her friend and benefactor but who is falling into debt in order to keep his wife in the lap of luxury. Desperate to pay off his own bank loans, he steals the money Selma's been saving for Gene's operation. She confronts him and in a dramatic scene ends up shooting him. She is soon caught and thereafter tried and sentenced to death.

The fact that this would be a musical constituted another radical departure for von Trier. It was also something of a departure for Danish film, as it would be the first musical produced in Denmark since 1967. Musicals were certainly more of an American genre, and von Trier was greatly inspired by *West Side Story* (1961) and *The Sound of Music* (1965), which he had seen as a youngster, although *Dancer in the Dark* would resemble neither.

In the autumn of 1997 he convinced the waifish Icelandic pop singer, Björk Gudmundsdottir, to write the music for the film. According to her, von Trier had sought her out after seeing her music video, *It's So Quiet*.[1] He also wanted her to play the lead role of Selma, and that she was much less enthusiastic about. Even though she had previously acted in a couple of smaller films, she considered herself a songwriter, not an actress, and normally turned down film work. She would claim that for two years she tried to convince von Trier to get himself a real actress before giving in after he presented her with a *fait accompli* – telling her he would simply abandon the whole project if she didn't play the lead role. In that case two years of work on the music would have been in vain.[2]

She agreed, 'for Selma's sake', having developed an attachment to von Trier's fictional character. The songs she wrote were Selma's songs, not hers, and she even knew which musical Selma liked best: *Singin' in the Rain* (1952). Von Trier's creation had established itself inside her head. And he used that to convince her to play the part. Selma was becoming a very real person to both of them.

But what kind of a person? According to Björk, von Trier saw Selma as a childlike figure whose musical musings would resemble nursery rhythms and children's songs. She, on the other hand, perceived Selma as a woman.[3] She came to feel that she knew Selma better than Lars did. As the shooting wore on over the summer of 1999 in Avedøre and in Trollhättan, Sweden, the two battled over the soul of Selma. And perhaps as a way for Björk to wrestle her away from Lars, she *became* Selma ... but too completely, without the distance a professional actor brings to the task, without the ability to leave the set at the end of the day and think about something else. When Selma, for example, was about to shoot her friend, officer Bill, Björk herself had a nervous breakdown.

Von Trier, for his part, had never been known for his professional detachment on the set, and the psychological battles between them were intense and violent, making for a very troubled production.

The film itself was a contradiction in terms: a social-realistic musical. Musicals were traditionally all about feel-good optimism and superficiality. About entertaining people. But *Dancer in the Dark* was not intended to entertain people.

Von Trier was again looking for an element of counterpoint that would give his film an edge, in the same way that he had given the melodramatic story in *Breaking the Waves* an edge of immediacy and realism by imbuing it with a documentary visual style. Contradictions were his stock in trade and could make a film come to life. Now he was once again searching for a way to subvert genre conventions in order to slip around the viewers' preconditioned expectations and reach their emotions. But here the challenge was much greater.

This would not be a traditional musical where people just started singing and dancing all of a sudden. These song-and-dance interludes usually had no organic connection to the plots, but in *Dancer in the Dark* the musical numbers were extensions of Selma's psychological state and the segues from reality to fantasy, predicated upon the gradual emergence of a dominating rhythm from the location soundscape, were key moments in the film.

This transformation was also accomplished by visual means: only fixed cameras would be used for the musical numbers and hand-held cameras for the rest; only bleak, washed-out, melancholy colours for reality, and radiant, happy colours for the song-and-dance interludes.

An additional twist on the photography had been worked out by Tómas Gislason who had often influenced the visual look of von Trier's films. This entailed the placement of a hundred small digital video cameras to record the musical numbers from just as many different angles. Footage from some of these hundred cameras, with colour heightened by electronic manipulation, would later be cut into the musical numbers. These 'hundred eyes of Lars von Trier' received a lot of publicity, but the technical implementation proved burdensome and the results were less than impressive.

Dancer in the Dark at Cannes

The start of May 2000 found Denmark in a patriotic mood, their Olsen Brothers pop duo having just won the Melody Grand Prix (European Song Contest) in Stockholm. Their winning song, *On the Wings of Love*, now echoed through Copenhagen's shops and cafés with a maddening frequency. And Cannes was coming up in a couple of weeks. If *Dancer in the Dark*, the only Danish film 'in competition', could win some kind of prize – not to say the Palme d'Or – that would prove that the country's star was on the rise.

The Festival opened on Wednesday, 10 May. On 11 May, Kristian Levring's *The King Is Alive*, the fourth Dogma film, screened in the 'Un Certain Regard' section.

The plot of Levring's film revolved around an international group of tourists who become stranded in the Namibian desert, and to kill time they stage an off-the-cuff production of Shakespeare's *King Lear*. It was shot in Namibia, in English, and, unlike the first three Dogma films, wasn't particularly Danish, but was, like *The Idiots* and *The Celebration*, an ensemble piece of the type that seemed ideal for Dogma treatment. It received mixed reviews but attracted considerable attention and even critics of the picture seemed to find it interesting in some way.

Von Trier arrived in his camper-van on Saturday, 13 May, nervous but in good spirits. *Dancer in the Dark* would premiere on Wednesday, 17 May, at which point most of the competition would have played its hand.

'Still Hope For von Trier' ran a lead piece in the 16 May issue of *Politiken*, which went on to report that thus far none of the films screened 'in competition' could be tipped as clear favourites. Liv Ullmann's *Trolösa* (*The Faithless*), with a manuscript by Ingmar Bergman, was generally considered one of the front runners, as was *Sånger från andra Våningen* (*Songs From the Second Floor*) , by fellow Swede, Roy Andersson. It was a good year for Scandinavian film.

On Sunday morning, *Dancer in the Dark* press screened. Sentiment was sharply divided. Pockets of squabbling broke out in the theatre during the screening, and after it ended there was a standing ovation, very rare for a press screening at Cannes. That evening at the gala premiere, a near riot broke out when a number of people were for some reason denied entrance to the theatre. *Dancer in the Dark* was clearly the festival's hottest ticket.

The next morning as Danes unfolded their papers, the superlatives jumped out at them in bold type. 'With enthusiastic lack of distance,' wrote Hans Jørgen Møller for *Politiken*, '*Dancer in the Dark* is a masterpiece of film art.' 'The Palm for von Trier,' gushed Per Dabelsteen. 'Extraordinary,' agreed Ole 'Bogart' Michelsen. And so on ... [4]

The French, always big von Trier fans, almost wholly concurred with their Danish colleagues. *Libération* praised the film's 'surrealistic elegance' and called it 'modern and stimulating'. 'A filmic horn of plenty overflowing with pain and joy,' said *Le Monde*. Reviewers from other countries added their voices to the chorus of praise, such as Ab Zagt of the Dutch daily, *Algemeen*: '*Dancer in the Dark* is an almost shockingly good film. It is absolutely the best film I have seen at Cannes this year, maybe the best I have ever seen at Cannes.'

After so much praise, the first slam, delivered the next day by Derek Elley of the influential American trade, *Variety*, was a shock. 'Artistically bankrupt on almost every level ... *Dancer in the Dark* will dance into box office darkness.'

It was the only review Aalbæk Jensen had read to that point. He later said:

> It was probably the meanest review I have ever read. It was great. I almost collapsed 17 times of laughter. The worst that can happen down here is that everyone starts thinking that the film is the favourite. The risk is then that the jury will go against it. ... The worst review is an indifferent one.[5]

Von Trier expressed indifference, noting that he was glad some people hated his film as otherwise he would think his career was over.

Battles on the set

Only now that the film had premiered did he feel free to publicly confirm the rumours of trouble on the set between himself and Björk. He admitted,

> It was simply dreadful ... a torment ... a sadomasochistic experience for both of us. An enrichment for the film but not for me personally. ... Every single second of the last two years has also been a strain for Vibeke Windeløv as well, due to the artistic incompatibility and temperamental battles.[6]

Windeløv later admitted that everyone on the crew considered it a 'doomed' project,[7] one that had clearly been on the brink of collapse at least once. A collapse that might well have dragged Zentropa down with it.[8] With von Trier about to have a nervous breakdown and Aalbæk Jensen totally out of the picture,[9] it was left to Windeløv to attempt to communicate with their star.

'Björk is very special,' commented Catherine Deneuve when queried about the affair. 'She is not an actor but plays on her feelings. And that is hard. At times she ran away for many days like a school kid. She is a very shy and private person, and in this situation it had a cost.'[10]

Björk hadn't been talking to the press (despite a clause in her contract saying she would promote the film as much as possible), but soon broke the silence to give her version. It tallied with what von Trier was saying, that the whole affair had been complete hell.

> Seen from every perspective, this experience has been a catastrophe for me. To be in the middle of the studio surrounded by hundreds of people, day after day, was a real nightmare. Every morning when I awoke, they were already there, right in front of my nose ... I found myself constantly besieged.[11]

Not only was she the star of a major film production but she was also the central focus of the aforementioned documentary, *The 100 Eyes of Lars Von Trier*, which was being filmed at the same time by Anders Lund Madsen. That was another camera being stuck in her face. At one point when he tried to film a violent argument, she stopped cooperating with him and he had to be replaced with another director, Katia Forbert Petersen.

To be the star of a major motion picture – what a difference from the egalitarian functioning of her Icelandic punk rock bands, Kukl and The Sugarcubes. Iceland itself, a Danish colony for 700 years, was not, generally put, a culture of power structures and hierarchies. Now suddenly she found herself at ground zero in the 'world of Lars von Trier'. *Danish Imperialism – The Sequel.* The struggles between the two seemed to take on historical dimensions. Von Trier felt himself unwillingly cast in the role of executioner, leading the condemned prisoner to her death, while she saw him as Napoleon Bonaparte and herself as Pippi Longstocking, battling for human rights.

Björk's performance was for many a central issue, especially since so much of the pre-release hype would centre on the battles between herself and von Trier. To some the film confirmed reports that he had brutalised her and that her tormented performance was no acting job, particularly in the scenes that took place in the prison. Here her suffering is deeply moving and/or disturbing. Was that the plan, to exhaust or torment her into such a performance? The way that, according to Hollywood lore, sadistic but brilliant directors like Preminger and Hitchcock had tormented great performances out of their actors? This would be highly unlikely in von Trier's case. He had been called a manipulator before, but this was not his style. And in any case, he seemed to have suffered at least as much as anyone else. But however he achieved it, and at whatever cost to the mental well-being of both parties, he got a rare performance from her. To repeat his own comment, the clashes were a 'berigelse' (enrichment) for the film if not for him personally.[12]

Total victory

These revelations didn't seem to hurt the film's chances, and if anything only increased the buzz around the picture. There was also some talk of a best actress award for Björk, but a jury half composed of professional actors hardly seemed likely to give the honour to a confirmed non-actor like her, however much she dominated practically every scene of the film. Lena Endre of *The Faithless* still seemed poised to win that award.

Sunday night finally arrived – the moment of decision. Von Trier was in the audience, head shaven, appearing a bit overweight and ill at ease, no doubt plenty nervous. His sixth time participating in Cannes, the fifth time 'in competition'.

When the winners were announced, even the film's biggest fans were stunned: *Dancer in the Dark* won both the Palme d'Or and the award for best actress.

On TV Danes could see von Trier, flanked by Björk, accept the award with typical awkwardness, only just managing a few barely audible phrases of thanks in an English much spottier than his norm. Flashbulbs popped and applause rained down on them. He hardly seemed functional, more embarrassed than happy. He mentioned his little son and said how he'd been vomiting all night long back home in Denmark. All he wanted to do was just to drive his little car back to his little home in little Denmark and be with his family. Humility Danish style, times ten.

'It's a shame that Lars von Trier is not better at saying thanks,' wrote Ebbe Iversen in *B.T.* shortly thereafter. 'It is not von Trier's modest style to hint that he is totally thrilled. He prefers instead to hide his feelings behind a mask of mild irony.'[13] Why couldn't he be more like Bille August, a lot of Danes wondered. Bille was *so* good at receiving big awards.

With his usual irony, von Trier went on to thank Gilles Jacob who was leaving his post as Festival boss that year. 'I want to thank Gilles. I don't know if he has much knowledge of film, but I am deeply grateful to him.' At the post-awards press conference he elaborated, saying what those who had followed his career already knew well: 'Gilles took my first film, *The Element of Crime*, down to competition here in Cannes. That was a difficult film. But participating in Cannes at that point was a great encouragement for me – it meant that I became known at home and in other countries. Otherwise I certainly never would have been able to make more than one film.'[14]

After all the trials and tribulations bound up in making *Dancer in the Dark*, here was the perfect opportunity for closure as von Trier and Björk sat together in good spirits behind a small forest of microphones, blinded by flashbulbs ... Björk caught once again in the gears of the movie machine, besieged from all sides.

It was the kind of scripted happy ending that movie folk expect. The pair had just received the ultimate reward that makes all the pain and sacrifice worth it, that heals all wounds. Justice had been done. So how on earth could this moment be anything else than perfect? The slick, tuxedo-clad Master of Ceremonies thrust a microphone into their faces so they could say that yes, it had all been worth it, and that they really, really did love each other after all. Even better, how about a quick but spontaneous and heartfelt embrace ... maybe some tears.

It was patronising and forced and they both displayed a singular reticence to follow the script. Millions of people waiting for them to say something but nothing to say. No, they didn't love each other, at least not yet and probably never, and neither of them ever retracted assertions that it had all been simply horrible.

But at least for an hour the rest of the world got the ending it wanted.

That night the Danish contingent partied hot and heavy at the Zentropa suite, a jubilant Aalbæk Jensen capping off the bash with his trademark naked plunge into the pool, a crowd of journalists and miscellaneous merrymakers quickly joining him. All this minus two prominent no-shows – von Trier and Björk.

A few days later Aalbæk Jensen and Vibeke Windeløv rolled into the Zentropa lot in an old black Bentley to hosannas, flower bouquets and photo-ops. The picture in *B.T.* showed a broadly smiling Windeløv in foreground, hoisting a bunch of flowers, while Aalbæk Jensen lurked in the background, one arm raised in victory, the other hand clutching beer and cigar.

What did he think of it all?

'It's just like when one has fucked: afterwards you just want to pull the quilt up over your head and sleep.'[15] Not a particularly outrageous comment from a man who routinely regaled journalists with reports of his sex life, but it nonetheless prompted at least one angry letter-to-the-editor about this 'pornification' of the language.

In the Danish media the win was hailed as a total triumph, not just for von Trier but for Danish film in general. It was seen as the crowning of the modern golden age of Danish film, initiated back in the late 1980s with the awards that Bille August and Gabriel Axel had brought home. In the same span of time mighty America had only managed to win one more Palme d'Or than Denmark!

But one had to pity poor Zentropa. According to Aalbæk Jensen, winning the Palme d'Or was the worst thing that could have happened to the company.[16] 'Zentropa has always been based on a childish "rasmus-modsat" mentality (being contrary for the sake of it), and suddenly we're world champions.' Horrors. Furthermore, the two had been acclaimed pillars of society: von Trier had received Danish, French and Swedish orders (been knighted) and been invited to royal balls; a year later his flamboyant partner would be inducted into the Danish *Blue Book* where only royalty and old money usually resided. It would take some spin on their part to continue to cast themselves as the scruffy upstarts of the film world. But they could always try. As Aalbæk Jensen claimed in a March 2000 interview in *Euroman* magazine, they both dreamed of launching into a project that was so politically incorrect that it would lose them all this respect in one fell swoop.

The euphoria over von Trier's victory lasted into June as the European Football Championship kicked off in Holland and Belgium. Although lodged in the 'Group of Death' with Holland and France, the Danish team seemed ready, prompting some patriots to predict total victory. Denmark had just won the Eurovision Song Contest and a Palme d'Or, they figured, so why not toss another trophy onto the heap?

Alas, it was not to be. Quite to the contrary, in fact, as the Danish football team finished dead last. (That kind of thing can happen when your over-the-hill goalie is being hailed as your best player.)

Danish response

Average Danes who couldn't afford to fly to Cannes or weren't film critics would have to wait until September to see the movie and make up their own minds, but in the meantime there was another more pressing issue to engage them – the national referendum on European Monetary Union, which was coming up on 28 September.

As the rainy summer of 2000 wore on, political debate intensified, with most government and business leaders coming out for the Euro. The two head honchos of Zentropa were also both 'pro Euro'. Von Trier had even contacted the pro-Euro Centrum Democrat Party and offered to make a gratis 'vote yes' campaign commercial for them. This was a position that many Danes fiercely opposed. Von Trier had also previously been dead against it, but no longer. Since Denmark was to all intents and purposes already a part of the EU, he said, it would be stupid not to go in for the monetary union as well. He was furthered swayed when he learned on television that all the new Euro notes would feature a 'national side' which depicted either the national seal or the royal crown heads of all the participating countries. That fired him up: 'The Danish Queen must be on the note, god-damn it!'[17]

On 23 September Zentropa and the Social Democrat Party held a Vote Yes rally at the studio. Visitors could mingle with various celebrities including von Trier, Aalbæk Jensen, comedian Jacob Haugård and even the Danish prime minister himself, Paul Nyup Rasmussen. Von Trier was forced to play host when Aalbæk Jensen, who had arranged the whole thing, was re-routed to New York to attend the American premiere of *Dancer in the Dark* at the New York Film Festival. 'The Eel called me this morning,' von Trier reported, using Aalbæk Jensen's nickname. 'He's having a good time. He was very drunk.' He himself hadn't thought much about voting, he claimed – this whole thing was the Eel's department. When all the speeches were over, some visitors departed the auditorium to take a tour of

Zentropa's facilities while others stayed to hear the cover band, the Tina Turner Jam.[18]

As it turned out, Danes voted overwhelmingly against the Euro.

*   *   *

The 100 Eyes of Lars Von Trier was scheduled to premiere at the Odense Film Festival in late August, and was generating considerable buzz. It came as a surprise, then, when it had to be withdrawn at the last moment. Björk had seen the final edit and had refused to be a party to it. It now had to be completely re-edited.

After Katia Petersen had taken over the director's reins, she had focused on the hundred-cameras-angle, but that was soon overshadowed by the stormy relationship between the two principals. The final edit included, among other scenes, the moment when Björk broke down as she/Selma was about to shoot officer Bill, and the scene where she, in a fit of fury, bit and ripped her blouse into pieces before stalking off the set and vanishing for days, to leave the whole production hanging.

Rather than continue to battle and argue with Björk over every frame of film, it was decided to simply call a halt to negotiations, cut out all the scenes that contained her and fill in the holes with additional explanatory narration by von Trier and more interviews with cast and crew. Zentropa Real boss Carsten Holst said,

> We would have a solid basis to insist on using the interviews, which she obviously willingly recorded, but we've decided, on humanitarian grounds, and for our own mental survival, to stop battling with Björk, finish this film and get on with our lives … But all who have seen the original cut agree that one gets a fantastically good impression of her.[19]

Once again, nobody seemed to know where the real ending in the film – or in real life – lay. It all just seemed so perfect that the ending should be that magic and deeply moving moment when Lars and Björk stood side by side at Cannes, lifting the Palme d'Or together over their heads and smiling broadly while flashbulbs popped and eyes misted up. That scene was in the documentary but unfortunately they couldn't freeze it, and life went on, and the battles with Björk continued. 'That was a euphoric moment we experienced,' said Holst, '... but then it became "the everyday" again.'

After all the many months – years, in fact – of hassles with Björk, and after giving countless interviews to the world press over the course of the summer to hype the film, von Trier must have been sick to death of it all by the time the Danish gala premiere at the Imperial rolled around on 31 August. 'I believe I just might fall asleep during the film,' he quipped.

All the surprises in a film that had been full of surprises appeared to be over.

Not quite.

When the film opened a week later, Danish critics trashed it.

'Unforgivably boring', ran bold heads in the *B.T.* tabloid review. 'The film left a worse taste in my mouth than if I had eaten 20 boxes of Kleenexes,' wrote the paper's scribe, Brigitte Grue, who went on to slam *Dancer* as an insult to the viewer and a pollution of their feelings.[20] Henrik List, writing for *B.T.* had, like most other Danes, high expectations for the film and voiced disappointment that Denmark's otherwise courageous, uncompromising and provocative director had botched the chance to make the kind of musical that would have been successful in the traditional sense as well as subversive enough to send Fred Astaire and Ginger Rogers spinning in their graves. Instead he found it to be a 'psychological snuff film', a piece of emotional pornography.[21] (A year later at Zentropa's Cannes 2001 bash, this review would win him the 'Surmulerpris' [sulky person prize] – a lemon.)

The Danish monthly magazine, *Blender*, called it von Trier's most bizarre film, while Anders Rou Jensen of *Politiken* called it his most disappointing.[22] 'There's a gaping hole in the story,' observed Morten Piil of *Information*,[23] which also printed a pro-review by Eva Jørholt, headed 'Shameless Masterpiece', in acknowledgment of the wildly divided nature of critical response. In fact several other Danish papers reconfirmed positive first impressions, but it was the pans that stuck in people's minds.

Aalbæk Jensen shrugged off the surprising attacks by his fellow Danes.

We didn't expect anything else. We know the Danish soul very well. Most of the papers which now attack the film enthusiastically sounded their trumpets for it in Cannes, but now they have apparently set other reviewers to the task. That is Denmark for the good and bad. Now that things have gone well for one of the nation's sons, they figure he should be knocked back into place.[24]

This was a direct reference on his part to what is known as the Jante Law, a mythical code of conduct that supposedly encapsulates the negative aspects of the Danish mentality, and is invoked by Danes practically every time one of their countrymen gets 'knocked back into place' or gets a comeuppance.

The term originates from the novel, *A Refugee Crosses His Tracks*, penned in 1933 by Norwegian writer, Alex Sandemose, who had lived for some years in a town in northern Sealand. In Sandemose's fictional town of Jante, moral and social behaviour was prescribed by ten firm rules, including 'You shall not think you are special. You shall not think you are good at anything. You shall not think you can teach us anything. Don't imagine you are better than us and so on, all of which can basically be condensed into 'Don't think you are somebody.'

Danes supposedly begrudge any success or fame that isn't leavened with great doses of almost apologetic humility. This represents the negative side of the famous Danish sense of egalitarianism. This egalitarianism certainly has its good points: it's the impetus behind one of the most fair-minded and progressive social systems in the West, and in a historical context might explain why Denmark never had a 'strongman' or dictator. Had such a person ever appeared on the scene and tried to get Danes to follow him, they would have just laughed and said 'Don't think you are somebody.' Now that Danes had a couple of strongmen in the film world, the same response apparently applied, the Jante Law being constantly invoked in regards to von Trier and Aalbæk Jensen. They constantly invoked it themselves. In fact it seems to be the Eel's mission in life to break each and every rule every single day.

*   *   *

After reading about *Dancer in the Dark* in the press for almost half a year, it was now time for the Danish public to judge for themselves. Released in a massive (for the Danish market) forty-nine prints, the film opened wide in big city and small provincial town alike as ticket-sellers waited for the block-long lines to form.

The lines never formed. *Dancer in the Dark* would go on to be a pronounced disappointment in Denmark, especially in light of the fact that it had received more free press than anything since World War II. 'Word of mouth', for its part, never took off. The film finished a distant third at the box office that year, selling 'only' 195,000 tickets,[25] a figure dwarfed by the previous year's blockbuster, Susanne Bier's *The One and Only* which sold 840,000 tickets. Björk won the best actress trophy at the Bodil awards (and predictably stayed away), but otherwise *Dancer in the Dark* received only minor awards at both the Bodil and the Robert ceremonies, shut out by *The Bench* on both occasions, a little social-realist film about a terminal alcoholic. A bit of a comedown it must have been for von Trier, who used to own those awards. But not for Zentropa. They had produced *The Bench*.

International release of *Dancer*

About a month after the Danish release of *Dancer in the Dark*, it opened internationally to predictably polarised response.

Critics of the film frequently focused on its lack of credibility in both setting and language.

The exteriors, shot in Trollhättan, imparted no sense of a specific place or period. Reportedly second-unit director, Anders Refn, took one location shot of Selma and Kathy on a street in Arlington, Washington, but it is almost impossible to spot. And aside from a few old American cars driving around (which at one point seem to be of 1940s vintage), there is little visible evidence that the story takes place in the mid-60s.

Regarding language, Björk dominated the film to such a degree that if one couldn't buy her dialogue, delivered in a 'hideous faux-cockney accent', as one London critic expressed it,[26] it was impossible to buy the film. Catherine Deneuve, for her part, playing Selma's friend and co-worker, Kathy, delivered her lines with the strongest of French accents, leading many to wonder how a beautiful French woman with patrician airs ended up working in a grimy small-town factory in the state of Washington. Von Trier had originally intended Kathy to be a black woman, but Deneuve, who had sent a fan letter to him after seeing *Breaking the Waves*,[27] ended up with the part. Udo Kier plays a doctor of Czech origin, but after a brief exchange of Czech with Selma, he drops back into heavily German-accented English. Finally there was Joel Grey, an American faking a Czech accent. The hand-ful of American actors (David Morse, Cara Seymour, Peter Stormare and Vincent Paterson) could hardly 'right the ship' in this respect. It seemed that von Trier took none of the pains he had taken with *Breaking the Waves* to ensure that the film was authentic from a linguistic perspective.

This was apparently not a drawback in countries like France and Japan, where *Dancer in the Dark* was a huge hit and drew over one and two million viewers respectively, but then again, prints in those countries were shown in dubbed versions and hence language was not a factor. In Britain, on the other hand, where the film was a flop, and where much to Aalbæk Jensen's fury some theatres offered viewers their money back if they walked out in the first half-hour,[28] it apparently was.

The popular conception, born at Cannes, that Americans hated the film didn't pan out. It got wildly mixed reviews in America, and did OK, if just, at the box office. But many US critics *did* hate the film with a special intensity and various theories were forwarded as to why.

Both Aalbæk Jensen and Anders Refn thought that the negative American press was probably due to the fact that the film was such a tough indictment of America's justice system. Other Danes, including the afore-mentioned von Trier scholar, Peter Schepelern, agreed. Such a supposition, however, ignores the fact that most Americans in the film milieu who would be watching and commenting on a 'European art-film' would overwhelm-ingly tend to subscribe to leftist viewpoints. They would hardly be commit-ted supporters of the death penalty, or in any case that would not be the issue to provoke their sense of patriotism.

Had any felt called upon to defend the death penalty, it would have been difficult. Shocking reports of condemned prisoners who had lawyers who fell asleep in court or showed up drunk to defend them were being featured regularly in the press. American jurisprudence appeared to have much to fear from the truth, but it had nothing to fear from *Dancer in the Dark*. With a defence attorney who never asked a single question and Joel Grey breaking out into song and dance on the Judge's bench, a tough attack this was not.

Furthermore, the courtroom scenes lacked credibility. An American jury in the mid-6os would be much more inclined to regard Selma as a heroic escapee from a brutal communist regime than the bad communist that the prosecutor so easily convinces them that she is. Had her defence attorney ever opened his mouth, he could have quickly had the jury in tears over how this poor little woman had escaped from a communist dictatorship to come to wonderful, free America with the simple dream of saving her son. At that time in America nobody *immigrated* from communist countries, only escaped and defected.

That von Trier had never been to America and got all of his impressions of the country from what he read or saw on TV was something he happily admitted. He and Aalbæk Jensen made much of the fact they never travelled to 'God's own country', and that when they dealt with Americans, they made them come to Denmark. But now that he was making movies set in America, his ignorance of the place was becoming something of an issue. There was talk about it in Cannes. 'People were offended that I would make films about places I had never been to, or make films in places I would not go to.'[29]

But hadn't Hollywood always done the same thing? If they could play loose with facts, why couldn't he?

'Creatively it's actually a privilege that I haven't been to America – so why not make more American films?'[30] Why not indeed. His next film, *Dogville*, would again be set in America. Had he not by now dismissed the concept of trilogies as a mere marketing gimmick,[31] maybe he would have proclaimed *Dancer in the Dark* to be not only the end of the Gold Hearted Trilogy, but the beginning of the American trilogy.

In the final analysis, *Dancer in the Dark* might well be the most polarising film ever made, proof of just how subjective film really is despite the public's seemingly insatiable appetite for rankings and ratings and neatly packaged judgments capped with five stars or two thumbs up, or whatever. And if von Trier had only succeeded in putting critics at each other's throats, he must have been happy with that, as it had never been his life's goal to make things easy for them.

Seven
Dogma – the Next Generation and *Dogville*

The new Film Town

With the filming of the *Quiet Waters* series, it became clear that Zentropa had outgrown the Ryesgade studio and they began searching for a new home that would give them more office and studio space. To shoot that series they ended up renting a disused military staging camp in a suburban area south of Copenhagen called Avedøre. They spent a small fortune to turn the main hall into a serviceable studio (which still doesn't manage to serve all their needs). Later, by stages, they bought most of the rest of the camp and in 1999 they and various affiliates and allies, like Nimbus – now partially owned by Zentropa via their equipment-sharing arrangement – moved in. Reports that the commune's mayor sold the camp to them for a single crown are dismissed by Zentropa financial boss, Peter Garde, but in any case, they got a studio complex and sprawling grounds at a dirt cheap price. After more reconversion work, Film Town, as it came to be known, now consisted of, among other things, three sound studios, tennis courts, a cafeteria, equipment sheds, editing facilities, a three-storey building for manuscript writers and a cottage specially designated for visiting Americans. The place still had a down-at-the-heels look to it, but more importantly they now had a self-contained film production centre that handled everything from concept development all the way through to distribution.

Zentropa was now the largest production company in Scandinavia when measured by output. It had grown to a workforce of seventy employees and according to Aalbæk Jensen cost 3 million kroner a month to run.[1] Between 1994 and 2001 they had produced over fifty feature films and had further increased their library by buying the rights for *Europa* from Nordisk with an aim to be able to sell von Trier's films as a package. They were or had been attached to over sixty companies all across Europe (although many were inactive rights-holding entities). Just like the Danish economy, their product line was extremely diverse. In addition to film production they dabbled in music and book publishing (Zentropa Edutaintments) as well as TV, Internet and multi-media projects. Their decentralised organisational structure was appreciated by the many producers and directors they were associated with, and also provided some amount of insurance that if a big production sank on them, it wouldn't drag everything else down with it. And if they did go bankrupt one day, von Trier and Aalbæk Jensen would have the rights to their back catalogue as a kind of pension fund when the sales contracts expired in fifteen to twenty years.

As for the future, they planned to focus on strengthening their ties with foreign production companies and entering into new markets in both production and distribution. They even had a company in the States now, ZentAmerica, established in the spring of 2001. The goal there, as spokesman, Thomas Mai, put it, was

> to produce American films with European feeling. That is to say, we'll offer American directors the possibility to make films as we do it in Europe – with greater artistic freedom and the right of final cut. At the same time, we'll try to send some of the post-production work over to Zentropa in Avedøre.[2]

Aalbæk Jensen, for his part, even had hopes of convincing American producers to *make* films in Film Town.

The move to Avedøre wasn't just to accommodate their expansion, but was also a concrete manifestation of their long-held desire to push film production in a more democratic direction, as laid out in Von Trier's 1999 text, *Open Film Town*. They wanted to create something akin to a socialist collective inside the brutally capitalistic milieu of film production. Their goal was to make film accessible, to demystify it, to engage people from the community in the process and to tap into that youthful energy. Zentropa even had an arrangement with Avedøre high school which made it possible for students to get hands-on film-making experience. In return Zentropa would get goodwill in the community, ideas, enthusiasm and, not least, cheap labour. And for all that, they needed a *place*.

While the new facilities lacked the glamour or history of that other famous European film factory, Cinecittà, in Rome, they were in any case aiming for something closer to the anarchy and idealism of Christiania, another converted army base well known to Danes,[3] a place close to the hearts of two old lapsed communists like Aalbæk Jensen and von Trier. Film Town certainly had hippies, concurred resident Thomas Vinterberg, but was just as much a den of Mafia as it was a collective. 'It's hippies but it's also businessmen with Kalasjnikovs under the desk.'[4]

The sprawling grounds in Avedøre soon became a hive of activity. Von Trier could often be seen navigating about in his camouflaged golf cart, while Aalbæk Jensen preferred to wheel around on his more macho motorcycle. Film Town was one of the places movie folk wanted to see when they came to Denmark, and after a tour of the place they usually left impressed.

Not everything that took place at Film Town was connected to film production and not all of it was profitable. According to Vibeke Windeløv,

> If Peter and I only concentrated on Lars, we would all be really rich, with the money he earns. On the other hand it wouldn't be nearly as much fun. Peter has really opened this place up and created a sanctuary with a mass of creative activities going on – a part of which are not necessarily intended to set film production in motion and which also don't necessarily make tons of money.[5]

In America some hot-shot consultant would have come in and told them to eliminate these unprofitable cells pronto, but this wasn't America, as the Eel no doubt would have happily enlightened the ignorant if anybody could be that stupid. To be sure, despite the guard booth and barbed wire fences that ringed the compound, it was a hippie commune compared to most studios, the kind of place perhaps only possible in Denmark. (On the other hand, in his public utterances von Trier often seemed to prefer the role of robber baron. Making a profit was not to be under-valued.)

Zentropa, house of mirrors

The relationship between von Trier and Aalbæk Jensen, and their operating style, was by now the central enigma of the Danish film world.

Aalbæk Jensen elaborated on their partnership in an interview in the March 2000 issue of *Euroman* magazine with Jens Vilstrup.

> Gradually Lars and I developed into a pair of Laurel and Hardy-like figures. I was the fat ugly idiot who delivered the goods, and von Trier was the strange little oddball ... the shy, strange film genius with the phobias. We played the roles better and better, and as a rule got positive publicity out of it, or in any case something that could be used for positive publicity.

In return, writers always knew that a good story was just a phone call away. It was, as the Eel put it, a case of mutual exploitation.

Not everyone agreed that all the publicity had a positive effect. Jesper Friis, an editor at *Politiken*, predicted that the continuation of Aalbæk Jensen's boisterous act could lead to a credibility problem.[6] Henrik Byager, who had previously worked with Aalbæk Jensen on commercials, found his style to be wearing thin. If he hadn't had Denmark's best film-maker behind him, added Byager, nobody would bother to listen to him.[7] Both had a word of advice for the Eel – relax!

No way. That just wasn't his or the company's style.

'Zentropa is run on a hot-air balloon strategy,' as Aalbæk Jensen expressed it, 'created to thrive in a circus atmosphere ... a hyperventilation that can only function through force of expansion and a great amount of boastful braying.'[8] – Relax? They had to be always in motion, always planning new films and carpet-bombing the DFI with proposals, always launching new ships, always out on the edge.

Von Trier's recurrent bouts of silence and reclusiveness (sometimes even to the point of hiding himself under the editing table[9]) obliged his partner to be all the louder for it, and Aalbæk Jensen became the ringmaster of the Zentropa circus. He was as one writer phrased it, 'both a gift and a pestilence to the media'.[10]

Who was the real Peter Aalbæk Jensen? Was he the financial wizard it appeared, or was he rather, as he himself claimed, so bad at maths that his own customers had to help him add up the numbers so he didn't cheat himself?[11] Was it possible, as he also maintained, that he had no feel at all for what made a good film and hardly ever read scripts or passed creative judgments on a project? Some said his greatest talent was purely on a social plain. He himself reckoned he had an ability to deal with people, to get a sense of where they were coming from and get them to go where he wanted them.[12]

To the casual newspaper reader, who after years of suffering his bombast probably didn't care anymore, he was pure caricature; a big studio boss American style who revelled in crass behaviour, who underpaid his employees and then bragged about it. His oft-photographed poses with a fat cigar were so studied and predictable that the picture could have been a cardboard prop. But beyond this self-invented public persona he could be hard to figure, not least due to his admitted penchant for misleading and confusing journalists.[13] He appeared to take nothing seriously, not even himself. It couldn't be real, one had to think.

Occasionally people got a fuller picture, like writer Henrik Vesterberg, who stuck by his side for three days on assignment for *Politiken* in December of 1999 and came to discover that the man actually had a sophisticated and nuanced sense of timing and diplomacy, and could even keep quiet when the situation merited.[14]

As for the famed brutishness with which he treated members of staff – assumedly with an element of irony firmly in place – it gave them, he claimed, good preparation for the real world they would encounter later on if they survived his pay scale and sense of humour. He had to be tough with them, he said, so they didn't waste their time like he did when he was young.

For some, Zentropa did in fact prove to be a way into the industry. They had been party to some very inspiring success stories. But for others, hired under their so-called 'småtter' ('Little Ones') system, where entry-level employees got a chance to see how the film business worked in exchange for no pay the first year and low wages the second and third, it was a dead end. It was, moreover, a system that had generated some amount of controversy in highly unionised Denmark where a general belief exists that people should be paid a living wage for their labour. According to journalist, Kirsten Jacobsen, there were many young people in the film milieu who were critical of it but dared not complain openly for fear of damaging their future prospects in the field.[15]

Nonetheless, Zentropa continued to get louder, bigger and maybe even better. All the buzzers, bells and canned laughter had made them the most talked-about studio in northern Europe, but it was sometimes hard to see through all the blue smoke and mirrors and tell which of their many projects succeeded and which didn't. Judging from their success at pulling the levers of the Danish and European funding machinery and all the awards, press and hoopla they attracted, it could seem that they never made a bad decision.

In fact they made their share. Or more. In 2000, the DFI filed a report that gauged the success of films going back to 1993, and the films by Zentropa collectively had the poorest attendance record.[16] Big press didn't always translate into big numbers. Pussy Power ApS was a good example of that. This company was launched in 1998 to make sophisticated, quality pornography, and von Trier's name if not direct involvement in production gave it instant hip-appeal. Their first film, *Constance*, released the same year, attracted massive press coverage throughout Scandinavia and Pussy Power appeared to be on a roll – another bold stroke from the naughty boys at Zentropa.

The public must have been surprised then, when after two more films – *Pink Prison* in 1999, and *Hotmen, Coolboyz*, a gay item from 2000 – they announced on 7 January 2001, that they were finished with porno. It had been a massive money-loser for them (not to mention a highly unpopular idea with Aalbæk Jensen's wife).[17] *Hotmen, Coolboyz* alone, totally ignored by the press, had lost Zentropa 1.1 million kroner.[18] And only nine months before, Aalbæk Jensen had been bragging to *Euroman* about all the great ideas he and von Trier had cooked up to generate press. Look at how much talk the porno film idea had produced, he boasted. In fact many writers had seen the idea as a publicity stunt from the word go.

It wasn't just Aalbæk Jensen's circus, though. Von Trier was still the creative engine behind Zentropa and even though other directors' films were occasionally bigger hits in Danish theatres, he was their most marketable name, and without him making a film approximately every two years, Zentropa would fold. (The English-language films and the *very* low-budget Danish films were the most profitable for them). Regarding all of Zentropa's other far-flung projects, he made his presence felt when necessary, particularly when creative questions arose. For example, another company called Innocent Pictures later took over the porno idea, but a clause was written into their contract with Zentropa stating that if Lars von Trier deemed the finished product to be garbage, it would never see the light of day.[19]

Total war

Despite the fact that Danish film was perceived far and wide as a great success story, there had been bad blood brewing between a group of producers and the DFI going back to 1997, and Zentropa had been right in the thick of it. While Aalbæk Jensen was no doubt still smarting over the Dogma funding fiasco, the object of his ire was now the new boss of the DFI – one Henning Camre.

In 1992, Camre had been head-hunted to London to reorganise the National Film and Television School, and now had been brought back to Denmark to run the new Film House, a big old refurbished building in central Copenhagen which housed the DFI, The Film Museum and Statens Film Central under one roof and one administrative structure.

There had never been any love lost between the Zentropa duo and authority figures. And now the old boss was the new boss.[20]

Camre's style could hardly be called relaxed or *laissez-faire*, and Danish producers quickly sensed the change in tone. He wanted more control over the issuance and use of funding and he wanted to see money back on films that had turned a clear profit, and that basically meant *Breaking the Waves*.

For his part, Aalbæk Jensen felt squeezed from all sides while masses of state money were being needlessly spent on other things … like the new Film House. Reconversion work on the grand old building on Gothersgade had gone horribly over-budget and the place, in his opinion, employed far too many people and wasted too much money on stuff like building a restaurant. After all, the success of Danish film owed to the *movies*, not to a building.

He proceeded to lash out in the press at his old headmaster over the course of the next four years, portraying him as an arrogant and intransigent bureaucrat who fostered a bad working atmosphere and was guilty of hubris and power abuse ... who was the boss of what he called 'The Evil Empire' – the DFI. Camre's old friend, Jørgen Leth, rising to his defence in an editorial,[21] admitted that his lack of diplomacy could resemble arrogance and dismissiveness, but claimed that his judgments were almost always right. That Camre had persuaded the government to increase film support by a whopping 75 per cent, bringing the budget for the year 2000 up to 350 million kroner[22], didn't impress the producers. Considering the success Danish film was having, they figured that was as hard as selling a sighted dog to a blind man.

In November 1999, Peter Aalbæk Jensen publicly accused Camre's deputy director, Thomas Stenderup, of taking an illegal decision to deny Zentropa support, and the next month was publicly forced to apologise to him to head off a defamation-of-character law suit.[23]

Aalbæk Jensen hammered away at the DFI's perceived lack of communication skills, at one point relating to a *Euroman* reporter that he had to call all of Zentropa's employees into the cafeteria and inform them he probably couldn't pay their wages on the first of the month because the DFI had not paid 5 million kroner that they had previously agreed upon in production support – all because Zentropa had not delivered the necessary paperwork.[24] Ridiculous, he thought, in a country where legally binding handshakes and letters of intent should be sufficient.

At other times he just seemed to be harassing the DFI for sport. When asked by *Euroman* magazine's Jens Vilstrup in March 2000 how he and von Trier could still be rebels when they had in fact become the 'establishment', he answered:

> If you have to fight with someone, it should be against someone who is bigger than you are. That is why we have been fighting with the DFI, biting the hand that feeds us. Business-wise it's rather stupid to feud with those who give us the most money, ... ha ha ha ... but now let's see what happens.

The feud even spilled over into *The Wall Street Journal*, which on 8 July 1999 wrote about the situation in a way that portrayed Aalbæk Jensen and von Trier as the heroes and the DFI as the villains. Whatever the truth, the steady attacks on the DFI created the impression that they were in chaos and reflected badly on the industry in general. There was a perception that all this would cause damage to Danish film, just when it had achieved so much momentum. Something had to be done, and the culture minister ordered an investigation into the functioning of the DFI.

The report landed on her desk on 1 November 2000. It praised some things about the Institute but criticised their lack of dialogue with the producers, giving credence to Aalbæk Jensen's attacks. He wanted heads to roll.[25] Instead, a series of meetings were arranged to try and reconcile the two parties, but things only got worse. At the end of the month the producers met to consider issuing a statement of no confidence in the DFI. This would have meant a cessation of every form of communication with Camre and his two deputies and thrown Danish film into a crisis. Secret meetings between the two parties were held and this was avoided, but the atmosphere of antagonism remained.

The DFI's position was and always had been that they weren't just a self-serve buffet to dish out money, and that they couldn't show favouritism to one company. As the numbers released in the spring of 2001 revealed, Zentropa had received 30 per cent of available state support (46.4 million kroner), almost twice as much as the next largest recipient, Nordisk film, which had received 17 per cent, so the DFI was hardly starving Zentropa to death. (On the other hand, Aalbæk Jensen claimed that *per film* Zentropa received less state funding than any other studio.)

Dispensing money to Zentropa and other Danish producers was, in fact, only one of the DFI's many tasks. They had to support the country's independent art-house cinemas, for example, and they had to find a way to save old Danish films. Prints were at present being stored in appalling conditions in an old fortress that had been built in 1892, and many of them were in the process of crumbling into nitrate powder. The imperilled state of the Danish film heritage was starting to get as much press as the feud between the producers and the DFI, and to some seemed a hell of a lot more important. The politicians were also starting to get tired of all the fuss. It made everybody look bad.

After all, the problems between the producers and the DFI seemed to hinge more on personalities than on policies. Camre wasn't the kind of fellow to end up taking a nude plunge into the pool with Aalbæk Jensen at one of Zentropa's Cannes bacchanalias. And Aalbæk Jensen, it seemed, wasn't about to shut up.

A truce of sorts was declared in October 2001 with the publication of *Without Cigar*, an oral biography of Peter Aalbæk Jensen wherein both he and Camre weighed in on the feud at length. While neither gave any ground, they both claimed that they had nothing against each other personally. Camre's stewardship of the Film School, readily conceded his former student, had been an important factor in the success that Danish film was now enjoying. For his part Camre singled out a number of what he perceived were Aalbæk Jensen's positive qualities, and sang the praises of Zentropa's importance to Danish film.

State of Danish film, post-*Dancer in the Dark*

Dancer in the Dark's success at Cannes diverted attention from the fact that up until that point the year 2000 had been a bad one for the Danish film industry. Ticket sales were far below that of the previous year when Danish films had captured a record 28 per cent of the domestic box office. This was due largely to the fact that the precious few Danish films that were released in the first half of 2000 drew poorly. On the production side, of the twenty features expected to be produced in 2000, only four were in production at the start of May – a disaster for the Danish film trades. And to make matters worse, Henning Camre's ambitious co-production funding arrangement between the DFI and DR to produce eighty features over four years now lay in ruins after DR, under pressure from politicians to increase their contribution even more, simply walked away from the deal. They preferred to spend their money on TV series.

Dancer in the Dark was a much needed morale booster, but it was no solution to these problems, and in fact was seen by some as part of the problem. As Erik Crone, foreman for the Danish Film and TV Production Centre, expressed it shortly after *Dancer*'s triumph,

> We are a small country and without public support we must realise that
> we won't have film production. At the moment it is hard to get purely

Danish films financed, and that is intrinsic for the development of talent. It
should not be the case that we make only English spoken films from here
on in.[26]

It was not a new issue, but in the current near-crisis situation, it was a
pressing one, both from a cultural and a financial perspective. What, in
fact, determined a film's 'nationality'? 'I think', von Trier would say, 'that
a film should be individual, not national. It should speak to the world, in
the world's language, but with the voice of the person who made it.'[27] And
the world's language, at least in terms of commercial film production,
seemed to be English. Thomas Vinterberg, Ole Bornedal, Nikolas Winding
Refn, Kristen Levring and von Trier himself were all currently asking the
DFI for financial support for films to be made in English, while Susanne
Bier and Bille August had done the same for films being shot in Swedish. If
all the money went to non Danish-language films, growth and development of Danish-language cinema would come to a halt. Of course funding
could be sought elsewhere, but state support was far preferable since a
director didn't have to give up rights or artistic control to get it, as was so
often the case with TV money or foreign money, particularly when it came
from America.

The issue came to a head later that spring when both Ole Bornedal
and Thomas Vinterberg were informed by the DFI that their upcoming
films, *I Am Dina* and *It's All About Love* respectively, were not considered
Danish films and qualified for only minimal support. They were both furious and threatened to leave Denmark and make films elsewhere, Bornedal
going on to declare on 4 June that he was giving up all DFI support, and that
if the film became a success he would make sure Denmark got no credit for
it.

Everyone seemed to agree that a new approach was needed and that successful Danish directors should not be penalised for seeking to make films
for an international audience, films that would in turn enhance Denmark's
reputation abroad. Film had become one of the country's most visible
export commodities: Danish features had sold over 6.5 million tickets in
other EU countries over the last four years, placing Denmark only behind

England, France and Italy, and ahead of Germany(!),[28] and they had reaped a ton of positive press in America.

In an editorial in *Politiken* on 10 June it was argued that film should now be viewed as a real and competitive export commodity, like beer, butter and pork. The old state-support system could no longer sustain it, and what was needed was a new policy geared to attract private investment capital to film production. That seemed to make sense. After all, the Danish 'culture business' had grown by 29 per cent in the 1992–8 period while the private sector in general had grown only by 15 per cent.[29]

But for the time being the DFI held firm to its position, articulated that autumn by consultant Vinca Wiedemann, that only in extraordinary circumstances would an English-language film qualify for substantial support. Vinterberg, Bornedal and others immediately protested.

As it turned out with Vinterberg's film, Wiedemann would step in in May of 2001 and save it with an 'emergency' grant of 2 million kroner after a French investor pulled out while the film was actually being shot. She maintained that she hadn't changed her position, but that this was an extraordinary circumstance and that if Vinterberg's film sank, the reputation of Danish film in general would suffer and adversely affect others who tried to make international films. 'With *It's All About Love*, Thomas Vinterberg has set himself a great artistic challenge and we will of course help when we can when unexpected problems arise in the middle of shooting.'[30]

On 22 November 2000, concrete steps were taken to redefine the status of Danish film when culture minister Cerner Nielsen and finance minister Pia Gjellerup issued a joint policy paper declaring that culture would now be regarded as a 'real' business. 'Danish Culture as a Wave-breaker against Hollywood', headlined an article in *Politiken* the next day, going on to quote key passages of their statement:

> We have need for a competitive Danish entertainment and culture industry to ensure the whole environment does not drown in Disney. Co-operation between the culture and business spheres is necessary to counter the trend towards global homogenisation. As Danes we need to recognise ourselves in the global landscape.

The two ministers went on to assure Danes that '... closer ties between the cultural and business sectors will in no way lead to a reduction of public support for the arts'.

Now the Danish culture 'industry' could expect the same kind of state support that had so successfully given impetus to the software and biotechnology industries. It was stated that by mid-2001, 50 million kroner would be injected into culture via the existing public-owned development/venture company, Vækst Fond (Progress Fund). Its purpose was to find venture capital for projects that investors were otherwise hesitant to invest in, and when it received a matching amount from private sources, the government money would be freed up. The goal of this project was to finance bigger Danish films that could compete in the global market place. On 21 February, much earlier than expected, the government dumped twice that much, 100 million kroner, into the fund, with Danish film slated to be the first area of culture to benefit when things got rolling. This was an attempt to establish the kind of regional film fund that had been so successful elsewhere in Europe.

The state, the private sector and the media were all bullish on film, oddly a lot more bullish than Danish film producers were. A reality check was needed, and on 12 June 2001 it arrived in the form of a producer's report which concluded that the money earned abroad by Danish films hardly justified all the self-congratulation trumpeted in the media.[31] Danish bacon had nothing to fear.

The reasons were multiple. Danish films in foreign markets only appealed on average to a narrow art-house public. It was expensive to compete in these markets and to get a film to 'cross over' to a more mainstream public. To promote a film aggressively in the US, for example, was incredibly expensive. As for the glowing reports in the Danish press of big ticket sales in foreign countries, this was misleading, since Danish producers often traded rights for production investment or sold foreign rights for 'up front' lump sums, thus precluding any participation in windfall profits that might result if the film became a big hit.

Dancer in the Dark was a case in point. In mid-2001, Aalbæk Jensen announced that the film had generated a total worldwide income (theatrical and video) of $1 billion. Yet only a tiny fraction of that money found its way back to Zentropa since they had to pre-sell so many rights and make so many unfavourable deals to finance it. The money it had made had mostly been for foreign distributors and investors. According to Aalbæk Jensen only 7 million kroner made it back to Denmark to be split up among the Danish investors. Nor were the Dogma films, with 33.3 per cent of their take going to Danmarks Radio, the gold mine they appeared to be for Zentropa.

'When the Progress Fund becomes a reality, we can finance much more of a given film much earlier, and thereby also get completely different and much more lucrative deals with foreign investors,' commented Zentropa finance chief, Peter Garde[32] on the harsh realities that still governed Danish film finance.

Danish distributors were forced to make these kinds of deals because, in addition to lacking clout, it was frequently difficult to get an accurate overview of what was happening in foreign markets. They had to trust their foreign distributors in a business where what happened in reality and what stood on a contract were often two different things. The Danish studios were not international conglomerates like the American majors, and were not able to dictate terms or check on the foreign numbers as they would have liked.

But if they organised, there was hope. 'The film world is a little family in Denmark,' commented Rikke Ennis, from Zentropa's aptly named Trust Film Sales. 'When producers are as good as they are at forming alliances and cooperating in all other possible areas, they should also be able to cooperate on the export of Danish films.'[33]

The Progress Fund project, for its part, faltered on the launching pad: in late August of 2001 it was announced that private investors had been unwilling to part with the necessary sums needed to reach the 50 million mark and thereby make the government money accessible. It had been the responsibility of the four leading film companies – Nordisk and Zentropa among them – to find the investors and they hadn't been able to do it. Apparently the prospective investors didn't like the odds: it was accepted wisdom that seven to eight out of every ten films ranged from average failures to out-and-out fiascos. And often profits weren't registered until the losses on all a studio's films were covered. The Progress Fund plan was put on hold, and in November suffered a further setback when Danes voted in a new right-leaning government that was much less committed to public support of the arts. How Anders Fogh Rasmussen's new administration, will deal with these issues is as yet unknown.

Dogma – the next generation

One of the films that saved the year 2000 from being a total disaster was the fifth Dogma film, *Italian For Beginners*, by Lone Scherfig. An ex-Film School graduate, Scherfig had a couple of feature films behind her but was best known for TV work, having directed several episodes of the popular show,

Scene from *Italian for Beginners* by Lone Scherfig (2001)

Taxi,[34] as well as later episodes of the aforementioned *Quiet Waters* series. *Italian For Beginners* was a romantic comedy ('No genre films' alert!) about six single Danes from different walks of life who all end up taking a class in Italian together and wrestling with common emotional problems, such as the lack of passion and love in their lives.

It didn't open until the start of December, but was rolled out wide in sixty prints and became an overnight hit. Now the block-long lines started forming. In just ten days, 131,000 Danes had seen the film. By Christmas it had sold 267,000 tickets, eclipsing the total of 193,623 tickets *Dancer in the Dark* had sold since its September opening. By February of 2001, it had attracted 600,000 viewers, helping to push the market share for Danish-made films up to a record 30 per cent. The film's success was capped by a slew of prizes at the 2001 Berlin Film Festival.[35]

Up until the release of *Italian For Beginners*, the momentum of Dogma seemed to have come to a halt. It had been declared dead or dying by von Trier, Søren Kraugh-Jacobsen, Aalbæk Jensen, a host of critics and pundits, and even by its official spokesman, Thomas Vinterberg, who was by now sick of talking about it and would do everything humanly possible to make his next film, *It's All About Love*, as un-Dogma as could be.[36] The first four films by the original Dogma brothers all seemed like ancient history by now, with the exception of Kristian Levring's *The King Is Alive*, which wasn't actually released until a month *after* Scherfig's film, and only in four prints. And now each of the brothers were engaged in very un-Dogma-like films, all to be shot in English.

A secret round-table was held by the brotherhood in November of 2000, but yielded no bold new declarations. They all agreed a pure Dogma film had not yet been made, and that that was good. Dogma brother without portfolio, Jesper Jargil,[37] was at the meeting and reported that no new manifesto or updating of Dogma 95 was in the offing.[38]

And that was too bad, according to some who felt that the concept was being polluted by the appallingly low quality of foreign Dogma films, the majority of which seemed to be cranked out by directors who sought Dogma certificates merely to gain exposure, particularly at film festivals that often played anything stamped 'Dogma'. These films had been almost universally savaged by critics and spurned by the public. This in turn inclined many to slam Dogma as a gimmick. Some even claimed this charlatanism was damaging the reputation of Danish film in general for which Dogma had become a virtual trademark.

Why was there such a gap, many wondered, between the home-grown and foreign product? Maybe because outside Denmark Dogma had largely come to be regarded as a way for anyone to make cheap films on video, with subsequent predictable lack of quality. In Denmark the films had been made by established studios, Nimbus and Zentropa, which were very professional operations despite the studied 'unprofessionalism' of the finished Dogma product. And, as noted by many, the first three films were very Danish. How this made them better films is hard to say, seeing as the purely technical implementation that was Dogma had no apparent link to a film's nationality. But it did seem to matter – maybe because the films by von Trier, Vinterberg and Kraugh-Jacobsen manifest a specific mentality and were grounded in a specific location and sensibility, while many of the non-Danish films seemed to lack character.

The main problem was that the certification process, criticised by many, including von Trier, now gave these foreign films the seal of approval, or at least the appearance of such. Yet after the Dogma brothers had signed off the original plan to collectively review them, there was no real way of policing them. Second, the Vows of Chastity had come to be interpreted purely as a technical blueprint, often with little regard given to the aesthetic or spiritual side of the process which was what Dogma had really been all about.

But perhaps the main problem was that the people making Dogma films were not the people Dogma had been created for, that is to say established film-makers who were looking for relief from the apparatus. The people making Dogma films (outside Denmark) were almost exclusively young, impoverished or first-time directors – or often actors (Jean-Marc Barr, Udo Kier, Jennifer Jason Leigh, etc.) who had fallen in love with Dogma as actors seemed to do.

'Today a technological storm is raging,' von Trier had written in the Dogma manifesto. 'For the first time, anyone can make movies.' But Dogma had proven that not everybody had the *talent* to make movies, or the commitment to finish them – or the money, judging by all the enquiries the Dogma secretary received as to whether Zentropa helped finance Dogma films (the answer was a quick 'no').

A lot of films simply disappeared from the Dogma radar scope. A case in point was Paul Morrissey and Udo Kier's *The House of Klang*. After so much hype, it had apparently been abandoned.

At the start of January 2000, Kier himself was reported to be shooting a Dogma film in Los Angeles. Entitled *Broken Cookies*, it was to be the seventh Dogma film. Kier was to play the lead, a wheelchair-bound transsexual called Lola, while Russ Meyer's old discovery, Kitten Natividad, also had a part. The film appeared nowhere on the official list of nineteen Dogma films issued in November of 2000, but mention of it popped up in the February 2001 issue of the alternative German culture magazine *Stadt Revue*, where Kier reveals in an interview that the title had been changed to *Outsiders on Wheels* – the name of the club in the film whose members, wheelchair-bound transsexuals, earn their money with telephone sex, posing as 'the most beautiful Swedish girls one could imagine'. But by that point Kier had run out of money and it seemed likely that the film would never be finished.

* * *

Dogma was a chimera, an amorphous commodity that seemed to shrink and expand at once, to defy quantification or definition, thanks in large part to the ambiguity and irony that was part and parcel of its conception. To some, it was still a potent antidote to the fakery of Hollywood film-making, while to its detractors, it was itself a slick PR trick, a fraud. And Dogma had its detractors.

Some viewers physically couldn't bear the grainy digital images jerking around on a big movie screen and had to flee theatres, while others couldn't accept it as a concept. 'With their vows of chastity,' commented the critic Philip French, 'they don't so much attempt to reinvent the wheel as to throw the wheel away and drag the cart down the dusty streets by hand.' British director Alan Parker, among others, voiced concern that this rough hand-held video look of the Dogma films would deprive audiences of a reason to come to theatres when they discovered that films looked just as good on their video monitors at home. Danish cinematographer, Hans Bonnesen concurred: this home-video style was killing the craft of cinematography. But others felt differently and credited Dogma for getting viewers to accept non-traditional looking movies into the mainstream.

The Dogma films had been big hits in Germany, but Germany's most influential critic, George Seesslen, didn't go along with it and issued a stinging rebuke to the Danes in an issue of *Die Zeit*.[39] He deplored what he saw as *The Celebration*'s fake-amateurishness. Of the first three Dogma films, Seesslen wrote, 'the "spontaneity" was constructed and the primitivism completely conscious'. With Dogma, 'the renunciation of an aesthetic turns into an aesthetic of renunciation'. Dogma was nothing but a PR trick he concluded.

Nonetheless, some of those who felt they had Dogma pegged after the first three films had to reconsider when *Italian For Beginners* and *The King Is*

Nikolaj Lie Kaas in Åke Sandgren's *Truly Human* (2001), Dogma film number six. Kaas also played the idiot, Jeppe in von Trier's *The Idiots* (1998)

Alive came out. They were two very different films that showed that Dogma could be adopted to different approaches and stories.

In April of 2001, the second wave of Dogma continued to roll with the release of number 6, *Truly Human*, by von Trier's old Film School collaborator, Åke Sandgren. A satiric fable in the Kasper Hauser mould, the film tells the tale of a little girl's imaginary big brother, played by Nikolaj Lie Kaas (Jeppe of *The Idiots*), who miraculously comes to life. Armed only with naïveté and goodness, he confronts the complexities of modern Danish life. It was the first Dogma film to explore contemporary social realities like racial prejudice, and did so with a mixture of fantasy and social-realism. As an outsider himself, the Swedish-born Sandgren was perhaps better able to perceive and critique these nuances of Danish life than a native. *Truly Human* got high marks from almost all the critics, with the performance of Nikolaj Lie Kaas invariably singled out for praise, but the film was not wildly embraced by the public and sold only 53,000 tickets.

Stine Stengade in a scene from Dogma film number seven: Ole Christian Madsen's *Kira's Reason – A Love Story* (2001)

The seventh Dogma film, entitled *Kira's Reason — A Love Story* was a bleak drama about a man struggling to preserve his love for his mentally disturbed wife. Directed by Ole Christian Madsen, it opened in Denmark on 26 October and was even more popular with critics than the sixth Dogma production, going on to reap almost all of the main awards at both the Robert and Bodil ceremonies in February and March of 2002 respectively. The film revealed not so much that Dogma was capable of going in new directions as that the Dogma concept was more elastic than first thought, and that it was not necessarily even the main ingredient in a successful 'dogma' film. It was marginally more popular than *Truly Human*, selling almost 70,000 tickets, although throughout 2001 both were still being somewhat over-shadowed by the fifth production which was proving to have a long life in theatres. (The fifth, sixth and seventh Dogma films helped make 2001 a huge success at the Danish box office. With 3.5 million tickets sold, it was the highest-grossing year since 1980 and represented a dramatic turn-around from the previous year's total of slightly over 2 million. With this boom at the box office and the market share for Danish films hovering at 30 per cent — approximately 10 per cent over what is considered normal — criticism of Henning Camre, as *Politiken* scribe Per Dabelsteen put it, had been silenced.[40])

The filming of the eighth Dogma film, *Elsker Dig For Evigt (Open Hearts)*, wrapped just before the new year, 2002. Directed by Susanne Bier, the film is a romantic drama about a marriage put under enormous strain when a man falls in love with the girlfriend of the fellow his wife has just run over in her car. The date of release has been scheduled for Autumn 2002.

Zentropa's main competitor, Nordisk, has in the meantime also come up with a Dogma-like project called 'Director's Cut' which was conceived by producers Åke Sandgren and Lars Kjeldgaard. Unveiled for the press on 9 August 2001, Director's Cut seeks to speed up and simplify the process of making a film, and concerns itself with logistics rather than the aesthetic side of film-making, as Dogma had. It contained nothing resembling the Vows of Chastity, but rather laid out clear guidelines intended to liberate the director from the time- and energy- consuming complications of financing and shooting a film, including limiting budget and crew size and making financing contingent upon presentation of only a synopsis, not a finished manuscript – important practicalities that Dogma had never formally addressed. Four directors, Morten Arnfred among them, were now embarked upon Director's Cut films to be completed by 2003.

Dogville

Von Trier had been thinking about the storyline of his next film, *Dogville*, for a long time, but when he finally put pen to paper, the writing went quickly. On 6 December 2000 he had submitted a thirty-page synopsis to Windeløv, and by the New Year he had completed the 150-page script which thereafter was translated into English.

The film would be, according to Windeløv, 'experimental' … very scary, a psychological drama, but not a 'thriller'. Plot details were leaked to the press. One day a woman who is 'on the run' arrives in a mountain village. In the beginning she is left alone, but gradually her new neighbours begin to exploit her. When it is discovered that there is a reward out for her, they make her life hell. In the meantime it is revealed that her father is a Mafia boss, and he eventually takes over control of the town. Now it is up to her to decide the fate of the townspeople. 'You shall treat these people the way they have treated you,' she is told, with dramatic consequences to follow.[41]

Set in an American Rocky Mountain village in the 1930s, yet filmed entirely in an empty studio with just a few props, *Dogville* bodes to be von Trier's most technically innovative, not to say risky, film to date. Locations like a prison, a factory, and so on would be indicated by chalk marks on a black floor. The suspenseful atmosphere would be created almost entirely by the interplay between light and shadow, but he would also make full use of music and effects. And it would be ambitious: A DFI publicity booklet published in January 2002 declared that von Trier's new concept is intended to reconstruct the entire known language of the cinema!.

A theatre lighting expert and two of the Danish actors began tests on a sound stage in Film Town in great secrecy at the start of 2001 to see if this daring technical approach would actually work. The DFI granted its largest development support sum yet, 1.3 million kroner, to pay for the tests. They revealed the need for a few changes, such as the use of more props and a larger studio, but otherwise the innovative filming technique was deemed a success. Zentropa showed an eight-minute test film to potential buyers at the 2001 Berlin and Cannes festivals, with Aalbæk Jensen attempting to lower expectations after his own fashion.

> I said far and wide at Berlin that they should stay away from the film. Of course that made them extremely curious. Because of that they reckoned it was really, really awful. So then after they saw it they were so relieved that they protested that they would willingly buy it – but for a sensible price.[42]

In March von Trier was granted 9.3 million kroner in support from the DFI for *Dogville*, somewhat less than they had asked for but still a very large sum, and one that was bound up in some controversy as it was given by consultant Vinca Wiedemann[43] who, as noted earlier, had declared that only in extraordinary circumstances would English-language films get substantial support. Von Trier himself was apparently an extraordinary circumstance, although she denied it.

> Lars von Trier doesn't get special treatment, but his project is in a special class … therefore I am happy to be able to grant money to this film, which I believe can be completely fantastic, and which at the same time can help advance Danish culture and Danish film in the wider world.

It was clear that 'Lars von Trier must have support,' concurred Erik Crone.[44] Maybe some eyebrows were raised, but no controversy here. Von Trier's status was no longer a point of debate.

Nicole Kidman was first choice for the lead. Negotiations stretched on through the spring and into the summer until Aalbæk Jensen finally lost patience and announced in late July that enough was enough with this waiting game and that Kidman was out. This might even be a godsend, he speculated, like it had been with *Breaking the Waves* when the last minute substitute, Emily Watson, turned out to be perfect. A couple of days later he had to retract it all when it turned out that Windeløv actually *had* received a signed contract from Kidman some time previously. Kidman was back in.

Edward Norton was originally rumoured to be the male lead, but since the film was mostly financed with European capital, that meant that one of the leads had to be played by a European actor and Norton was dropped in favour of Stellan Skarsgård. Later Chlöe Sevigny, James Caan, Lauren Bacall and Ben Gazzara were also signed. Shooting finally started on 7 January 2002 in Trollhättan, and it was now predicted that the film wouldn't premiere until the 2003 Berlin Film Festival.

On 30 January, about midway through the shoot, von Trier and his stars met the press. He was asked if rumours were true that there were parallels in the film with the tougher immigration policies that the new Danish government was putting into effect. His disgust with the policies of Anders Fogh Rasmussen's government were no secret; during the election he had taken out a newspaper ad urging Danes to 'vote decency'.

'Maybe there are,' replied von Trier. 'I am very worried about the rightward swing in Denmark. It's not good. We also see that in other places in the world, like in America, for example. ... But I will not make a political film, even though I might touch upon some political topics.'[45]

During the Berlin Film Festival in early February, reporters caught up with Aalbæk Jensen and he elaborated on von Trier's plans beyond *Dogville*, reporting that Lars had already sought manuscript development support from the DFI for his next film. The working title was *Dear Wendy*. 'It'll be a kind of *The Kingdom* meets *A Clockwork Orange* and takes place in the present in Harlem, USA, among a crowd of irritating young white people – intellectuals who have a great passion for their firearms. It will be cast exclusively with relatively unknown international actors.'

'The third part of Lars' so-called USA-trilogy will eventually take place during the American Civil War,' he added, tongue very possibly planted firmly in cheek.[46]

Regarding other future plans, von Trier had managed to raise eyebrows when he had announced back in late 2001 that he would direct the Richard Wagner opera *Nibelungens Ring* in Bayreuth in 2006. In addition to cementing his reputation as the consumate maverick, he also managed to embroil himself in the feuds that raged among Wagner's surviving family members, with the composer's great-granddaughter, Nike Wagner, recommending that he stay home.

By 2001 it seemed a given that any Danish director with some success behind him would shoot a film in English and go for the biggest (usually

American) star he could get in an effort to break his film internationally. By mid-2001, Thomas Vinterberg was shooting *It's All About Love* with Claire Danes, Joaquin Phoenix and Sean Penn. Ole Bornedal was shooting *I Am Dina* in Norway with French superstar, Gérard Depardieu. At 130 million kroner, that film had snatched the mantle of Scandinavia's most expensive film away from *Dancer in the Dark*. And Nicolas Winding Refn had signed Tom Sizemore to star in his new English-language film, *Fear X*, co-written by American author, Hubert Selby – only to later replace him with John Turturro. Søren Kraugh-Jacobsen, for his part, is presently working on an English-language class drama, entitled *Skagerrak*, to be shot in Scotland, with Lone Scherfig also shooting her next film, *Wilbur Wants to Kill Himself*, in Scotland and in English. *Innocence*, Kristian Levring's upcoming movie, will also be English.

But if Danish directors were going abroad in greater numbers, Danish actors for the most part were not going with them.

*   *   *

Conclusion

It is tempting to conclude that von Trier and his posse are today being challenged by a 'new guard' of young film-makers who have new things to say and no use for old idols, but that would be simplistic not to say misleading. First of all, this 'posse', which includes the likes of Sandgren, Gislason, Bier, Arnfred, Scherfig and the Dogma boys, is no homogeneous group, nor are they all even from the same generation. Second, as for the young film-makers who are coming up through the ranks and scoring hits (and helping to keep a sense of Danishness in Danish film), their films are more often than not being produced by Zentropa or one of its affiliate companies. For example, Nicolas Winding Refn's *Pusher* (1996), which was at the forefront of a new very 'un-Trieresque' wave of gangster films and dark comedies, was produced by Balboa, a Zentropa daughter company.

How, specifically, has von Trier's influence been felt? As discussed in these pages, he is a catalyst and an instigator who by his actions and his attitude has helped to diversify Danish cinema and given it momentum. He can

Mads Mikkelsen (l) and Kim Bodnia in a scene from *Pusher* (1996)

hardly be accused of being a 'cork' in Danish film life the way that many accused Bergman of being for decades in Sweden. Yet his influence has been felt more from a business and idea perspective than from an aesthetic perspective. Nobody is trying to copy his film-making style or stealing his themes or subject matter. Young Danish film-makers seem to be more inspired by Quentin Tarantino than Lars von Trier. Purely as a film-maker, he remains alone. Like Bergman. The great genius. As to whether that lofty adjective can be applied to von Trier is still a question that hangs in the air, still divides and still polarises the debate about him.

What von Trier thinks about this is not known. Surely in all his evasiveness and irony he would never dignify the question with a straight answer, but if he at this midway point in his life and career possesses the same ability to evaluate himself as he does to provoke himself, he can only come to one embarrassing conclusion – that he really is one. He has that very rare quality of being thoroughly human, he never ceases to explore and work with his own duality, his inner schisms. It all comes together – past, present, future; childhood, adolescence, manhood; business, art, private life – and he demands that you see it as a whole. And if you don't 'get it', what does he care? He offers you his entire life as a work of art. There is not much more he can do, and yet that is perhaps a greater challenge than many a 'customer' can cope with because it requires that you, like him, provoke yourself into dealing with *yourself* honestly.

Most of us find that frightening. We compartmentalise: work goes in one little box, spiritual issues in another and basic instincts in the smallest, almost forgotten box way back in the darkest corner of the closet. And that just won't do with Lars von Trier. In order to perceive his genius, you must get in touch with your own.

NOTES

Introduction

1. During the silent film era, Denmark was a 'film power' rivalled only by France and America. Its films were exported around the world, and actors like Asta Nielsen and Valdemar Psilander were renowned. This all ended after World War I, and the subsequent advent of sound (exposing the limited reach of the Danish language) further restricted export of Danish films.

2. *Ekstra Bladet*, 12 June 1996.

3. *Politiken*, November 1997.

4. Annelise Bistrup, 'Mask Play', *Berlingske Tidende (B.T.)*, 28 May 2000, sec. 2, p. 1.

1 – The Early Years

1. *Politiken*, 5 July 1996.

2. *B.T.*, 1 September 1996.

3. 'Jeg Er Nærmest Lidt Latterlig', *Alt For Damerne*, 19 May 1988, pp. 5–8.

4. *Politiken*, 5 July 1996.

5. *Politiken*, 27 May 2000.

6. School in Denmark, as a rule, starts at the beginning of August.

7. HF is the equivalent of American high school plus the first year of college, hence grades 11, 12 and 13.

8. The Free Exhibition was founded in 1891 by a group of painters who rejected the established norms of art sanctioned by the Charlottenborg gallery which displayed, among other artists, Hammershøi and Willumsen.

9. Palle Schantz Lauridsen, *Sekvens: Lars von Trier – Filmvidenskabelig Årbog 1991* (Copenhagen: Institut for Film, TV & Kommunikation, 1991), p. 11.

10. Lars von Trier, *The Idiots: Manuscript and Diary* (Copenhagen Gyldendal A/S, 1998), p. 238.

11. *Jyllands-Posten*, 11 December 1994.

12. *B.T.*, 26 May 1984.

13. Mette Hjort and Ib Bondebjerg, *Instruktørens Blik* (Copenhagen: Rosinante Forlag A/S, 2000), p. 219. Published in English as *The Danish Directors: Dialogues on a Contemporary National Cinema* (Bristol: Intellect Books, 2001), p. 212.

14. Ibid., pp. 219–20.

15. Paul Hammerich, *Opgang og Nedtur* (Copenhagen: Gyldendal Publishers, 1980), pp. 62–5.

16. On the other hand, the School has also been criticised by some for being *too* professionally oriented; too geared to preparing students for entrance into 'the industry', with insufficient emphasis placed on artistic, creative or spiritual development.

17. Peter Schepelern, *Lars von Triers Film: Tvang og Befrielse* (Copenhagen: Rosinante Forlag A/S, 2000), p. 41.

18. Niels Krause-Kjær, 'Rigets Herre', *Jyllands-Posten*, 11 December 1994.

19. This subject is referred to much more extensively later in the book.

20. *Information*, 21 May 1996.

21. Modern State support for film production in Denmark began in 1964 with the Danish Film Fund, which distributed money raised from a kind of ticket tax. This system proved insufficient, and in 1972 the Danish Film Institute was founded to administer funds allocated directly by the Culture Ministry. In 1973, two consultants were employed to sift through the hundreds of funding requests and shepherd the worthy few into production. The system remains in place today with up to six consultants now employed. Their job, which lasts between three and five years, has many aspects: they advise on style and content, edit scripts, point producers towards additional sources of funding and just generally try to keep the film-maker's spirits up through the long process of getting a film made and onto screens. Although sometimes controversial, the consultant system is popular in Denmark despite the great number of applications that must be rejected. The strength of the system is that film-makers negotiate with individuals, not a faceless institution or a committee, and if rejected, a film-maker can apply again to another consultant. The fact the consultants can and have approved films that had virtually no public can be considered either a drawback or advantage of the system depending on one's viewpoint. A second way by which film-makers can obtain funding is known as the 60:40 arrangement. It's basically a 'matching

funds' deal in which consultants are not involved although evaluation of the project is still made. In either situation, the money is supposed to be paid back if the film turns a profit.

22. *Politiken*, 5 July 1996.

23. *Jyllands-Posten*, 23 May 1998.

24. *Politiken*, 27 May 2000.

25. *Jyllands-Posten*, 11 December 1994.

26. The island upon which Copenhagen is located (Denmark being composed of hundreds of islands).

27. *Jyllands-Posten*, 11 December 1994.

28. *Politiken*, 7 January 2001.

29. *B.T.*, 28 May 2000.

30. *Information*, 21 May 1996.

31. Kirsten Jacobsen, *Uden Cigar: Faderen, Sønnen og Filmkøbmanden* (Copenhagen: Høst & Son, 2001).

32. Vilhelm Hammershøi, 1864–1916, was an exceedingly famous Danish painter particularly renowned for his depictions of interiors and his work with light and space.

33. *Politiken*, 5 July 1996.

34. Eva Jørholt and Martin Drouzy, 'Thou Shalt Honor Thy Wife: Dreyer and His Family', *Kosmorama*, issue 215, Spring 1996, pp. 22–3.

35. Zoran, Petrovic 'Lars von Dreyer?', *Kosmorama*, issue 217, Autumn 1996, p. 21.

36. 'Jeg Er Nærmest Lidt Latterlig', *Alt For Dameme*, 19 May 1985, p. 8.

37. Schepelern, *Lars von Triers Film*, p. 53.

38. Ibid., pp. 53–5 .

39. Lauridsen, *Sekvens*, p. 13.

40. *Information*, 21 May 1996.

41. This film has been listed as both 'Images of a Relief', and 'Pictures of a Relief', but it's original Danish title,

Befrielsesbilleder, translates more appropriately into 'Images of a Liberation' since the film deals with the World War II Liberation, not a relief.

42. Novels: *J.B. – En Teori (J.B. – A Theory)*, 1975; *Tegninger I Mørket (Drawings in the Dark)*, 1977; *I Envision a Book and this is How It Goes*, 1977. Radio play: *Transistor*, 1977.

43. *Politiken*, 23 November 1982.

44. *Aktuelt*, 13 April 1985.

45. *Politiken*, 23 November 1982 .

46. *Politiken*, 30 June 1982.

47. Thanks in part to the publication of a number of books and studies on the subject, prominent among them Peter Øvig Knudsen's 'Efter Drabet' ('After the Killing'), 2001, which is to be made into a documentary film series.

48. *Ringkjøbing Amts dagblad*, 22 November 1982.

49. *B.T.*, 30 June 1982.

50. *Politiken*, 30 June 1982.

51. *Politiken*, 23 November 1982.

52. *Epidemic* manifesto booklet, 1997, p. 6.

53. Lauridsen, *Sekvens*, p. 12.

2– From *The Element of Crime* to *Europa* and Zentropa

1. *Morgen-Posten Fyn*, 13 May 1984.

2. Peter Schepelern, *Lars von Triers Film: Tvang og Befrielse* (Copenhagen: Rosinante Forlag A/S, 1997, 2000), p. 72.

3. Henning Carlsen's *En Lykkelig Skilsmisse (A Happy Divorce)*, co-produced by a French company and shot in French, had been chosen for competition in 1975, without winning. The last time a Danish film had won a prize in Cannes was back in 1966 when Per Oscarsson had received the Best Actor award for *Hunger* by the same Henning Carlsen.

4. *Information*, 21 May 1996.

5. *Jyllands-Posten*, 11 December 1994.

6. As revealed in a made-for-TV portrait of Lars von Trier directed by Frans Horwitz in 1991.

7. Palle Schantz Lauridsen, *Sekvens: Lars von Trier – Filmvidenskabelig Årbog 1991* (Copenhagen: Institut for Film, TV & Kommunikation, 1991), p. 14.

8. *Aktuelt*, 16 August 1991.

9. The Bodil awards, named after Danish actresses, Bodil Kjer and Bodil Ipsen, were established in 1948 by the Association of Danish Film Writers and became known as the 'Danish Oscars'. The Robert awards, established in 1982, were chosen by members of the Danish Film Academy, which represented the film trades and industry perspective, and it quickly established itself as competition to the Bodil awards.

10. *Weekendavisen*, 20–26 July 2001.

11. *Ekstra Bladet*, 26 July 1984.

12. Schepelern, *Lars von Triers Film*, p. 92.

13. *Weekendavisen*, 18 September 1987.

14. Gitte Merrild (ed.), Kim Foss (contrib.), *Copenhagen Culture: A Cultural Manual* (Copenhagen: Copenhagen Cultural Capital 96 Foundation, 1996), interview with Lars von Trier, p. 147.

15. *Weekendavisen*, 26 June 1987.

16. Mesmer being a reference to the Edgar Allen Poe character: the doctor who artificially keeps people alive between life and death.

17. Bendtsen had filmed both *Ordet* (1955) and *Gertrud* (1964) for Carl Th. Dreyer. He was about to retire for good when von Trier got him to change his mind. He even wanted Bendtsen to use the same camera he had used on the Dreyer films, but that proved impossible as it drew on an incompatible electrical current.

18. *Politiken*, 27 May 2000.

19. Second Manifesto, 1987:

> Seemingly all is well. The young men are encouraged in their steady relationship with a new generation of film. The anti-conception which is supposed to contain the epidemic only makes the birth control more effective: no unexpected creations, no bastards – the genes are intact. There exist those young men whose relationships resemble the endless stream of Grand Balls of an earlier era. There are also those who live together in rooms devoid of furniture. But their love becomes expansion without soul, reduction without bite. Their 'wildness' lacks discipline and their 'discipline' lacks wildness. ... LONG LIVE THE BAGATELLE! (LONG LIVE THE INSIGNIFICANT DETAIL.) The bagatelle is humble and all-embracing. It exposes a corner without making a secret of eternity. Its setting is limited but magnanimous and therefore gives space to life. *Epidemic* manifests itself in the legitimate/serious relationships of the young men as a bagatelle – for among bagatelles the masterpieces are numbered.

20. *Weekendavisen*, 26 June 1987.

21. *Aktuelt* (n.d.).

22. *Weekendavisen*, 26 June 1987.

23. *B.T.*, 15 May 1987.

24. *Politiken*, 11 September 1987.

25. *B.T.*, 11 September 1987.

26. *Information*, 12 September 1987.

27. *Information*, 19 May 1987.

28. *Aktuelt*, 11 September 1987.

29. *Jyllands-Posten* (n.d.).

30. *Kristeligt Dagblad* (n.d.).

31. Danmarks Radio (known as DR) is the Danish public service broadcasting conglomerate that dominates in the field of radio and television broadcast and production. Formed in the 1920s as a radio broadcasting company, it entered the field of television in 1954, and until 1986, when TV2 was founded, it was the only TV station in Denmark. Not only is it one of the country's most important producers of radio and television programming, but it is also very active in the co-financing of feature films.

32. Søren Frank, 'Lars von Trier: I Lynch-Stemning' ('Lars von Trier: In a Lynch Mood'), *Euroman*, 1994, p. 78.

33. At the time of *Epidemic*'s rerelease, another Danish film, *Stjerner Uden Hjerner (Stars Without Brains)*, was being called the worst film ever made in Denmark. With his typical sense of irony, von Trier took umbrage at this, became jealous and claimed that his very own *Epidemic* had been the most critically despised film ever. Of course this wasn't true: as noted, the film got some very positive reviews. Rather, it is indicative of von Trier's and Aalbæk

Jensen's desire to generate press – *any* press – and their need to be seen, and to portray themselves as rebels who survived and flourished 'in spite of' all who were against them. But while it hadn't been the most critically savaged film, it had been one of the least seen, and he understandably wanted to give the public another chance to view it.

34. Schepelern, *Lars von Triers Film*, p. 141.

35. Ibid.

36. Ibid.

37. *Politiken*, 1988.

38. Interview with Arne Notkin, *Audio Visuelle Media*, 17 June 1988.

39. Ibid.

40. Ibid.

41. Lauridsen, *Sekvens*, p. 19.

42. Kirsten Jacobsen, *Uden Cigar: Faderen, Sønnen og Filmkøbmanden* (Copenhagen: Høst & Son, 2001), p. 190.

43. Richard Kelly, *The Name of this Book is Dogma 95* (London: Faber and Faber Ltd, 2000), p. 84.

44. Ibid.

45. *B.T.*, 16 April 2001.

46. Schepelern, *Lars von Triers Film*, p. 113.

47. *Ekstra Bladet*, 7 July 1996.

48. Schepelern, *Lars von Triers Film*, p. 134.

49. *Ekstra Bladet*, 7 July 1996.

50. *Politiken*, 11 August 1991.

51. *Weekendavisen*, 26 May 1987 .

52. Von Trier would go on, in 1992, to make *Change* in France for the group Manu Katche, and a pair of videos that same year for the Danish rock star, Kim Larsen (founding member of the seminal Danish rock band, Gasoline);

Dana's Have (*Dana's Garden*) and *Leningrad. The Shiver*, with music by Joachim Holbek, in 1994, and *You're a Woman*, from 1998, were made in connection with his own films, *The Kingdom* and *The Idiots* respectively, and round off his videography to date.

53. *Ekstra Bladet*, 20 May 1991.

54. Schepelern, *Lars von Triers Film*, pp. 118–19.

55. *Politiken*, 22 May 1991.

56. *B.T.*, 22 May 1991.

57. Schepelern, *Lars von Triers Film*, p. 119.

58. Ibid.

59. Peter Jeppesen, Ebbe Villadsen and Ole Caspersen, *Danske Spillefilm 1968–1991* (Esbjerg: Rosendahl Forlag A/S, 1993), p. 63.

60. *Aktuelt*, 2 March 1991.

61. The Swedish daily, *Dagens Nyheter* (n.d.).

62. *B.T.*, 24 December 1991.

63. Ibid.

3– *The Kingdom* and *Breaking the Waves*

1. *B.T.*, 27 May 2000.

2. Søren Frank, 'Lars von Trier: I Lynch-Stemning' ('Lars von Trier: In a Lynch Mood'), *Euroman*, 1994, p. 77.

3. This was the nickname that von Trier's favourite teacher at university, Martin Drouzy, had been dubbed with.

4. *Kosmorama*, issue 211, Spring 1995.

5. Gitte Merrild (ed.), Kim Foss (contrib.), *Copenhagen Culture: A Cultural Manual* (Copenhagen: Copenhagen Cultural Capital 96 Foundation, 1996), p. 148 .

6. *Ekstra Bladet*, 23 March 1995.

7. Bornedal, for his part, would shortly go on to Hollywood to direct the American

remake of *Nightwatch*, which starred
Nick Nolte. Upon his return he reported
that it had been an awful experience,
and the film flopped into the bargain. So
much for Denmark's big hope to
conquer Hollywood. For all it's lustre on
the international stage, the country still
didn't have a world-class director (as
Holland had Paul Verhoeven and
Germany had Wolfgang Petersen) who
had made it big in America.

8. *Ekstra Bladet*, 8 November 1994.

9. *Kosmorama*, issue 211, Spring 1995,
    'Mediernes Morgenluft?' by Lars Bo
    Kintergård.

10. The money had originated with the
    Sonning Prize which had been given to
    Bergman by the Danish university in
    1989. He had returned the grant with the
    stipulation that it be parcelled out to
    deserving Danish film and theatre figures.

11. *Ekstra Bladet*, 6 February 1995.

12. Ibid.

13. 'Said yes to a man she hardly knew',
    interview with Bente Trier by Merete
    Holger Storli in *Søndag*, issue 2, January
    2000, pp. 12–13.

14. *B.T.*, 11 April 1997.

15. *Jyllands-Posten*, 26 May 1996.

16. Peter Schepelern, *Lars von Triers Film:
    Tvang og Befrielse* (Copenhagen:
    Rosinante Forlag A/S, 1997, 2000),
    pp. 207–10.

17. Kirsten Jacobsen, *Uden Cigar: Faderen,
    Sønnen og Filmkøbmanden* (Copenhagen:
    Høst & Son, 2001), p. 117.

18. *Jyllands-Posten*, 26 May 1996.

19. *Politiken*, 5 July 1996.

20. *Politiken*, 19 May 1996.

21. *Politiken*, 27 May 2000.

22. *Aktuelt*, 22 May 1996.

23. *Information*, 11 September 1997.

24. *Ekstra Bladet*, 25 June 1998.

25. *Politiken*, 4 March 2000.

26. *Ekstra Bladet*, 7 July 1996.

4 – The Birth of Dogma and *The Idiots*

1. This date was pinpointed by scholars to
    be 22 March, when the brothers
    Lumière held their first private
    screening of *La sortie de l'usine Lumière à
    Lyon*, rather than the generally assumed
    date of 28 December when the first
    public screening of the film took place
    at Café Grand.

2. *Weekendavisen*, 26 June 1987.

3. There has been some debate in the
    Danish media about the lack of films
    made by immigrant film-makers, and
    the cloistered nature of the film milieu
    no doubt contributes in some fashion to
    the situation. For example, almost all of
    the graduates of the Film School who
    come from other ethnic backgrounds
    go on to make careers outside
    Denmark. When the immigrant
    experience in Denmark is conveyed in
    film (*The Pizza King*, *Pusher*, etc.) it is
    usually Danish film-makers who are
    directing them.

4. 1. Shooting must be done on location.
    Props and sets must not be brought in
    (if a particular prop is necessary for
    the story, a location must be chosen
    where the prop is to be found).
    2. The sound must never be produced
    apart from the images or vice versa.
    (Music must not be used unless it
    occurs where the scene is being shot.)

3. The camera must be hand-held. Any movement or mobility attainable by hand is permitted. (The film must not take place where the camera is standing; shooting must take place where the film takes place.) [Ed. What is rightly meant by this oddly translated last phrase is that the film must not take place in front of a *stationary* camera, and that shooting must take place where the film takes place, ruling out cranes, helicopter shots and other techniques used to convey distant point-of-views.]

4. The film must be in color. Special lighting is not acceptable. (If there is too little light for exposure, the scene must be cut or a single lamp be attached to the camera.)

5. Optical work and filters are forbidden.

6. The film must not contain superficial action. (Murders, weapons, etc., must not occur.)

7. Temporal and geographical alienation is forbidden. (That is to say that the film takes place here and now.)

8. Genre movies are not acceptable.

9. The film format must be Academy 35mm (later clarified to be the *exhibition* format).

10. The director must not be credited. Furthermore I swear as a director to refrain from personal taste! I am no longer an artist. I swear to refrain from creating a work , as I regard the instant as more important than the whole. My supreme goal is to force the truth out of my characters and settings. I swear to do so by all means available and at the cost

of any good taste and any aesthetic considerations.'

5. Richard Kelly, *The Name of this Book is Dogma 95* (London: Faber and Faber Ltd, 2000), p. 153.

6. *LA Weekly*, 2 March 2000.

7. Kelly, *The Name of this Book is Dogma 95*, p. 89.

8. *Ekstra Bladet*, 8 September 1999.

9. Kelly, *The Name of this Book is Dogma 95*, p. 137.

10. *Jyllands-Posten*, 10 December 1996.

11. Kelly, *The Name of this Book is Dogma 95*, p. 92.

12. *Information*, 5 October 1996.

13. *Ekstra Bladet*, 18 October 1997.

14. Ibid.

15. *Ekstra Bladet*, 23 September 1997.

16. Lars von Trier, *The Idiots: Manuscript and Diary* (Copenhagen: Gyldendal Forlag A/S, 1998), p. 282.

17. *Politiken*, 27 October 1997.

18. *B.T.*, 14 October 1997.

19. *Politiken*, 5 July 1996.

20. *Information*, 6 November 1997.

21. *Ekstra Bladet*, 14 October 1997.

22. *B.T.*, 12 April 2000.

23. *B.T.*, 24 July 2001.

24. *B.T.*, 15 January 1997 .

25. Ibid.

26. Von Trier, *The Idiots*, p. 160.

27. This diary was eventually published in French and Danish to coincide with the premiere of *The Idiots* in Cannes and its theatrical release in Denmark (see Bibliography).

28. *Weekendavisen*, 11–14 May 1998.

29. *Politiken*, 27 May 2000.

30. Ibid.

31. Ibid.

32. Von Trier, *The Idiots*, p. 270.

33. *B.T.*, 22 May 1998.

34. *Weekendavisen*, 11–14 May 1998.

35. Von Trier, *The Idiots*, pp. 184–5.

36. Ibid., pp. 248–9.

37. Ibid., p. 187.

38. *B.T.*, 17 May 1998.

39. *Jyllands-Posten*, 22 May 1998.

40. *B.T.*, 20 May 1998.

41. *Jyllands-Posten*, 22 May 1998.

42. Eva Jørholt and Martin Drouzy, 'Thou Shalt Honor Thy Wife: Dreyer and His Family', *Kosmorama*, Spring 1996, p. 24.

43. Even though, ironically, he had renounced his identity as an artist in the Dogma manifesto.

44. Autonomes are young radical leftists descended from Denmark's early-80s 'BZer' (Squatter) movement. They frequently engage in street protests and actions, sometimes violent, and resemble punks in appearance. They often live in collectives, Copenhagen's Nørrebro district being their 'home turf', and are perhaps the most pronounced example of a segment of Danish society that has broken with 'The Group'.

45. Von Trier reported in his diary that the visit by the real mongoloids caused his actors to fall completely out of character. The were overcome by sympathy. The illusion of the game was shattered and they even began calling each other by their real names.

46. *Jyllands-Posten*, 17 July 1998.

47. Kelly, *The Name of this book is Dogma 95*, p. 87.

48. Ibid.

49. *Politiken*, 12 May 2000.

50. Kirsten Jacobsen, *Uden Cigar: Faderen, Sønnen og Filmkøbmanden* (Copenhagen: Høst & Son, 2001), p. 113.

51. Ibid., p. 104.

52. *Aktuelt*, 25 August 1999.

53. *Ekstra Bladet*, 25 August 1999.

54. Jacobsen, *Uden Cigar*, p. 112.

55. *Weekendavisen*, 11–14 May 1998.

56. *Politiken*, 6 February 1999.

57. *Ekstra Bladet*, 17 February 1999.

58. Pity the poor distributors, then, when the film later failed to take off, selling more tickets in Denmark (351,000) than Holland, Italy, France and Germany combined.

59. One such group in Oslo wrote their own anti-Dogma manifesto requiring, among other things, that all possible effects be used in a film, that the crew should keep themselves out of the picture and that the director must be credited to avoid false modesty.

5 – Projects and Provocations

1. *Jyllands-Posten*, 26 May 1996.

2. Taken from promotional literature for *Quiet Waters* published after the start of the series by Trust Film Sales APS in English.

3. *Politiken*, 27 May 2000.

4. Mette Hjort and Ib Bondebjerg, *Instruktørens Blik* (*The Director's View*) (Copenhagen: Rosinante Forlag A/S, 2000), p. 288.

5. Ibid., p. 232.

6. *Pølse vogns* are canopied grilled-sausage wagons, unique to Denmark and Danish street culture,

that dispense meat of such horrid quality that it is actually prohibited in Germany.

7. Jørgen Leth is regarded as one of Denmark's foremost directors of documentary and experimental films. His credits include *The Perfect Human Being* (1967), *66 Scenes From America* (1981 and currently being remade) and *From the Heart to the Hand* (1994), a portrait of von Trier collaborator, Tómas Gislason. Some of his films in the 1960s were made in cooperation with the experimental film group, ABCinema.

8. *B.T.*, 3 April 2001.

9. The Dogumentary Manifesto reads: **Dogumentarism** relives the pure, the objective and the credible. It brings us back to the core, back to the essence of our existence.

The documentary and television reality which has become more and more manipulated and filtered by camera people, editors and directors, must now be buried.

This takes place with the following documentarist content guarantee:
The goal and content of all Dogme documentary projects must be supported and recommended in writing by at least seven people, companies or organizations who are relevant and vital. It is content and context which plays the primary role in Dogumentarism. Format and expression are secondary to this process.

Dogumentarism will restore the public's faith as a whole as well as the individual's. It will show the world raw, in focus and in 'defocus'.

Dogumentarism is a choice. You can choose to believe in what you see on film and television or you can choose **Dogumentarism**.

The Documentarist code for Dogumentarism:
1. All the locations in the film must be revealed. (This is to be done by text being inserted into the image. This constitutes an exception of rule number 5. All the text must be legible.)
2. The beginning of the film must outline the goals and ideas of the director. (This must be shown to the film's actors and technicians before filming begins.)
3. The end of the film must consist of two minutes of free speaking time by the film's 'victim'. This 'victim' alone shall advise regarding the content and must approve this part of the finished film. If there is no opposition by any of the collaborators, there will be no 'victim' or 'victims'. To explain this, there will be text inserted at the end of the film.
4. All clips must be marked with 6 to 12 frames black. (Unless they are a clip in real time, that is a direct clip in a multi-camera filming situation.)
5. Manipulation of the sound and/or images must not take place. Filtering, creative lighting and/or optical effects are strictly forbidden.
6. The sound must never be produced exclusive of the original filming or vice versa. That is, extra soundtracks like music or dialogue must not be mixed in later.
7. Reconstruction of the concept or the directing of the actors is not acceptable. Adding elements as with scenography are forbidden.
8. All use of hidden cameras is forbidden.

9. Archived images or footage that has been taken for other programs must never be used.

10. *Film*, issue 19, November 2001 (Danish Film Institute), p. 30.

6 – *Dancer in the Dark*

1. *Politiken*, 20 May 2000.
2. Ibid.
3. *Politiken*, 15 July 2000.
4. Quotes taken in the wake of the Cannes premiere of the film and all reported in *Politiken*, 18 May 2000.
5. *Politiken*, 20 May 2000.
6. *Politiken*, 18 May 2000.
7. *Jyllands-Posten*, 28 August 2001.
8. *Politiken*, 18 May 2000.
9. According to an interview in the DSB Magazine, *Ud Og Se*, February 2001, Aalbæk Jensen claimed he never exchanged a single word with her, and that he had later heard that she had told an American director that he was an evil person – 'even more evil than Lars von Trier', she had reportedly said. 'There can be no greater honour than that,' he reflected (p. 24).
10. *Politiken*, 18 May 2000.
11. *Politiken*, 20 May 2000.
12. *Politiken*, 18 May 2000.
13. *B.T.*, 23 May 2000.
14. *Politiken*, 22 May 2000.
15. *B.T.*, 23 May 2000.
16. *B.T.*, 27 May 2000.
17. *B.T.*, 15 July 2000.
18. *Politiken*, 24 September 2000.
19. *B.T.*, 26 August 2000.
20. *B.T.*, 8 September 2000.
21. Ibid.
22. *Politiken*, 8 September 2000.
23. *Information*, 8 September 2000.
24. *Ekstra Bladet*, 8 September 2000.
25. *Politiken*, 15 December 2000.
26. Antonia Quirke, *The Independent*, 15 September 2000.
27. Peter Schepelern, *Lars von Triers Film: Tvang og Befrielse* (Copenhagen: Rosinante Forlag A/S, 1997, 2000), p. 245.
28. *B.T.*, 27 January 2000.
29. David E. Williams, 'Waiting For von Trier', *The Hollywood Reporter*, November 2000, pp. 107, 148.
30. Ibid.
31. Mette Hjort and Ib Bondebjerg, *Instruktørens Blik* (Copenhagen: Rosinante Forlag A/S, 2000), p. 224. To package his films as trilogies, says von Trier,

> was a rationalization after the fact. It was first when Niels (Vørsel) and I wrote *Epidemic* that we hit upon the idea. But trilogies have always been good. Bergman also made trilogies with his films, with nobody being able to figure out why they were called trilogies. It is a way to advertise a less fortunate film. That's called a package deal, just like in TV where films are sold in a package.

7 – Dogma – the Next Generation and *Dogville*

1. Kirsten Jacobsen, *Uden Cigar: Faderen, Sønnen og Filmkøbmanden* (Copenhagen: Høst & Søn, 2001), p. 56.
2. *Politiken*, 5 March 2001.
3. Only a fifteen minute bicycle ride from the heart of Copenhagen, Christiania was

founded on 26 September 1971, when six rebellious Danes, entered a recently evacuated military encampment on the island of Amager through a hole in the fence. They envisioned it as a place where new thoughts and ways to live could flourish, a self-sufficient town for one thousand people. In 1972 the defence ministry agreed to supply water and electricity to the area, and Christiania has survived ever since. Today, known mostly for 'Pusher Street' where hash is openly sold, this self-proclaimed Free State is one

of Copenhagen's biggest tourist attractions and one of the few remaining vestiges of 1960s idealism left in the western world.

4. *Politiken*, 16 January 2000.

5. *B.T.*, 27 May 2000.

6. Jens Vilstrup, 'Aftalt Spil' ('Arranged Play'), *Euroman*, March 2000, p. 38.

7. Ibid.

8. Ibid., p. 34.

9. Molly Stensgaard, 'En God og Nærværende Dreng: Afslappet', ('A Good and Attentive Boy: Relaxed'), *Politiken*, 27 May 2000, sec. 2, p. 6. In her contribution to this portrait of the many-sided von Trier, film editor, Stensgaard, tells how he could be disrespectful to people in a humorous way.

    Aalbæk Jensen sometimes came into the editing room with one big investor or another and Lars would crawl down under the table and hide. And so they would stand there and chat, and I was sometimes a little in doubt as to whether I should tell them that he in fact was hiding right there under the table.

10. Henrik Vesterberg, *Politiken*, 26 December 1999.

11. *Politiken*, 24 June 2000.

12. *Politiken*, 24 June 2001.

13. Vilstrup, 'Aftalt Spil', p. 37.

14. *Politiken*, 26 December 1999.

15. Jacobsen, *Uden Cigar*, p. 224.

16. Ibid., p. 219.

17. Ibid., p. 254.

18. *Politiken*, 7 January 2001.

19. *B.T.*, 14 May 2001.

20. It has been said that one advantage of the small, close-knit Danish film community – often described as a family – is that you could never get really angry at anyone or cheat them, since sooner or later you would have to deal with that person again. On the other hand there were 'family feuds' that seemed to go on for ever.

21. Jørgen Leth, 'Filmlovens Mand', *Politiken*, 7 November 2001.

22. *B.T.*, 13 June 2001.

23. *Aktuelt*, 13 December 1999.

24. *Politiken*, 27 May 2000.

25. *B.T.*, 8 November 2000.

26. *Politiken*, 23 May 2000.

27. *Film*, May–June 2001, issue 15 (published by the Danish Film Institute).

28. *Politiken*, 9 February 2001.

29. *Politiken*, 23 November 2000.

30. *Politiken*, 2 May 2001.

31. *B.T.*, 13 June 2000.

32. *Politiken*, 15 July 2001.

33. *B.T.*, 13 June 2001.

34. *Taxi* was created by Rumle Hammerich, the young Film School student who

wrote the *The Last Detail* which von Trier had directed. They both went on to survive that film: Hammerich going on to considerable success in the Danish film and TV world, working for DR-TV and now employed as a producer for Nordisk where he was involved with the 'Director's Cut' concept (more on that shortly).

35. Cæcilia Holbek Trier was also 'in competition' at the 2001 edition of the Berlin Film Festival, in the esteemed Kinderfilm (Children's film) sidebar with her feature, *Susanne Silleman*. After her split with Lars, she had recovered her health and gone on to resume a successful directing career – and was never referred to in the press as 'the ex-wife of Lars von Trier'. Agnes and Selma would spend every second weekend with Lars and Bente who ended up having an amicable relationship with Cæcilia.

36. *Politiken*, 1 June 2001.

37. For his part, Jargil was hard at work on a documentary about Dogma entitled *The Putrified* that would be released in August 2002. It would cap his triology (*The Humiliated, The Exhibited*) on Lars von Trier which he would call *The Kingdom of Credibility*.

38. *Politiken*, 25 November 2000.

39. *Die Zeit*, 8 September 1999.

40. *Politiken*, 20 December 2001.

41. *Politiken*, 9 June 2001.

42. Jacobsen, *Uden Cigar*, p. 92.

43. This was the same Vinca Wiedemann who had previously been employed by Zentropa (as scriptwriter on the Morten Korch project). Such apparent conflicts of interest weren't rare: an article by Per Dabelsteen in *Politiken*, 27 October 2001, revealed that of the approximately 100 million kroner Zentropa had received in DFI funding since 1992, 90 million of that was granted by consultants who have since been employed by Zentropa. Some would no doubt argue that this situation was unavoidable in a film milieu as small and in-bred as the Danish one, and that if this 'coziness' produced conflicts of interest, it also produced synergy.

44. *B.T.*, 29 March 2001.

45. *Politiken*, 1 February 2002.

46. *Politiken*, 8 February 2002.

BIBLIOGRAPHY

Danish

Hjort, Mette and Ib Bondebjerg. *Instruktørens Blik* (*The Director's View*)(Copenhagen: Rosinante Forlag A/S, 2000). Also published in English as *The Danish Directors: Dialogues on a Contemporary National Cinema* (Bristol: Intellect Books, 2001).

Jacobsen, Kirsten. *Uden Cigar: Faderen, Sønnen og Filmkøbmanden* (*Without Cigar: the Father, the Son and the Film Merchant*) (Copenhagen: Høst & Son, 2001).

Jeppesen, Peter, Ebbe Villadsen and Ole Caspersen. *Danske Spillefilm 1968–1991* (*Danish Feature Films 1968–1991*) (Esbjerg: Rosendahl Forlag A/S, 1993).

Lauridsen, Palle Schantz. *Sekvens: Lars von Trier – Filmvidenskabelig Årbog 1991* (*Film Theory Yearbook 1991: Lars von Trier*)(Copenhagen: Institut for Film, TV & Kommunikation, 1991).

Schepelern, Peter. *Lars von Triers Film: Tvang og Befrielse* (*The Films of Lars von Trier: Compulsion and Liberation*) (Copenhagen: Rosinante Forlag A/S, 2000).

von Trier, Lars. *Manuskript og dagbog* (The Idiots: *Manuscript and Diary*) (Copenhagen: Nordisk Forlag A/S, 1998).

English

Kelly, Richard. *The Name of this Book is Dogma 95* (London: Faber and Faber Ltd, 2000).

Merrild, Gitte (ed.), Foss, Kim (contrib.). *Copenhagen Culture: A Cultural Manual* (Copenhagen: Copenhagen Cultural Capital 96 Foundation, 1996).

FILMOGRAPHY

Youth films

1967 – 71, all directed, written, photographed and edited by Lars von Trier

Turen Til Squashland
(*The Trip to Squashland*, circa 1967)
Format: 8mm (animation)
Running Time: 1 minute
Colour

Nat, Skat (*Good Night, Dear*, or *Night, Treasure*, circa 1968)
Format: 8mm
Running Time: 1 minute
Colour

En Røvsyg Oplevelse
(*A Dead Boring Experience*, circa 1969)
Format: 8mm
Running Time: 1 minute
Colour

Et Skakspil
(*A Chess Game*, circa 1969)
Format: 8mm
Running Time: 1 minute
Black and White

Hvorfor Flygte Fra Det Du Ved Du Ikke Kan Flygte Fra? Fordi Du Er En Kujon
(*Why Try to Escape From That Which You Know You Can't Escape From? Because You Are a Coward*, 1970)
Format: 8mm
Running Time: 7 minutes
Colour

En Blomst
(*A Flower*, circa 1971)
Format 8mm
Running Time: 7 minutes
Black and White

Films made while attending Copenhagen University

Orchidégartneren
(*The Orchid Gardener*, 1977)
Director and Writer: Lars von Trier
Production: Film Group 16
Format: 16mm
Running Time: 37 minutes
Language: Danish
Black and White

Menthe – La Bienheureuse
(*Menthe – The Blissful*, 1979)
Director and Writer: Lars von Trier
Production: Film Group 16
Format: 16mm

Running Time: 31 minutes
Language: French
Black and White

Films made
at the Danish Film School

Nocturne (1980)

Director and Writer: Lars von Trier
Production: Danish Film School
Format: 16mm
Photography: Tom Elling
Editing: Tómas Gislason
Running Time: 8 minutes
Language: Danish
Colour and Black and White

Den Sidste Detalje
(The Last Detail, 1981)

Director: Lars von Trier
Screenplay: Rumle Hammerich
Production: Danish Film School
Format: 35mm
Photography: Tom Elling
Editing: Tómas Gislason
Running Time: 31 minutes
Language: Danish
Black and White

Befrielsesbilleder
(Images of a Relief, 1982)

Director and Writer: Lars von Trier
Production: Danish Film School
Format: 35mm
Photography: Tom Elling
Editing: Tómas Gislason
Running Time: 57 minutes
Language: Danish and German
Colour

Commercial feature films

Europa Trilogy
The Element of Crime (1984)

Director: Lars von Trier
Screenplay: Lars von Trier and Niels Vørsel
Cast: Michael Elphick (Fisher), Esmond
    Knight (Osborne), Me Me Lai (Kim),
    Jerold Wells (Police Chief Kramer),
    Ahmed El Shenawi (therapist)
Production: Per Holst Film in cooperation
    with the Danish Film Institute
Format: 35mm widescreen
Photography: Tom Elling
Editing: Tómas Gislason
Running Time: 103 minutes
Language: English
Colour

Epidemic (1987)

Director: Lars von Trier
Screenplay: Lars von Trier and Niels Vørsel
Cast: Susanne Ottesen, Allan de Wall,
    Ole Ernst, Michael Getting, Colin Gilder,
    Svend Ali Haman, Claes Kastholm
    Hansen, Gitte Lind
Production: Element Film in cooperation
    with the Danish Film Institute
Shooting Format: 16mm and 35mm
Projection Format: 35mm, 35mm sequences
    photographed by Henning Bendtsen,
    16mm by various
Editing: Lars von Trier and Thomas Kraugh
Running Time: 106 minutes
Language: Danish and English
Colour and Black and White

Europa,
(released in America as
Zentropa, 1991)
Director: Lars von Trier
Assistant Director: Tómas Gislason
Screenplay: Lars von Trier and Niels Vørsel
Cast: Jean-Marc Barr (Leopold Kessler),
Barbara Sukowa (Katharina Hartmann),
Udo Kier (Lawrence Hartmann),
Ernst-Hugo Järegård (Uncle Kessler),
Erik Mørk (priest)
Production: Nordisk Film in cooperation
with the Danish Film Institute, the
Swedish Film Institute, PCC, Telefilm
GMBH, Gunnar Obel, WMG and
Gérard Mital Productions
Format: 35mm CinemaScope
Primary Photography: Henning Bendtsen
Editing: Hervé Schneid
Running Time: 113 minutes
Language: English and German
Colour/Black and White

The Gold Hearted Trilogy

Breaking the Waves (1996)
Director: Lars von Trier
Assistant Director: Morten Arnfred
Writer: Lars von Trier, co-written by Peter
Asmussen and David Pirie
Cast: Emily Watson (Bess),
Stellan Skarsgård (Jan), Katrin Cartlidge
(Dodo), Jean-Marc Barr (Terry),
Adrian Rawlins (Dr Richardson),
Jonathan Hackett (the minister)
Production: Zentropa Entertainments in
cooperation with other production
entities
Shooting Format: 35mm and digital video
Projection Format: 35mm CinemaScope
Photography: Robby Müller

Editing: Anders Refn
Running Time: 158 minutes
Language: English
Colour

Idioterne (*The Idiots,* 1998)
Director and Writer: Lars von Trier
Cast: Bodil Jørgensen (Karen),
Jens Albinus (Stoffer), Anne Louise
Hassing (Susanne), Troels Lyby
(Henrik), Nikolai Lie Kaas (Jeppe),
Louise Mieritz (Josephine), Henrik Prip
(Ped), Luis Mesonero (Miguel),
Knud Romer Jørgensen (Axel), Trine
Michelsen (Nana), Anne-Grethe Bjarup
Riis (Katrine)
Production: Zentropa Entertainments in
cooperation with other production
entities
Shooting Format: digital video
Projection Format: 35mm
Photography: Lars von Trier (Kristoffer
Nyholm, Jesper Jargil and Casper Holm
assisted on photography)
Editing: Lars von Trier and Molly Malene
Stensgaard (on Avid)
Running Time: 111 minutes
Language: Danish
Colour

Dancer in the Dark (2000)
Director and Screenplay: Lars von Trier
Cast: Björk (Selma Jezková), Catherine
Deneuve (Kathy), David Morse (Bill),
Peter Stormare (Jeff), Joel Grey (Oldrich
Novy), Vincent Paterson (Samuel, the
director)
Production: Zentropa Entertainments in
cooperation with other production
entities

Shooting Format: 35mm and digital video
Projection Format: 35mm widescreen
Photography: Robby Müller
Editing: Molly Malene Stensgaard and
    François Gédigier
Length: 139 minutes
Language: English
Colour

Forthcoming
Dogville

Dear Wendy (working title)

TV films and projects
Medea (1988)
Director and Writer: Lars von Trier
Screenplay: Carl Th. Dreyer and Proben
    Thomsen
Cast: Udo Kier (Jason), Kirsten Olsen
    (Medea), Henning Jensen (Kreon),
    Solbjerg Højfeldt (nurse), Baard Owe
    (Aigeus), Preben Lerdorff Rye (teacher),
    Ludmilla Glinska (Glauce)
Production: Danmarks Radio (TV and
    Theatre Department)
Format: shot on video, copied onto film and
    copied back to video
Editing: Finnur Sveinsson
Running Time: 75 minutes
Language: Danish
Colour

Riget (The Kingdom, 1994)
Directors: Lars von Trier and Morten Arnfred
Writers: Lars von Trier and Niels Vørsel
Cast: Ernst-Hugo Järegård (Stig G. Helmer),
    Kirsten Rolffes (Mrs Sigrid Drusse),
    Ghita Nørby (Rigmer), Søren Pilmark
    (Krogen), Otto Brandenburg (Porter

Hansen), Jens Okking (Bulder), Holger
    Juul Hansen (Dr Einar Moesgaard)
Production: Zentropa Entertainments and
    Danmarks Radio TV in cooperation with
    other European production entities
Shooting Format: 16mm (blown up to 35mm
    for theatrical release)
Photography: Eric Kress (steadicam: Henrik
    Harpelund)
Editing: Molly Malene Stensgaard and Jacob
    Thuesen
Running Time: 4 episodes of 63, 65, 69 and
    75 minutes' duration
Language: Danish
Colour

Lærerværelset
(The Teacher's Room, 1994)
Concept: Lars von Trier
Directors: Lars von Trier and Rumle
    Hammerich
Production: Zentropa for TV2
Running Time: 6 episodes at 25 minutes
    each
Language: Danish

Marathon (1996)
Concept: Lars von Trier
Production: 8 episodes by Zentropa
    Entertainments for Danmarks Radio

Riget II (The Kingdom II, 1997)
Directors: Lars von Trier and Morten
    Arnfred
Screenplay: Lars von Trier and Niels Vørsel
Cast: Ernst-Hugo Järegård (Stig G. Helmer),
    Kirsten Rolffes (Mrs Sigrid Drusse),
    Holger Juul Hansen (Dr Einar
    Moesgaard), Søren Pilmark (Krogen),
    Ghita Nørby (Rigmer), Jens Okking

(Bulder), Birthe Neumann (Miss
Svendsen)
Production: Zentropa and Danmarks Radio
in cooperation with other production
entities
Photography: Eric Kress (steadicam: Henrik
Harpelund)
Editing: Molly Malene Stensgaard and
Pernille Bech Christensen
Running Time: 4 episodes of 63, 79, 76 and
78 minutes' duration
Language: Danish

Morten Korch
(Quiet Waters, 1998–9)

Executive Producer: Lars von Trier
Directors: Henrik Sartou, Finn Henriksen
and Lone Scherfig
Writers: Peter Thorsboe, John Stefan Olsen
and Ole Meldgaard
Production: Zentropa Entertainments for
TV2
Running Time: 26 episodes produced
Language: Danish

D-Dag (Project D-Day, 2000)

Experimental TV project made in
cooperation with Thomas Vinterberg,
Søren Kraugh-Jacobsen and Kristian
Levring
Production: Nimbus Film in cooperation
with Zentropa, DR, TV2, TV3, TV
Danmark
Format: digital video
Running Time: 70 minutes
Language: Danish

INDEX

Films indexed by title are by von Trier unless otherwise indicated
Page numbers in **bold** type indicate detailed analysis; those in *italics* denote illustrations
n = endnote (indexed only for background information, not citations)